W9-BTP-904

When Sparks Fly

Igniting Creativity in Groups

DOROTHY A. LEONARD

WALTER C. SWAP

Harvard Business School Press

Boston, Massachusetts

Printed in the United States of America
03 02 01 00 99   5 4 3 2 1

Library of Congress Cataloging-in-Publication Data

Leonard-Barton, Dorothy.
    When sparks fly : igniting creativity in groups / Dorothy A.
  Leonard, Walter C. Swap.
        p.   cm.
    Includes bibliographical references and index.
    ISBN 0-87584-865-6 (alk. paper)
    1. Creative ability in business.   2. Teams in the workplace.
  3. Social groups.   I. Swap, Walter C.   II. Title.
  HD53.L46   1999
  658.4'036—dc21   99-20608
                                                         CIP

The paper used in this publication meets the requirements of the
American National Standard for Permanence of Paper for Printed
Library Materials Z39.49-1984.

To the primary assets in our own merger and acquisition:

Cliff and Alison;
Gavin;
Michelle, Michael, and Scott

Contents

Preface

This book was born of a belief, a challenge, and a request. The belief is that creativity can be encouraged, enhanced, and enabled by managers. Although so much innovation today emerges through *group* processes, most literature on creativity focuses on creative *individuals*. We maintain that any group can be more creative, even if its members individually wouldn't score highly on tests for creativity. If you are a manager seeking better ways to harness the talents of your group members and to ignite creativity, we've designed this book with you in mind. We believe your leadership can make a real difference.

The challenge motivating the book was to merge perspectives from two thought worlds that usually avoid each other, but which provide complementary insights into human behavior: basic research in psychology, particularly social psychology; and practical experience in management. The venues for knowledge building are very different in these two worlds: the controlled conditions and careful experimental designs in the psychologist's laboratory, versus the often chaotic, time-pressured environment in management. We aimed to integrate the insights of both into a useful perspective on group creativity. We therefore dived into psychological literature to identify solid, research-based findings. Then we tested the relevance and realism of our conclusions through interviews with dozens of leaders, from entrepreneurs running small businesses or midlevel managers of creative groups to CEOs of long-established companies. We also drew on our own years of prior study and research—Walter on social psychology, and Dorothy on innovation. But we have not hesitated to build as well upon the work of colleagues in management, such as Rosabeth Moss Kanter, Kathleen Eisenhardt, and John Kao, whose writings on innovation parallel and support many of the ideas contained herein. We owe a special debt to Teresa Amabile, whom we have cited extensively because of her original social psychological research on creativity and complementary applied managerial perspective.

Finally, we have responded to requests from some readers of the senior author's 1995 book, *Wellsprings of Knowledge*, for an in-depth treatment of a topic introduced in a chapter in that earlier work, namely knowledge *generation*. Group creativity is all about producing new, useful knowledge—or innovations. We analyze each step in the creative process and provide practical suggestions for managing each of these steps. But depth, we trust, does not preclude brevity nor demand ponderous prose. Our objective was to write a book that you could pick up in the airport, read during a couple hours' flight, and deplane at a new mental as well as physical destination. We wanted to have a *conversation* with you, our reader—so the tone of the book is not particularly academic (except in the research sidebars, which you can skip or skim with little loss of overall flow of ideas).

As is usual with undertakings such as this book, more people contributed than are represented on the title page. Three anonymous reviewers and our editor, Marjorie Williams, made suggestions for improving earlier drafts. Research Assistant Anne Conner sleuthed out materials for Chapter 5. Robert Irwin labored to uncover references and Laurie Calhoun to rediscover some—after we thought we had been *so* careful to keep them all. We also greatly appreciate the help of Irene Nelson, without whose domestic contributions this book would have taken much, much longer to complete.

For the deficiencies remaining in the book, we of course hold each other responsible! (That's one of the joys of co-authorship.)

When Sparks Fly

1

What Is Group Creativity?

Jeri Davis, vice president of R&D for the company, glanced around the room. The product managers and the team leaders for current development projects were all in attendance. Stan, Marian, Kirk . . . there must be at least 150 years of cumulative experience with the board games industry in the room. Surely with all that knowledge they could come up with a creative new product to challenge the electronic games taking over the market. She checked the clock, noted that it was six minutes past the announced starting time. Where the heck was Kevin? But even as she cleared her throat and said, perhaps a bit too loudly, "Okay, maybe we'd better get started," she realized that everyone else was also waiting for Kevin. Kevin—the "Creative." "Twenty-one good people in the room," Jeri thought, "and we all think it's one man's job to provide the creative spark. What a waste."

Deadlines. Budgets. Downsizing. Time-to-market pressures. And now you need to deliver innovation as well. Perhaps you, like Jeri, are leading a group of intelligent, hard-working people—who don't think of themselves as particularly creative. What to do? Jeri's minor epiphany would be useful for many managers because it illustrates a number of myths about creativity. Myths may have roots in some

deep truth that has accumulated over years of experience and observation. But myths also exaggerate, oversimplify, and can seriously
mislead. So let's scrutinize a few.

Myths about Creativity

Myth # 1: Creative output depends on a few, often flamboyantly different individuals.

Not all organizations have officially designated "creatives," but certainly there *are* especially creative individuals, and their potential
contribution to groups should not be minimized. For such individuals, some combination of temperament and life situation has given
them idiosyncratic lenses through which to view the world. They
make connections and spy opportunities others don't, turn questions
upside down, and are as curious as a four-year-old or an Arctic
explorer. For them, creativity is a way of life. We would certainly
like a few of them around.

However, "Everyone is creative," says Bill Shephard, director of
programs for the Creative Education Foundation in Buffalo, New
York.[1] So—nature or nurture? Must we rely for creativity solely on
those individuals who are destined by personality and upbringing
to see the world differently? Or can creativity be nurtured in an
organization? We suggest that innovation results from a creative
process that inevitably includes people who would not define themselves as either creative or flamboyant. They may never have sculpted
or composed music and may not have a single ring piercing any
part of their anatomy. Nonetheless, as we shall see, their individual
contributions may be essential to group creative output. A creative
group is not the same as a group of "creatives."

The second myth is closely related.

Myth # 2: Creativity is a solitary process.

As even a cursory glance through the stacks of books on creativity
will reveal, most research and writing on creativity has focused on

the individual—how to unlock each person's creative potential, the "secrets" of really creative people, and the relationship between individual intelligence and creativity. In cartoons, a lightbulb appears over a character's head to indicate that a sudden inspiration has illuminated the way to a creative solution. As we shall see, the kinds of insight and intuition symbolized by the lightbulb are important elements in the creative process. The problem with the lightbulb metaphor, however, is that it suggests that insight emanates only from individuals. In reality, we dare not relegate responsibility for innovativeness to single individuals, nor to discrete functions such as research and development. Our organizations are parched for creative output from boardroom to basement and financial office to factory. Creativity in business is a *group* exercise. As Warren Bennis has noted, "The Lone Ranger, the incarnation of the individual problem solver, is dead."[2]

A variant on this myth is that groups are inherently conservative; that really creative ideas get watered down in groups: The protruding nail gets hammered down. Most of the world-altering inventions of the twentieth century emanated from groups of people with complementary skills—not just the inventor toiling as a lone genius. For instance, the name of William Shockley is most closely associated with invention of the now-ubiquitous transistor. However, that remarkable act of creativity actually derived from his joint work with two others—Walter Brattain and John Bardeen. Together this small group discovered the "holes" (the absence of electrons) that carried electric currents in silicon.[3]

Myth # 3: Intelligence is more important than creativity.

Many leaders certainly believe in stocking their teams with the most intelligent men and women available, and letting creativity take care of itself. We agree that intelligence is important. However, intelligence and creativity are modestly associated only up to an I.Q. of about 120. Beyond that level, all individuals seem equally capable of creative thinking.[4] So while we certainly advocate selecting for intelligence, a group of smart people does not always translate to a smart—or creative—group.

Myth # 4: Creativity can't really be managed.

Creativity is frequently regarded as an art—an unknowable and ad hoc process for each project, a process that "just happens." Some would carry this myth even further, and argue that by attempting to manage creativity we would dampen or even destroy it. Wordsworth warned:

> Sweet is the lore which Nature brings;
>> Our meddling intellect
> Misshapes the beauteous forms of things:—
>> We murder to dissect.

Perhaps, as with the beauty of nature, there is a certain amount of magic involved in creativity that never can be fully understood. In almost all groups, however, managers can shape the creative process, design the group composition, enhance the physical environment, provide the tools and techniques to move things along, and lead the creative charge. Far from murdering creativity, such managerial efforts may resuscitate a moribund process or enhance the creativity of an already productive group. It isn't easy. Managers have to redesign the ship while they sail—innovate while they keep the normal enterprise operations running. But, as we shall see, creativity is required and occurs even in these routine organizational activities.

Myth # 5: Creative groups are found only in "The Arts" or in high-technology companies.

We can learn a lot from the free-wheeling Silicon Valley high-technology companies and from Los Angeles power luncheons, where both creativity and profitability are legitimate discussion topics. But creativity thrives in the nooks and crannies of management everywhere, and the same general principles for promoting creativity apply in pharmaceutical companies, banks, higher education, the military, and even the government. Truly. And there could be a lot more creativity in *all* of our organizations if managers challenged themselves to stimulate it.

Myth # 6: Creativity is relevant only to Big Ideas.

The innovation that results from creative processes can range from incremental (redesigned tools, derivative or follow-on products, new interaction modes with existing customers) to radical (new strategic direction, new market, reconfiguration of businesses). Thus, we find creativity in small improvements that advance the organizational cause as well as in visionary leaps that reshape the future. While the *scope of change* obviously varies along this continuum, as do the challenges, the *creative process* is the same. Whether the group challenged to produce an innovation comprises three people with money left over from the office holiday party as a resource, or three hundred people working on the latest word-processing software platform, the stages and activities associated with creative output will be the same.

Myth # 7: Creativity only involves coming up with new ideas.

Well, sure, novelty is an important part of creativity. But only part of the complex creative process is coming up with new ideas. Before that can happen, the people have to be selected who will generate those ideas. They have to be given the tools to stimulate their divergent thinking and the time—and space—for reflection. And at some point the process has to be redirected to arrive at one or a few options that should prove useful.

From this brief consideration of creativity myths, we draw a number of conclusions that will guide much of our later discussion:

* Creativity is a *process*, and the process is similar regardless of the magnitude or industry location of the project.

* Creative individuals are important to creative groups. But not *all*-important.

* The right group composition *is* important.

* Creativity is a process that can be learned by groups. As a result, it can—and must—be managed effectively.

* The creative process goes beyond just generating novel ideas, although divergent thinking is critical.

* Creativity involves more than just being different or unusual.

What Is Creativity?

We know it when we see it, right? Not always. We may stand in awe in front of a Monet painting of water lilies or delight in the (obviously highly original) storybooks produced by our small children—but creativity in management contexts demands an additional descriptor besides *novel* or *unusual*. The creativity must also be *useful*; that is, must have at least the potential for utility. Clearly, we do not always know at the outset whether a creative idea is going to prove useful. Does anyone recall, much less use, the leg-powered snow shovel, the wet diaper indicator, the cigarette umbrella, the scent-awake clock and trained attack-rocks?

This leads us to the definition of creativity that will guide us throughout this book:

> Creativity is a process of developing and expressing novel ideas
> that are likely to be useful.

There are four important features of this definition. First, creativity involves *divergent thinking*, a breaking away from familiar, established ways of seeing and doing. Divergent thinking produces ideas that are novel. As we shall see, novelty for its own sake may actually be important in early stages of creative efforts, when you want lots of options—even wacky ones—but if the effort ends there, nothing has been accomplished besides some possibly exhilarating mental aerobics. Second, these novel ideas must be expressed or communicated to others. This expression provides a reality check on whether the ideas are really novel—or simply bizarre. Third, creativity must also include *convergent thinking*, some agreement that one or more of the novel ideas is worth pursuing. Fourth, this agreed-on option must have the potential for being useful, for addressing the problem that initiated the development of options.

The end result of the creative process is an *innovation*. More specifically:

> *Innovation is the embodiment, combination, and/or synthesis of knowledge in novel, relevant, valued new products, processes, or services.*

The task to be accomplished, the scope of the desired innovation, dictates the amount of creativity needed. Routine tasks and well-defined, well-understood problems may require a modicum, whereas novel situations and problems require maximum strength.

This book, then, is about a creative process that leads to a potentially novel, useful solution or process or product. Whether you lead a group of three in a nonprofit foundation or 30,000 in a Fortune 500 business, the basic *process of creativity* is the same. The scale differs, the societal implications differ, people differ from each other. But the process derives from some basic interactions among the members of our quirky, infinitely variable, but at the same time surprisingly predictable species.

And we are especially focused on *groups* as the creating body. Teams (self-managed or otherwise), task forces, councils, cabinets, and parliaments—all share some essential characteristics, captured in our final definition:

"A group may be thought of as two or more people, existing in an arrangement that permits some degree of interaction, and sharing some sense of identity as members."[5]

This definition is broad enough to encompass all of the types of groups likely to be encountered by readers of this book. It is also restrictive enough to exclude both those who interact but who have no common mission (e.g., a group of friends convening over dinner) and those with a common mission but who do not interact (e.g., all New York Yankee haters). However, face-to-face interaction is not a necessity for a group. Ten stamp collectors communicating

SOME DEFINITIONS OF CREATIVITY

"Creativity is that process which results in a novel work that is accepted as tenable or useful or satisfying by a group at some point in time."[6]

"A product or response will be judged as creative to the extent that (a) it is both a novel and appropriate, useful, correct or valuable response to the task at hand, and (b) the task is heuristic [not having a clear and readily identifiable path to solution] rather than algorithmic [the path to the solution is clear and straightforward]."[7]

"A company is creative when its employees do something new and potentially useful without being directly shown or taught."[8]

"Creativity is . . . the production of something that is *both* new and truly valuable."[9]

"Creativity . . . involves a process that is extended in time and characterized by originality, adaptiveness, and realization."[10]

Note that while each author has a distinctive spin on the concept of creativity, all agree that creativity is a *process,* that it involves the generation of something *novel* or *unusual,* and that the outcome of the process is something *useful.*

and trading via the Internet might constitute a group. A group may also be transient; for example, two workers who sit down together at a "hot desk," hook up their computers, and brainstorm some ideas for new products, then go their separate ways. Groups come in all sizes. However, we find it useful to focus on smaller, interactive groups that reside in those big groups we call organizations.

The Creative Process

Creativity is inherently messy, but despite Wordsworth's warning, we do need to dissect—or at least to structure—in order to enhance creativity. A physical model of the process would look more like a plate of spaghetti than the linear stages we lay out below. However, we need an organizing scheme for our discussion, and these five steps (as shown in Figure 1-1) capture the essential features of the creative process.

1. Preparation

2. Innovation opportunity

3. Divergence: Generating options

4. Incubation

5. Convergence: Selecting Options

Step 1: Preparation

The dead and the survivors of the devastated town of Guernica in Picasso's famous painting have strangely elongated necks, eyes on the same side of the face, and disproportionately large hands and feet. A man standing in front of it, apparently for the first time, was overheard to mutter to his companion, "Maybe he just couldn't draw." Yet in the same museum, the Reina Sofia in Madrid, one can see examples of the skilled, anatomically faithful portraits Picasso drew long before he started abstracting and exaggerating bodily

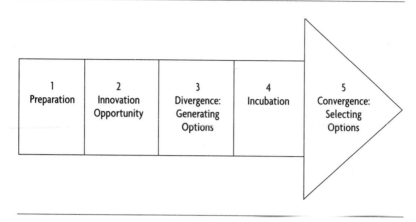

1-1 The Five Steps in the Creative Process

features to communicate stark emotions. In his remarkable late works, Beethoven anticipated the romanticism that would dominate nineteenth-century Western music, but his roots were in the classicism of Mozart and Haydn. Newton, Einstein, and Hawking were all grounded in deep knowledge of mathematics and put in years of work on gravity, motion, and cosmology before they each went on to revolutionize physics. There are no shortcuts. Creativity blooms when the mental soil is deep, rich, and well prepared. Deep relevant knowledge and experience precede creative expression. Groups have a potential advantage over an individual because multiple reservoirs of deep expertise can be tapped. Two (or more) heads are better than one, however, only if (1) there is useful knowledge inside the heads; (2) all that useful knowledge can be accessed; and (3) all that accessed, useful knowledge can be shared, processed, and synthesized by the group.

Step 2: Innovation Opportunity

Moreover, there has to be an opportunity for innovation—some need to exercise creativity. How is a group launched on a creative voyage? Some groups are born to be creative. Designated as explorers, they innovate or die. Research organizations such as Xerox's Palo

Alto Research Center or Hewlett-Packard's laboratories are mandated to continuously create; their members are challenged to reject the routine, the obvious, the known. Design firms, which exist to innovate, encounter opportunities for invention walking in the door daily. People in such organizations get up every morning knowing that their job, individually and collectively, is to be creative. We will include examples of such organizations throughout the book because their structures and routines reveal a lot about managing creativity.

However, most groups lack this single-minded focus on innovation. Far more have the need for creativity thrust upon them. The trigger for creative activity may knock at the door in the guise of a fairy godmother—a chance to improve conditions—or it may look more like a chainsaw murderer—a threat requiring immediate response to survive. Depending on the perspective of the company, the advent of the Internet is opportunity or crisis. Often the call for creativity comes as a problem to be solved. As recounted at greater length in Chapter 2, the group at Genzyme Corporation dealing with government regulators saw an opportunity to turn a liability into a competitive advantage when they negotiated a recategorization of one of their products.

One innovation often engenders the need for another—an opportunity for creative thinking. In 1845, when Sir John Franklin hauled one of the new-fangled "tin cans" of veal to the Arctic, he had to be sure to have a hammer and chisel on hand to open it. Contemporary consumers were using everything from pick axes to revolvers for opening cans! The British Army and Navy Co-operative Society, whose catalog was the Wal-Mart of the time, responded somewhat belatedly by offering its first can opener in 1885.[11] When Xerox copier machines were invented, a marketing innovation was required before the technological invention was useful. The original problem was that the machine offered no apparent advantage over carbon paper (remember what that was?). The advantage not foreseen was being able to make *multiple* copies—copies of copies, with no reduction in quality. Since this could not be done with carbons, no one saw the demand. The marketing innovation was to make money on user fees. People could try out a machine at minimal cost, "without requiring a leap of faith, unfathomable foresight, or monumental risk taking."[12]

Step 3: Generating Options

Once the opportunity or problem appears, the temptation in this rush-hour, info-snack world we occupy is to grab an option and run with it. But creative solutions are usually selected from a menu of alternatives, and the higher number of options we start with, the more likely one will be novel. So, we want some divergent thinking before we converge on the best solution. If you are thinking, "yes, but that sounds inefficient," you are right. We aren't after pure efficiency in group process here. We seek the novel and useful, and we are willing to sacrifice some efficiency in the name of creativity. The organizations whose livelihoods depend on innovation are masters at constructing menus of choices before they converge on a single selection.

Generating options is a surprisingly social activity—even people renowned for their personal creativity cite interaction as important. In one study of creative individuals, a typical respondent said:

> I develop lots of my ideas in dialogue. It's very exciting to have another mind that is considering the same set of phenomena with as much interest as one is. It's very exciting, the sparks, and dynamic interaction, and very much newer . . . ways of looking at things, that come out of those conversations.[13]

In a group, the sparks can fly. But the manager may have to provide the flints—and show group members how to use them—as well as bank some of the resulting fires.

Step 4: Incubation

Showers, it turns out, are useful for more than cleanliness. Shaving also. Even driving (though possibly not in Boston or Mexico City or Jakarta, where unusual attention to driving is essential to well-being). Apparently, we need "time out" from struggling with a problem or issue. While our conscious attention is focused on the task at hand, our subconscious is still busily digging around the issue, like a terrier after a buried bone. Then, when we are engaged in some fairly "mindless" task such as washing or driving, the terrier triumphantly produces the bone—a possible solution to the problem. We all have had the experience of returning to a problem, perhaps as mundane as the daily crossword puzzle that had us stumped, and solving it easily.

But is incubation just a fancy name for inaction? It depends on what you mean by "action." You have probably heard the story of the efficiency expert who reported to the CEO an individual whose services were clearly unneeded. "I found him with his feet up on his desk, staring out the window," the expert declared. "Young man," the CEO replied, "that man has brought millions of dollars into the firm, and when he came up with his last invention, his feet were in that exact position."

Groups, like individuals, need time to mull over the opportunity they have identified or crisis they have been presented with to consider various courses of action and test them mentally—particularly if the group members feel "stuck." Successful managers of innovation often deliberately interrupt a stalled group process so as to break mental wheel-spinning and force incubation. Indeed, the group need not be stalled to require managerial intervention. Surprisingly, a group that is hotly pursuing a tempting solution may need to be interrupted midgallop in order to pause for incubation. The invisible fermentation that occurs when group members reflect seems integral to the creative process.

Step 5: Convergence: Selecting Options

Achieving convergence is often the trickiest part for the manager. You have successfully fired up the group and ideas for solutions or avenues of exploration are as numerous as apples on a laden tree.

What to choose? How to reach consensus or at least acquiescence from group members? Group dynamics can vary in character from the coordinated moves of the Chicago Bulls or the Bolshoi Ballet, to the disorganized, acrimonious interactions of members of the U.S. Congress. The manager has multiple roles: referee and coach, lobbyist and statesman, conductor—even ringmaster of the circus at times. The skills needed for guiding convergence are very different from those for stimulating divergence. As we will see, the same people whose "off-the-wall" approach benefits the group or organization during creation of options can be perceived as a pain in the collective neck when the time comes to agree on action.

Beyond Convergence

Converging on an option does not mean, of course, that the fount of creativity is shut off at that moment. The selected alternative has to be assessed and implemented, and each of these group activities can stimulate new innovation opportunities. This is why the creative process is spaghetti-like rather than neatly structured as we have portrayed it here. Midcourse or even end assessments may throw the group back to a prior stage. Formal innovation projects, such as development of new products and services, often have elaborate gates and screens with clear-cut financial, strategic, and technical feasibility hurdles.[14] A group whose innovation fails to clear a hurdle will have to return to divergent thinking and elaborating new options. The discipline imposed by such evaluations is not antithetical to creativity—unless it forces premature closure or reflects an environment unable to tolerate any degree of risk.

Creative groups are understandably paranoid about financial Storm Troopers searching out and destroying infant innovations before they have a chance to grow. (If, as in one organization we know, every dollar spent on product innovation must return an *immediate,* provable three dollars in revenue, many creative ideas will not survive.) However, as we said earlier, creativity for managers has to result in something potentially useful, and usefulness depends on the needs and desires of the group or organization.

Moreover, the usefulness of the innovation resulting from the creative process often depends as much on the creativity expressed in its implementation as it does on the creativity harnessed in its inception. Implementation is almost never the four-lane highway envisioned when the group converged on an innovation concept. Sometimes it is more like a jungle path, to be reshaped or rerouted with machetes. In fact, any group members *implementing* an innovation will follow the same five steps in the process that they, or their predecessors, did in *creating* the innovation to begin with. No innovation enters a vacuum. There is always a need to creatively alter behavior, attitude, infrastructure, organizational norms— *something*.[15] As noted before, the output from one creative process usually stimulates the need for more creativity. Therefore, innovation opportunities abound not only in product development but in manufacturing, sales, and technical support, not only in service design but in operations, not only in the lesson plan but in its delivery in the classroom.

Road Map to the Book

Any manager responsible for innovation would greet the assertion that creative groups are easy to design or manage with a snort of derision. Challenging?—yes. Fun?—most of the time. Easy?—never. Ken Iverson, chairman of Nucor Steel says that when his company took on a new, extremely high-risk creative project, he slept like a baby—he woke up every two hours crying! The main reason that creative groups are hard to manage is that creativity is stimulated by diversity of perspectives. Chapter 2 describes why and how such diverse groups are designed—how the manager can compose a group to maximize its potential advantage over individual members. Chapter 3 describes how one manages that diversity to produce light rather than heat—to stimulate the divergent thinking that inspires a wide variety of options. Then, in Chapter 4 we turn to the challenge of selecting the best options through convergent thinking.

But understanding the steps in the process is not enough to enable managers to build a superior creative capability in their group. Processes flow within an environment—both physical and psychological. An ill-structured physical environment or badly misaligned psychological one can throw unreasonable barriers in the way of group creativity. In Chapters 5 and 6, we challenge managers to design a creative ecology—one in which knowledge flows like water and people are more likely to consider action than inertia.

To return to Jeri Davis . . .

To her own surprise, and the definite consternation of the managers and team leaders in the development meeting, Jeri voiced her thoughts out loud: "Twenty-one good people in the room," she said, "and we all think it's one man's job to provide the creative spark. What a waste. Instead of waiting for Kevin, let's think of ourselves as the creative group *that needs to come up with a new product idea. After all, we have tremendous experience in this room, and lots of brain power."*

"We weren't waiting for . . ." Stan started to protest, but his words drifted off and he glanced around the room nervously.

The rest of the group members just stared at Jeri like so many trained seals, awaiting further instructions. For a moment of panic, Jeri regretted her impulsive outburst. Despite her optimistic words, she had no idea if these people, intelligent as they were, could come up with something truly original.

Key Points

* Creative *people* can be important to an organization, but group creativity depends more on managing the creative *process* than on a few "creatives."

* The creative group process—developing novel, useful ideas—involves a series of steps, each of which is crucial for the final innovation. These steps include:

    * Preparation (selecting group members to maximize creativity)

    * Innovation opportunity (identifying the problem requiring creativity)

    * Generation of options (promoting divergent thinking)

    * Incubation (taking time to consider options)

    * Convergence on one option (moving from many options to one innovation)

* The creative process is not as linear as this list implies; within any step, a smaller cycle of some or all of the five steps can occur.

2

Creative Abrasion

"Surprise me," the CEO said to John, who had just assumed the newly created title of Director of Business Development. "You can hire six new people. Get some young blood in here and find us some new products—ones we can bring to market in, say, three or four years. Let's see what possibilities a creative group of people can identify in eighteen months." John was thrilled; what an opportunity at age thirty-four! He recruited three of the best financially minded, calculator-wielding MBAs he could find and set them to work sifting through the hundreds of possibilities in the research pipeline. With three job openings left, he pawed through dozens of impressive resumes before selecting three highly qualified young engineers. Eighteen months passed in a whirl of financial and technical analyses. To John's delight, the group members worked well together and became good friends. However, at the end, John was the one surprised—and out of a job. The group had rejected every idea in the pipeline on the basis of either financial or technical unfeasibility; they had identified not a single new idea worth pursuing. As John moved on to a different company, he was baffled: How could such a smart, well-qualified bunch of people have failed?

John's bewilderment may be shared by many managers who, presented with an innovation opportunity, hire or select intelligent people, throw them together—and expect creative miracles. Sometimes miracles do happen, but a randomly identified group of people is not likely to be especially creative. Managers are organizational designers. The composition of a group is as critical in creativity as it is for a choir. Can you imagine trying to sing Handel's *Messiah* with no baritones—or sopranos? Or perhaps worse, forcing half the baritones to try singing soprano? John's mistake was to hire six people whose formal training and personal thinking styles made them essentially a chorus of monotones. If you want creativity, you need intellectual diversity—the kind that leads to creative abrasion. We will talk later about how to manage the chaos that inevitably ensues from such intellectual ferment. First, why is diverse thinking useful? And how can you get that diversity?

Diversity and Creative Abrasion

You want your group to produce creative options. Where to start? Think for a minute about where those creative options are likely to come from. A modern-day Leonardo da Vinci might conceivably have all the different kinds of knowledge and skills needed, and if so, congratulations on landing him on your team. Short of that, you'll need to try something else to produce what scientists have called "requisite variety"—enough different options from which to choose that at least one is likely to be both novel and useful. This means that you must select group members who, in combination, will provide you with the requisite variety. Second, those group members must somehow be induced to *do something* with that variety, including debating—sometimes vigorously—the options. Group members will need to challenge one another and to welcome differences in intellectual background. Through this process, dubbed "creative abrasion" by Jerry Hirshberg,[1] the group can unleash the creative potential that is latent in a collection of unlike-minded individuals. Let's figure out first how to incorporate intellectual diversity into groups so we'll have the requisite variety, and then

CONFLICT AND INNOVATION

Kathleen Eisenhardt and her colleagues have examined the deter-
minants of performance and innovation in technology-based
companies. Some companies experienced virtually no conflict.
They tended to have little group diversity (e.g., consisting entirely
of engineers), created fewer options, and generally suffered in
effectiveness (e.g., time to market). Other companies had lots
of conflict, but it was frequently *personal* in nature. These companies were also relatively ineffective, because as their interactions (when they occurred) were divisive and angry. A final
group of companies was able to minimize interpersonal conflict
while effectively managing *substantive* conflict. "Such conflict
provides executives with a more inclusive range of information,
a deeper understanding of the issues, and a richer set of possible
solutions."[2] As a result, they emerged as the most productive
and innovative.[3]

turn to ways of promoting and managing the resultant creative
abrasion.

There are advantages to beginning with a *cognitively* heterogeneous group: people who are capable of providing a set of novel,
potentially useful alternatives. If you have heard the phrase, "think
outside the box" so often that just reading it makes you queasy,
consider this: Each individual has a wealth of idiosyncratic experience
and knowledge in his or her box. From that individual box, the
worldview is unique; problems and opportunities are seen through
a particular lens. Put enough *different* individual lenses together,
and you have a kaleidoscope of ideas. The great advantage of a
highly diverse group over an individual is that even if individual
members are still thinking within the boundaries of their own experience, *collectively* they will have numerous perspectives and those
perspectives can combine in wonderfully novel and useful ways.

Each person's preparation for the creative act—what is inside our individual box, if you will—consists of *what we know* (our expertise born of education, job experience, and practice) and *who we are* (our inherent abilities, cultural background, thinking-style preferences). One of the problems in composing a group whose members reflect a variety of perspectives is that none of us has our sources of deep expertise or our problem-solving approaches emblazoned on our foreheads. You can't be certain of what someone truly *knows* from reading a resume any more than you can detect someone's cognitive biases from visual cues. Of course these two sources of intellectual diversity overlap considerably, since our innate abilities and interests (as reinforced or inhibited by our cultures and family background) drive us to select certain educational and career experiences.

What We Know

Think of an expert you know—expert in the Spanish Civil War, in piano playing, in public speaking. How long do you think it took that individual to develop deep knowledge in the topic or activity? Five years? Seven? Research on expertise suggests at least ten. So even if we start young and delve deeply into a variety of subjects, most of us will not be able to claim expertise in more than a few fields. There have been a handful of twentieth-century "Renaissance men" who were remarkably fluent in different intellectual languages (e.g., Buckminster Fuller or Bertrand Russell). But most of us will need to create a diverse-brained group whose members collectively can draw on deep reservoirs of knowledge and create the collision of ideas underlying creative output.

The preparation that makes us into experts in our profession often starts in childhood. Imagine, for a moment, leafing back through the pages of personal history of two individuals. When they were toddlers, the little boy is over by the window, tugging on the long drapes, apparently fascinated by how the sun glints differently as the drapes billow. The girl is sitting on the floor intently lining up her blocks and building careful structures. When they are teens, she is hunched over a computer late in the night, giggling because she has just rigged her brother's computer to make the sound of a toilet flushing when he boots it—2,000 miles away at college. Our other teen is asleep, having spent the day sketching or experimenting with multilayered photographs, superimposing images on one another. By the time they are adults, their skill bases are totally different. That is, their *preparation* for creative activity is very different. Moreover, their natural interests lead them to seek different training and follow different careers, one in art, the other in computer science.

Any group creating application software will need them both— and need them to feed off each other's different perspectives. The artist becomes a screen designer, talented in expressing his ideas visually, through drawing and use of color. What does a line on the computer screen mean to him? It has depth, width, contour, and perhaps texture—symbols that trigger relationships in the mind of the viewer and guide a computer user by indicating a boundary or a starting point. Our computer scientist is mathematically gifted. To her, a line is an algorithm, an expression of distance between points. Both perspectives are critical to creating the lines on the screen. R. J. Berg, producer at the games company Electronic Arts, in California, says,

> The complexity of software development and production today is such that even important individual contributions are not enough for success in the product. People who are wonderfully skilled at engineering or art, music, production itself, need to understand how their contribution intersects with those of the other members on the team. Success in the product absolutely depends on the synthetic ability to see your own expertise for what it is and the contribution it can make in conjunction with everyone else's piece.[1]

How often do we hear our colleagues disparage one another with eloquent waving of the hands: "Oh, he's from marketing," or "She's

REMOVING BARRIERS TO COLLABORATION

At the Beckman Institutes for Advanced Science and Technology at the University of Illinois, Stanford, and Caltech, disciplinary barriers to collaboration have been effectively removed. Chemists, biologists, behavioral scientists, engineers, and computer scientists work together, united through a common pursuit of "MRTs"—main research themes, such as biological intelligence or human–computer intelligent interaction. Jiri Jonas, the Illinois institute's director, believes that the focus on MRTs has resulted in a large number of interdisciplinary research proposals. According to one theoretical scientist, "There is an expert in just about any area you need somewhere close at hand and they do collaborate."[5] William Brinkman, vice president for physical sciences research at Bell Labs, talks about the cross-disciplinary groups that come together because the labs' culture encourages collaboration: "We call it 'spontaneous teaming'—you see an interesting problem that another group is working on and you want to be part of it."[6]

an engineer"—as if such statements equate to: "They're barbarians"? The truth is, barbarians can refresh a different culture. "Hybrid vigor" is important in fields other than horticulture. Interval Research's David Liddle considers the infusion of different disciplinary perspectives into projects as the herbs that spice the dish. "There is no chance of doing good, new work . . . in a sterile environment where there are no herbs allowed."[7] The intermingling of intellectual bloodlines can reinvigorate routine activities and create a wealth of options not otherwise available for selection. At Fisher-Price, Marilyn Wilson-Hadid (marketing) and Peter Pook (product development), who have teamed up to argue their way to winning concepts, talk about the "magic" that occurs, the "energy that explodes" from their creative abrasion.[8]

Stimulating creative abrasion is difficult and scary because we are far more comfortable being with folks like us. We prefer our barbarians tame—either people from disciplines close enough to the dominant one to fit in comfortably, or ones whose utility is obvious to all. Yet groups noted for creativity expend much energy (and it does take energy) in identifying, recruiting, and hiring real outsiders—or at least getting them to visit for a while. The more radical the combinations of functions, the more likely the creative abrasion we want. Xerox Palo Alto Research Center (PARC) has birthed an enormous number of creative ideas—everything from the graphical interfaces so common on all types of computers today to the mice we use to navigate around the screen. Although Xerox has not profited from every one of the inventions, PARC has always been an exceedingly fertile ground for creativity. It attracts intelligent, creative individuals, of course, but management also deliberately fosters cross-disciplinary encounters. One of the more unusual programs is PARC Artist-in-Residence (PAIR), in which an artist pairs up with a computer scientist. The combination has yielded some unusual multimedia technology that neither could have conceived alone.

Or how about mixing anthropologists in with computer scientists? Introducing social scientists into a laboratory of "hard science" where physics and mathematics have traditionally ruled is not an intuitive way to encourage creativity. However, observations by anthropologists have deeply affected the design of copier machines. The traditional inclination of Xerox engineers was to make the machines "idiot-proof," that is, to try to anticipate everything that could possibly go wrong and design such problems out of the system. The anthropological approach was to observe and deeply understand the interaction of people with the machine, beyond ergonomic factors. The anthropologists filmed a couple of leading computer scientists trying to use a new machine to do their own copying. The footage of some very smart people becoming increasingly frustrated led to an important insight. Some trouble in using the machines was inevitable because of the increasing scope of tasks covered.

The solution was to help users manage troubleshooting through customized instructions in the display panel, linked to particular procedures, and visuals depicting the location of the problem. Clearing paper jams now took 20 seconds, compared to 28 minutes before the redesign.

Okay, so that's in a research setting—and in far-out California to boot. What if you need innovation from a group traditionally focused on rules, standards, and conformance?

At biotech Genzyme Corporation, Russell Herndon set up the corporate group dealing with regulation—a profession not exactly famous for creativity. Regulatory groups (called in some companies the "sales prevention group") are usually matched in temperament and outlook with the federal bureaucrats with whom they deal. After all, how much creativity do we want in the federal regulations governing drugs? Surprisingly, the answer is quite a bit, if we don't want to shackle biotechnology inventions with rules designed for medical devices. Genzyme products were new to the world, including Washington, D.C.—and for some, there was no extant regulatory path.

The usual job description for a position in regulatory affairs called for a law degree and focused on a very narrow segment of the process—labeling, for example. Herndon wanted his group members to take responsibility for a product from inception through market, and to influence regulation rather than mindlessly submit to government dictates. Although he did hire a couple of unusual lawyers, he also deliberately selected members for his regulatory group from nontraditional backgrounds such as liberal arts (English and History majors), straight biology, and chemical engineering so that they would bring new and diverse perspectives to the regulatory environment. This investment in building a creative group paid off in brainstorming sessions when the purely legal perspective was complemented by both highly scientific and nonscientific approaches.

One of the group's early innovation opportunities was the commercialization of Carticel, a process by which cartilage cells taken

---

DIVERSITY OF PROFESSIONAL BACKGROUND AND CREATIVITY

Laboratory research has consistently demonstrated that groups that are heterogeneous with respect to abilities, skills, and knowledge perform more creatively than homogeneous groups.[9] To verify this finding in work settings, Susan Jackson contacted the CEOs of 199 banks and asked them to assess the level of innovation in their organizations and to identify up to eight people who were key players in their top management teams. Jackson found a significant relationship between the extent of innovation (in products, programs, and services) and the degree of heterogeneity in "functional background" in the top management teams. That is, teams made up of people with different professional backgrounds and experiences were more creative than those made up largely of, say, marketing people.[10] In general, the empirical research has found that "when working on complex, nonroutine problems—a situation that presumably requires some degree of creativity—groups are more effective when composed of individuals with diverse types of skills, knowledge, abilities, and perspectives."[11]

---

from a patient are cultured, grown, and reimplanted in the knee. Since Carticel did not fit neatly into any of the regulated categories, no clear guidance existed on how to govern its application. Under the threat of having the process regulated as a standard biologic, which would have required ceasing production while the company ran prospective clinical studies, the Genzyme regulatory group came up with an innovative proposal that allowed Carticel to stay on the market in response to strong patient demand. As there were no immunological concerns and the tissue came from the same person receiving it back, Genzyme argued the procedure should be viewed more as a practice of medicine. However, the group suggested that the Food and Drug Administration (FDA) license the facility in which the cells were grown, and use historical data and surrogate markers (indicators of health benefits) to justify their approval. This novel proposal accomplished two major objectives at once: it protected Carticel from inappropriate regulation and erected a barrier to competitors.[12] It's unlikely that a traditional regulatory group would have been so creative.

Who We Are

We partially define ourselves by what we see in the mirror. Our mirror reports on our gender, our ethnicity, our age. Unfortunately, visible cues of difference among group members (gender, race, age) frequently merely add abrasion without creativity. So much depends on how differences are handled—and what differences we are talking about. But who we are is more than what people see when they first glance at us across a conference table. The kind of culture and family in which we have been raised, the ways our genes have predisposed us to think, and our distinctive personalities all shape the lens through which we see the world.

Cultural Diversity When we think of cultural differences, we are mostly aware of the dangers—violating local taboos can lose you anything from a business deal to a piece of your anatomy. If you are in Thailand, don't point the sole of your foot at peoples' heads. If you are in a fundamentalist Muslim country, don't touch the opposite sex—even on the hand. And you have probably heard of some egregious, if humorous, stories about miscommunication. How about the baby food company that pictured a smiling tot on their label? In some developing nations, the company discovered, only pictures of *contents* were traditionally portrayed on food jars. Consumers in those countries were understandably reluctant to buy jars that appeared to advertise cannibalism. An Asian company wanting to introduce a locally popular fermented cow's milk drink into the U.S. market started off on the wrong hoof when they named the drink "Calpis." (Think about it.) And for a car selling into a Spanish-

"DEMOGRAPHIC" DIVERSITY AND CREATIVITY

The experimental evidence strongly suggests that people prefer to associate, interact, and work with those who are similar to them. The "similarity-attraction" effect has been demonstrated in literally hundreds of studies.[13] People seem remarkably willing to seize upon virtually any basis for similarity, including age, gender, or race. How does this play out in terms of group process and creativity? *Age diversity* leads to low levels of group cohesiveness or integration, which in turn lead to high turnover. *Mixed-sex groups* have been found to be somewhat (although not statistically significantly) more creative than single-sex groups,[14] although, again, turnover tends to be high. Results for *mixed-race groups* do not form a coherent pattern. However, a recent study found that within an organization widely viewed as supporting diversity, creativity in mixed-race groups was high, particularly for mixed white–Asian groups. The results were attributed to a strong identification with the group task, which prevented the formation of same-race cliques.[15]

speaking culture, the name "Nova" ("No Go") is literally a non-starter. Panasonic committed an infamous gaffe in its 1996 worldwide ad campaign for its Japanese Web Browser, which featured Woody Woodpecker. The accompanying slogan was "Touch Woody—The Internet Pecker."

Cross-cultural misunderstandings go beyond communication; decisions in different cultures may rest on completely different assumptions. Western architects working in Asia, where different rules of design apply, soon discover that one does not place a stairway to the upstairs directly opposite the front door because this configuration invites Bad Luck to rush right into the family quarters.

Despite the possibility of cross-cultural misunderstandings, the mingling of cultural differences can also aid creativity. Commenting

CULTURAL FACTORS IN INNOVATION

In his study of innovation during and immediately after World War II, J. F. O. McAllister contrasted British and Nazi science efforts. "German war science was hierarchical and compartmentalised, discouraging free-wheeling interchange between scientists and soldiers. Hence while German radar was beautifully engineered, achieving signal stability 'that was better than that of the best instruments that [Britain] had available,' the German method of displaying aircraft position was awkward for air defence controllers to use."[16]

Geert Hofstede's classic study of IBM employees in forty countries illustrates the importance of culture on work-related values and attitudes. Child rearing and other socialization practices create a "collective mental programming" that sets us apart from our counterparts in other countries. Hofstede considers four primary dimensions along which cultures differentiate us: (1) power distance (how much people accept as natural and permanent the unequal distribution of power and influence), (2) individualism–collectivism (people viewing their selves and immediate families as sources of loyalty, as opposed to thinking in terms of larger work and societal units); (3) uncertainty avoidance (how much

on the innovation that flourished in fifth-century B.C. Greece, fifteenth-century Florence and eighteenth-century Paris, Csikszentmihalyi has noted, "centers of creativity tend to be at the intersection of different cultures, where beliefs, lifestyles and knowledge mingle and allow individuals to see new combinations of ideas with greater ease."[19] Nissan Design International (NDI) designers from California presenting their Japanese counterparts with the design for the Infiniti J-30 found that they had omitted a very important consideration— what the "face" of the car, viewed from the front, looked like. A downturned grill ("frowning mouth" as the Japanese characterized

people desire the reduction of ambiguity); and (4) masculinity–
femininity (strength of traditional gender roles). Hofstede's analysis clusters the forty countries in terms of how similar they
are to one another along these dimensions. Knowing, for example,
that your team members are from Denmark, the United Kingdom,
Belgium, and France, suggests that the former two might welcome
ambiguity, while the latter two would likely wish to avoid
uncertainty. This, in turn, might imply that your Danish and British
colleagues would be more interested in open-ended strategic
problems, while the Belgian and French members would be more
comfortable with operational problems.

Of course, as Hofstede takes pains to point out, it would be
a mistake to rely on group averages to characterize individuals,
but group trends can be useful in gaining insight into how different
people select and deal with problems.[17] While asserting the importance of cultural differences, Fons Trompenaars and Charles
Hampden-Turner issue a similar warning against stereotyping. They
see cultural differences as overlapping bell curves, in which each
culture has the full range of behaviors, but the *most predictable*
behavior will be different for the two.[18]

it) and narrow rectangular headlights ("squinty eyes" according to
the Japanese) gave the car an unhappy, even rude appearance! The
U.S.–based designers were less sensitive to this perspective because
they tended to follow their cultural predilection for viewing the car
from the side more than from the front. By slightly cheering up the
face of their car, the NDI designers felt they moved the design to
a higher level of cultural intelligence.[20] We also have the Japanese
to thank for a design adjustment to the toilet seats in the next Boeing
airplane. Sensitive to embarrassing others, the Japanese suggested
that hydraulics could eliminate the harsh sound of the seat slapping

down, an unnecessarily public communication of personal activities to people awaiting their turn outside the toilet.

Guido Arnout, CEO of CoWare, a company with corporate headquarters in Santa Clara, California and R&D in Belgium, is keenly aware of the need for cultural sensitivity. "By creating cultural diversity, you open employees' scope, make them sensitive to the fact that the world is *one* world. It is natural in the U.S. to think of the Far East as connected to U.S. markets and products—not so natural in Europe, where people tend to feel connected only to those countries on their borders (if at all). You can't grow a world-class company by staying in one ethnic culture."[21]

How did Tommy Hilfiger—a forty-five–year-old white man from Connecticut, designing prep-school clothes—become the designer of choice for urban black America? A writer in search of the answer came up with several hypotheses, including endorsement by Grand Puba, a hip-hop artist. The writer also had lunch with one of Hilfiger's designers, who was

> a twenty-six–year-old named Ulrich (Ubi) Simpson, who has a Puerto Rican mother and a Dutch-Venezuelan father, plays lacrosse, snowboards, surfs the long board, goes to hip-hop concerts, listens to Jungle, Edith Piaf, opera, rap, and Metallica and has working with him on his design team a twenty-seven–year-old black guy from Montclair [New Jersey] with dreadlocks, a twenty-two–year-old South Asian guy from Fiji, and a twenty-one–year-old white graffiti artist from Queens [New York]. That's when it occurred to me that maybe the reason Tommy Hilfiger can make white culture cool to black culture is that he has people working for him who are cool in both cultures simultaneously.[22]

As these examples illustrate, our cultures imprint preferences and perspectives. Show a cross-cultural group of consumers different design concepts, and it is likely that the Japanese will talk first about shape in describing objects, and only later about color, whereas

Europeans will do the reverse—or at least that was the experience of one group of consultants. To draw from a very different field, a medical professional remarked that the U.S. approach to inconvenient ailments was "just cut it out." (He noted the high number of cesarean sections and gallbladder operations.) The European approach he characterized as more systemic and conservative, and the Asian as including mind and body interactions more. A combination of the best from all three cultures, he believed, would result in the best possible treatment. Are these stereotypes? Yes—and subject to the usual dangers. Clearly not every U.S. doctor is a knife-wielding cowboy, and many are very sensitive to the effects of the mind, if not necessarily believers in the importance of *ch'i*, or spirit, in healing. The point is that the clash of cultures can be creative.

Think about the last time you were at a company meeting, a convention, or a social gathering with different cultures represented in the room. Did you view that time as an opportunity to explore, to identify some new perspectives, to learn? Or did you avoid talking about mutual problems for fear of controversy? (Or because it is hard work to speak slowly and really listen to someone with a pronounced accent?) Toy maker Fisher-Price has recently started a "Fisher-Price College in Reverse." After spending a couple of days in the traditional explanations of corporate history, identity, and culture to new hires (the usual "college" format), the "instructors" turn the tables on their "students" and ask to be taught about what the toy business is like in the countries outside the United States. What do East Aurora, New York employees learn from such sessions with their new European and Asian colleagues? Such things as that Japanese consumers want every toy to have an educational component, from baby rattles to pirate ships. Exchanges with their Milan, Italy contract design house have stimulated important product innovations for Fisher-Price. The Italian designers are less experienced in designing for the preschool market, while the U.S. designers are less exposed to European trends. The Europeans altered a toy western frontier fort they were building when the U.S. designers suggested a small but money-saving change. One of the actions a tot could instigate was rolling barrels out of the fort on a chute. The European zigzag path for the barrel was sophisticated and fun to watch, but expensive and relatively slow for children of this age. American counterparts suggested replacing the zigzag path with a straight chute that would give the young child immediate satisfaction—and would save three dollars on production. The Europeans, in turn, suggested a significant addition to a line of toys for infants when they emphasized the popularity of velour and striking colors over pastel-colored corduroy and gingham-covered playthings.[23]

So diversity based on culture *may* engender useful disagreement and alternative perspectives. However, individuals from a particular subset of society, be that based on gender, race, or nationality, may not represent the stereotype of that group. This cuts both ways: people who appear very different can be intellectual twins. We have a photograph of a heavily bearded, turbaned Sikh from India standing beside a woman from Minnesota—laughing together about the fact that their scores on a diagnostic instrument measuring intellectual preferences were identical. Moreover, people who look alike can have very different skills and approaches to problem solving. So adding an Asian American female or an African American gay man to your group may add diversity—but not *necessarily* the type we are talking about. (Of course, there can be other important reasons for "balancing" the group's membership.) The major point is that you can't judge the intellectual diversity of your group by *looking* at the members.

Yet the human tendency seems to be to aggregate upward to the highest level of abstraction—or the most visible difference. Personality differences we may attribute to culture or nationality. When an individual displays some behavior that is distinctive enough to attract our conscious attention, we may think, "That's because he's French," even if the real reason that his behavior is "different" is that he is more of an extrovert. We see gender when we might more reasonably notice profession. "Isn't that typical of a woman" may more accurately describe the fact that she's an artist, and a male artist would likely behave the same. The more sophisticated we are about all the different possible sources of abrasion, the more we can address them appropriately and include—or exclude—them in our groups. Judgments about intellectual diversity can be made only by a careful assessment of peoples' background, experience, and, as explored in the next section, their thinking styles.

Thinking-Style Preferences Ever wondered why an intelligent, well-meaning, and respected colleague annoys you almost any time that you work with him or her? Maybe you think this individual is always too deep into the details to understand the big picture—all trees and no forest. Or perhaps the opposite is true: he seems to be flying over a problem at 30,000 feet and ignoring critical data, perhaps labeling decisions as "strategic" because—from your point of view—he doesn't have the detailed information to back up the decision. And surely you have been in meetings where some of the participants sit on the edges of their chairs, pressuring for closure, with frequent glances at the clock and pointed comments about schedule, whereas others are clamoring for more information before a decision can be made—or, even more extreme, asking to revisit a decision made yesterday. These two groups of people can drive each other crazy! A prolific source of creative abrasion is the natural differences that occur among people in their preferred ways of thinking—problem solving, information processing, selection, and evaluation of data.

Take a moment to do a simple physical exercise. Cross your arms across your chest, in your normal posture—one arm over the other. (Even if you are on a plane, your companions won't think you odd!) After you have them solidly crossed, now cross them the other way, so that the arm that was underneath is now on top. How does that feel? Awkward? Did you have to stop and think about how to do it? Here is another exercise. (You will learn more if you actually do these rather than just read about them—come on, take a risk.) Take out a pen or pencil and write your first name down. Okay? Now, put the pen in your other hand and do it again. (If you are in public, you probably won't do this because it embarrasses you.) How did that feel? Worse than awkward, right? Maybe you had to move your whole arm to write. Your signature is probably two to four times bigger than usual! Why does this feel so much worse than just crossing your arms the opposite way from usual? What people usually say is: "It was much harder—this takes skill." "The signature looks stupid." "Takes me back to age eight." Writing with your nondominant hand is difficult because you have a natural preference for the other hand, reinforced by years of practice and experience. Perhaps most critically, your ego is involved in the production of your signature—you feel silly that the output is so visibly inferior.

Just as you have strong and weak preferences for body movements, you also have inborn *thinking-style preferences*, as "hardwired" as left- or right-handedness, reinforced by years of practice in your chosen profession and the way you interact with others in your private life. Some of these preferences are very strong and unlikely to be altered by circumstances. Others are relatively weak— even weaker than your arm-crossing preference. In choosing between two aspects of thinking styles we can be mentally ambidextrous (i.e., relatively indifferent between the two), but for other aspects, a switch is as difficult as trying to write with our nondominant hand. Since most of us don't spend much time or effort in analyzing why we approach problems the way we do or, for that matter, why others do so differently, we cannot identify our thinking preferences without systematic examination. However, there are dozens of diagnostics that can help people understand their own preferences. The most widely used such diagnostic is the Myers-Briggs Type Indicator, but there are many others.[24]

In the early-twentieth century, psychologist Carl Jung discovered that people had preferences in three aspects of their thinking styles: Sensing versus Intuition, Thinking versus Feeling, and Extroversion versus Introversion. Later researchers added a fourth discriminator: Judging versus Perceiving. The diagnostics based on Jung's work allow us systematically to reenact with pencil and paper our daily, often unconscious behavioral choices, and our responses to questions reveal patterns that identify our strong and weak preferences. If you are asked to fill out such a diagnostic—relax. It reveals no deep, dark secrets about your personality. But it can be quite useful, for example, in helping you recognize when you need to seek complementary preferences from partners and fellow team members, or in order to balance your own biases and strengths, or to design more cognitive variability into your groups.

Think back to the situation described at the beginning of this chapter. John limited himself by hiring people who all approached problems from similar perspectives. Although three were from financial backgrounds and three were engineers, all six preferred essentially "left-brained" tools and approaches. They all wanted lots of data, relied on solid analysis as a basis of reasoning, sought a definitive decision, and were temperamentally unwilling to revisit each other's decisions. Their analysis paralysis was predictable, given that no one in the group was inclined to seek out relatively imprecise but novel product concepts or talk to people outside their usual customer base.

The activities of our brains aren't really neatly divided between left and right cortexes, as once was thought. Nature is far more sophisticated—complex and messier. However, the left-brain, right-brain distinction is useful metaphorically because it helps us understand the complementary nature of thinking styles. The left-brained approach tends toward the highly detailed, analytical, and logical, whereas the right-brained tends toward more intuitive, emotion- and values-based reasoning. Any group of individuals focused on creativity and innovation rather than routines and efficiency profits from a mixture of thinking styles. When Jerry Hirshberg first set up the Nissan Design International studios in San Diego, he challenged himself to design the organization for creativity. He resisted the temptation to select and retain only people in his own image—highly intuitive, big-picture, visually oriented right-brained individuals. Instead, he also deliberately hired a few left-brained individuals who sought structure and always questioned "why" before proceeding. Initially, however, these individuals annoyed him; they seemed to be "anticreative" and threatened by novelty. However, he soon came to realize that he was wrong in that assessment: "They simply come to the table with a different set of preparations and expectations."[25] He needed such individuals to complement his own inclination to leap first and ask why and how later. In thinking-style diagnostics, Hirshberg found that he was "somebody who is likely to leap off a cliff with a joyous intuition and halfway down, scream up to the rest of the group, 'Hey, let's build a parachute—*now!*' And thank God, the [left-brained] people were there. I might have told them beforehand that I was having this impulse, and I thought we were going to jump off a cliff tomorrow morning about seven. If I did that, they would say 'thank you, Jerry,' and they would go home that night and think about it and come in with some ideas about how to make it work."[26]

What Hirshberg discovered was the opposite of John's experience—whereas John needed a few right-brainers to help him put aside the analysis for the moment in favor of unfettered exploration, Hirshberg needed a few left-brainers to help him consider the implementation of his bright ideas before he committed to them. Hirshberg came to think of this as *creative abrasion*—and to encourage it. Under his leadership, Nissan Design International hired designers in complementary *pairs*—as unlike as possible "so we keep from becoming a harmonious choir, all singing the same tune." So, for example, they hired a "breathtakingly pure artist who is passionate about colors" the same year that they hired a "Bauhaus, Teutonic, rational, clear-headed" designer with "a function-form orientation," who is "passionate about clarity and logic."[27] Such a managerial practice not only invited disparity but also virtually guaranteed that there would be conflict. This intellectual conflict Hirshberg willingly tolerated, believing that if the energy thus generated were channeled correctly into creativity instead of into anger, it would be a power plant of innovation.[28]

People who see the world differently, require different kinds of information, and have different levels of tolerance for ambiguity do annoy each other. The artist who has spent a lifetime thinking visually processes information differently from the accountant who has immersed herself in data. And recall that these choices of profession were likely based on a very early preference for certain kinds of problem solving. When you see the conflict of different preferences, you may think that there is an unavoidable "personality clash." Sure, such clashes do occur—and they may be based on antagonisms having little or nothing to do with thinking styles (e.g., two big egos). But identifying those clashes that *do* originate in different thinking-style preferences can transform conflict into opportunity for creative interaction. We should be no more irritated by someone who asks for more data when we have been sketching out the big picture, or someone who insists on suggesting far-out scenarios when we are intent on the details at hand, than we are by an accidental elbow jostling at a dinner party because we are right-handed and seated next to a left-handed guest. The reasons the physical jostling is less offensive than the mental are likely twofold: we know the guest next to us cannot help his preference any more than we can. Moreover, there is no ego involvement in which hand holds the fork! It therefore helps to understand that thinking-style preferences are similarly natural and not deliberate.

It helps even more if we can regard the resulting abrasion as an opportunity for a better solution than would have evolved from a comfortable process of compatible styles. When Fisher-Price moved to a cross-functional team structure, a thinking-styles preference diagnostic was part of the training. Director of Marketing Lisa Mancuso found understanding others' preferences enlightening. "One man on the team had been driving me nuts," she said. "He wanted to give me every little detail about why a schedule had slipped or what was going on in the factory—and all I wanted was the bottom line. [After taking the diagnostic] it turned out that he had thought me really rude because I wasn't interested in all the details, and just wanted him to get to the point. It really helped us communicate to understand that we just approached things differently."[29]

Recognizing thinking-style preferences also allows complementary staffing. Paul Horn, senior vice president and director of IBM

CREATIVITY AS A BALANCING ACT

Psychologist Robert Sternberg considers creativity a balance among three types of intelligence: creative, analytical, and practical. *Creative intelligence* is the ability to generate new and unusual ideas. *Analytical intelligence* is the ability to analyze those ideas and make decisions based on that analysis. *Practical intelligence* is the ability to see the connections between the ideas and real-life situations. It is certainly possible—but unusual—that one person might excel in two or even all three types of intelligence. More typically, a "creative" person would shine in only one. So a group composed exclusively of "creative" types would likely excel in coming up with lots of ideas but be hopeless in separating the good ideas from the worthless or in seeing practical implications of their creativity. And a group that also has members capable of elaborating novel ideas and others who can explore their applications will be more than a collection of creative individuals—it will be a creative *group*.[30]

Research, advises: "Pair your visionaries with implementers. The obvious fact here is that an idea won't succeed unless it is implemented. By pairing implementers with visionaries from the outset of the process, you reap two rewards: first, you get an end product, and second, implementers learn the craft of vision and visionaries learn the craft of implementing, which makes your team more valuable. Both skills need to be recognized, cultivated, and rewarded."[31] Carol Snyder, director of product design at Fisher-Price, makes a similar observation.

> "If I could compose a creative group from scratch," she says, "I would want three different kinds of people: ones that are really, really good at providing the seed of an idea, but get totally bored beyond the seed; some who love to

LOCATING CREATIVE ABRASION

At what level of the organization should creative abrasion be fostered? The easy answer is "everywhere." But this ignores the nature of the creativity process, in which divergence and convergence may depend on different abilities. Some managers, or groups of managers, may excel in their positions not because they are highly creative but because they are excellent promoters of creativity in those who report to them. Creative abrasion is more essential in fostering divergence, while the smooth interpersonal relations that characterize a homogeneous group facilitate convergence. In a study of forty-seven firms across eleven manufacturing industries, Sylvia Flatt found that *homo*geneity in length of service in the top management team (the CEO and direct reports) combined with *hetero*geneity in the vice presidential and senior management team led to highest creativity (number of patents awarded annually). The latter team was the source of new ideas and creative alternatives (divergence), and the CEO's team chose wisely among those (convergence).[32]

take the seed and build on it, once the idea is out there—massage it, make it into something; and finally, the ones who are really good at getting the idea through the system. That takes as much creative thinking as coming up with the idea in the first place.[33]

Designing Creative Abrasion into Your Group

There are many ways to introduce divergent thinking into your group, ranging from virtually cost-less to highly expensive, and there are degrees of creative abrasion, from mild to Tabasco-hot. The objective is to increase the level of stimulation and variety, to multiply the number of newcomer "dumb" questions that can stump your smartest people—and lead to innovative thinking. But let us not equate creative abrasion with simple conflict. The idea is not, of course, just to irritate group members. Personal conflict or basic incompatibilities over interpersonal styles can poison a group. Rather, you want to design appropriate cultural, disciplinary and thinking style diversity into groups, and then manage effectively the resulting abrasion for creativity.

Hire People Who Are "Not Like Us"

Look around you. How did recent hires hit the organizational radar screen? Did they submit resumes to a human resources department that is skilled at selecting people who "fit"? Top schools? Best experience base? Or perhaps they were identified by friends or relatives in the organization. Whatever your hiring practice, you are unlikely to interview, much less hire, someone who is very different in educational or cultural background unless you make a concerted effort to do so. The body politic rejects foreign transplants. If your hiring goes through the usual channels, your future workers will inevitably be cast in the image of those who have made your organization successful in the past.[34] And "different" people, whose abrasion could generate creative light, will head elsewhere. The hotshot computer programmer heads for Microsoft. A whiz at Finance? Destination: Wall Street.

So what, you say? Well, as long as you expect the world to stay pretty much the same, no problem. However, suppose you suspect environmental changes may build superhighways over your prior roads to success. Maybe the Internet will outdate your distribution system. Perhaps an aging population means taking aim at a different audience. Possibly the fact that consumers are increasingly sophisticated about "spin" changes your communication strategy. If you believe that some radical change is inevitable, you want to inject into the organization people whose preparation for creative activity (i.e., their deep knowledge bases) differs from the usual. If you wish to attract a top-notch recruit from an educational background not usually associated with your company, you will have to work at it.

Unless you are in the military, you probably do not have an *official* "dress code," but employees in your organization are accustomed to certain personal profiles and manners of speech and dress. (Ever think of wearing a brightly colored floral sports shirt to an important business meeting? See what we mean?) People who look different or act differently make us uncomfortable. The usual hiring channels screen out people whose cultural backgrounds differ. Picture this: a woman with a tongue stud and with hair striped with various shades of red applies for a position as accountant at your organization. Will she get hired? Probably not, but she was at *Wired*, the ultramodern journal that follows the Internet world. Unusual haircuts and pierced body parts are also the uniform at many entertainment-related companies where a man sporting a conservative suit and close-cropped hair would be the eccentric.

Hiring people who are very different from the norm does not guarantee creative output—especially people who just *look* different. As we said earlier, you can't always judge the book from the cover, the corporation from the Web page. To the relief of most of us, our appearances are not an infallible guide. However, hiring *everyone* with the same background and preparation bounds the employee pool in predictable ways—and therefore limits the types of creative abrasion likely to occur.

But wait, you say. What about the highly successful, even creative companies that select employees precisely because they *are* alike? Federal Express looks for "risk taking and courage of conviction." Disney wants people with an "up personality."[35] What Southwest Airlines seeks "first and foremost, is a sense of humor," according to CEO Herb Kelleher. "Then we are looking for people who have to excel to satisfy themselves and who work well in a collegial environment. . . . We hire attitudes."[36] Two points: First, these companies are looking for common personality factors that may be found in a wide variety of *intellectually diverse* people. Optimism (being "up"), for instance, isn't limited to detail-oriented people or big-picture folks, to accountants or to artists. Second, as we will discuss in Chapters 4 and 6 in some detail, homogeneity in the sense of sharing the organization's vision, goals, and values can aid creativity.

Invite Alien Visits and Perspectives

Perhaps, you say, after the "downsizing, right-sizing" era, you aren't hiring—period. That doesn't let you off the hook for inviting stimulation into the group. Even if you can't hire someone, you can bring people in on a temporary basis. Professors and employees from other companies take sabbaticals. Students and others are often willing to serve as paid or unpaid interns. Local colleges may have field-based studies or co-op programs through which students can work for a time in your organization and hold a useful mirror up to your operations for reflection. Fisher-Price finds room for ten or more "co-op" design-school students every year. Notes Senior Vice President Kevin Curran, "Not only are they a big help to designers and bring a fresh perspective, but we get to look them over as prospective hires."[37] At Integrated Systems Design Center (ISDC) in San Diego, cofounder Marco Thompson has taken the concept of internships a step further. "Each one teach one" is one of seven principles in the corporate "mantra." At any given time, ISDC has ten to fifteen interns among its 120 employees. Originally conceived to ensure that the company had a stream of well-trained engineers available for hiring, the internship program has become a profit center, as the students have proven so productive that their time can be billed to clients. The program succeeds because successful mentoring is an important element in employee performance reviews. Engineers and project managers are judged by how well their interns do. "No one can become a manager at any level in this company," says Thompson "unless you have proved yourself as a mentor."[38] ISDC also imports another kind of "alien": the customer's own engineers, who work on product development teams. For example, when ISDC was designing a set-top box for Mitsubishi, six of the twenty-person team were from Japan.

Consultants are another, if more expensive, option. The point is to introduce alien perspectives—people who will challenge the group by asking "dumb" questions and making ingenuous observations. A newly appointed director to the board of a company providing chickens to supermarkets asked a naive question: "What is fresh?" that provoked an industry review of the common practice of labeling frozen chickens "fresh."

And at many companies, returning "alumni" can bring with them the perspectives they learned from working at other organizations. American Management Systems keeps in touch with employees who have left because often the best return to the fold. At Gensler, the international architectural design and planning firm, a number of designers have a boomerang hanging on their wall. CEO Arthur Gensler values the fact that creative designers sometimes want to leave the firm to try their luck elsewhere. But they are always welcome to return, and the gift of a boomerang symbolizes their homecoming. The return rate of 12 percent is one of the highest in the field.[39]

The Manager and Creative Abrasion

If you have designed your group or organization with some of the suggestions above in mind, you have diversity. Plenty of it. And probably abrasion too. Now, let us consider the implications of creative abrasion for your personal management style.

Know Thyself

The starting point for all management is understanding yourself, and managing creativity is no exception. Your thinking style affects your ability to lead your group in creativity as surely as your vision affects your ability to walk. As the section above on thinking-style preferences indicates, each of us is hard-wired and highly proficient in some modes of thinking and relatively uncomfortable with others. Yet, if we are to spark innovation, we need the intellectual disagreement that raises options. If you are an enthusiastic, spontaneous, shoot-from-the-hip person, you *need* a cautious, detail-oriented person to ask the "how" questions—even if you choose to move ahead without answering them all. If you love protocol and the proven solution, you *need* that reckless think-from-the-gut individual who will push you to consider options that have never been tried before— even if you decide that none of them is feasible. So you need to know what your own biases are. Because so many of our biases are unconscious, the exercise of systematically exploring our preferences, using some reliable diagnostic such as the Myers-Briggs Type Indicator mentioned above, helps us understand how we make decisions. John (in our opening anecdote) loved working with highly analytical thinkers. "Right-brainers" gave him mental hives. Naturally (but unconsciously) he created a cozy, homogeneous, intelligent—but for his purposes, ineffective—group. Had he understood his own biases, he might have brought in some aliens, suffered the discomfort, and had better results.

Protect the Aliens

Suppose you have identified and recruited a useful "alien" who can challenge the group's prevailing world view. Any alien has to live with rules, reward systems, and most important, social norms that evolved to support *us*—that may be totally inappropriate for the alien. So your job does not end with hiring. If your new hire begins to feel as isolated and far from home as E.T., he or she is likely to "phone home" and leave unless you provide good reasons to stay. We humans are social animals, and we do not like being ostracized. The wise manager takes a number of measures to retain the alien perspective.

No Alien Should Have to Stand Alone If you are going to bring a data-driven individual into a big-picture group, or an artist in with engineers, or a hip youngster in with middle-aged traditionalists, try to bring in more than one frame-breaker—more than one very different person, even if the second or third individual differs along

---

THE IMPORTANCE OF ALLIES

In his classic study of conformity, Solomon Asch brought college students into a laboratory ostensibly for a study of "the visual perception of lines." A standard line was shown, along with three comparison lines, one of which was the same length as the standard; the other two were obviously different. Unknown to the naive subject, the six other students were experimental confederates who had earlier been instructed to respond incorrectly on certain trials. The subject would face a situation in which his eyes told him one thing, but the weight of six other judgments told him something entirely different. On these critical trials, most subjects went along with the erroneous judgment of their peers at least some of the time. However, when *one* of the confederates gave the objectively correct answer, while all of the others gave the incorrect answer, conformity was reduced nearly to zero. Just having that one ally was of crucial importance in resisting pressures to conform.[40]

---

alternative characteristics from the first. Aliens need some critical mass before they are effective.

Why the Alien Is There The alien's utility may be obvious to you and totally obscure to the other members of the group. A couple of psychologists invited to join a computer science group made the best of it by calling themselves "the psychos," emphasizing both their differences and reminding the group of why they were there—using humor to make both points. You may also need to prepare the aliens, inoculating them against the discouragement of initial rejection. The group may be pretty hostile—or may merely ignore them.

Make Sure the Alien Succeeds You were probably with us until that last point. Make sure the alien succeeds, you ask? How and why

HELPING ALIENS SUCCEED BY PREPARING THEM FOR REJECTION

During the Vietnam War, many men newly inducted into a combat unit were treated with hostility and derision by the veterans. The recruit felt stupid and inadequate, and psychiatric casualties among the new men were common. The psychiatrists named the effect the "FNG syndrome" (for the veterans' "fucking new guy" epithet). Rather than trying to treat these men after the fact, they intervened preemptively, preparing the new men for the hostility by helping them anticipate the reaction as being directed against the "FNG" rather than against them personally. "They don't hate you, they hate the FNG."[41]

should I do that? Ultimately, of course, it is up to the alien to succeed. However, it is important to ensure some small demonstrations of usefulness early in this individual's experience with your group. For example, some prominent male university professors in a university decided to launch a new executive education program in engineering management. They asked a younger female colleague whose background was in the social sciences to direct it. They had a number of reasons for wanting this alien in their midst—not the least of which was that they believed the program would be more innovative if they could include her different perspective. However, she was understandably concerned about the potential for failure. "Don't worry," they said. "We will make sure this succeeds." They carried through on their promise by personally recruiting excellent participants for the first run-through and agreeing to teach in it themselves so that the program would benefit from their prominence and reputation. They reviewed the curriculum to make sure that it would satisfy the engineering requirements, and encouraged the inclusion of social science materials about which their colleague was an expert. Once the program was successfully launched, they did not have to expend more energy helping the alien; she was integrated and productive.

The Limits of Heterogeneity

Imagine a group in which everyone is so different that they literally have no common language for communication. Members can be so grounded in their disciplines, cultures, or thinking styles that they refuse to listen to anyone else. As a result, creative abrasion is never ignited, and instead the group resorts to time-saving techniques such as voting and splitting the difference.

Managers of creative groups interviewed emphasized the need to select group members who are willing to "blur the boundaries," that is, those who are not territorial about their specialized knowledge and are not afraid to venture onto the intellectual turf of others. In fact, members of creative teams often emphasized that it was difficult to assign authorship for innovative ideas because everyone trampled down disciplinary boundaries in their eagerness to contribute. And more than one manager removed a team member who would not, or could not, leave his intellectual island for the good of the group. Therefore, just throwing different kinds of people together and expecting wonderful, creative results is unlikely. To manage a diverse group effectively requires some special skills that we will discuss in subsequent chapters.

To return to John...

To his relief, John did not have much difficulty finding another job. Since his whole group had been dissolved, managers in other companies interpreted his departure as part of downsizing. His former title as Manager of Business Development landed him a similar position in a new company. He recognized that at least part of his problem at his old job was that group members used very similar approaches to scrutinize ideas and all the same sources to identify potential product concepts. Determined not to make the same mistake, he added to his fledgling group of eight engineers at the new company, five people with very different backgrounds—two industrial designers, a market researcher, an industry expert, and an anthropologist who had worked on a number of highly successful consumer product lines. While all of them had some experience in new product development, they had all worked on different aspects. He knew a couple of them were going to annoy him personally because they were big-picture, idea people who were unlikely to present ideas as thoroughly backed with data as he would want. In fact, they sounded downright "touchy-feely." But he had worked with a very homogeneous, personally comfortable group before and look where it had gotten him! Better to have a group that would challenge him and each other. One thing he was sure of—the group meetings were going to be lively.

Key Points

* Creative groups need people who bring different, useful perspectives to the creative task. Selecting people with different *deep knowledge* as well as different *culture* and *thinking styles* provides intellectual diversity.

* Group diversity and the creative abrasion that results are most important when divergent thinking is needed.

* Selecting diverse group members is not the only way to promote creative abrasion. Visits to "aliens" and bringing in aliens with different perspectives are also crucial.

* Managing creative groups is particularly challenging because we want the benefits of *creative abrasion*—the clash of ideas—while avoiding *interpersonal abrasion*—the clash of people.

* Creative abrasion is most likely to flourish when managers understand their own thinking styles and ensure that aliens are protected and succeed.

* Creative groups select experts who can "blur the boundaries" of their disciplines.

3

Generating Creative Options

"I don't need to tell you how important this distance learning contract is," said Hazel as she opened the meeting. "If we get to design the ad campaign, we'll have a whole new line of business. That's why I've put our very best people on this team—including Fred from Sales and Tom—even though he's moved to our financial services account. I know some of you were a bit surprised at my bringing them in, but we needed a variety of backgrounds and knowledge to be creative. I was really pleased with yesterday's brainstorming session—we came up with a lot of cool ideas. Given our schedule and resource constraints, I've gone ahead and selected one to work on. The parody of university professors concept was funny—but I don't think we know enough about university teaching to pull it off. And I liked the notion of outreach to kids in developing nations, but we could offend some people with that one. So I suggest we go with the puppy training idea. If your dog can be trained to sit up and beg through the Internet, then for sure your kids can be taught calculus the same way. People like animals in ads; it won't offend anyone; we can make it funny and it's a low budget approach. I've divided you up into three subgroups; each group needs to get going on slogans, storyboards, budgets. We'll get together next Friday to see what you've come up with and select the best treatment. Any questions? No? Okay, let's move.

Hazel's heart is in the right place. She knows about creative abrasion and has convened a group that draws on different kinds of deep knowledge from its members. Unfortunately, if Hazel was using this book to guide her actions she apparently stopped reading after Chapter 2. She knows that she needs divergent thinking among group members in order to generate lots of options—but she thinks she has been there and done that after a single session of brainstorming. Maybe the group knows more about university professors than she thinks. Or maybe they don't need to. Maybe there is a way of making an advertisement about children in developing nations that will not offend. The ideas haven't been explored enough to know. After getting a few options on the table, Hazel is ready to go. The group has hardly paused at the intersection of ideas before she is blowing her horn to move them on.

How would you feel if you had been the one in Hazel's group to suggest the parody on university professors as the basis for an advertisement? Or the ad featuring small children in a developing nation schoolhouse? That not enough energy had gone into kicking the idea around? Even if the ad with the puppies *is* the best idea, it is far from developed. You wish there had been more time for debate, more time for building on each other's ideas, for pulling in knowledge from various people's heads. But you know Hazel. You had better "climb aboard because the train is leaving the station," as she is fond of saying.

Premature Convergence: The Urge to Merge

You need only one *super* solution, right? The trouble is, option #1 often seems so appealing that the group closes ranks around it, ignoring options 2, 3, and 4. And options 5 through 50 never arise. To be creative, a group must first be able to generate possibilities— lots of them. Then some of those options have to be elaborated and carefully thought through. Somewhere in this mix of generating and processing options, groups often run afoul of premature consensus, or "the urge to merge." What drives the urge? Lots of things, including:

* Perceived time pressures force the group's hand.
* The group's leader is overly directive.
* The group is insulated from outside opinion.
* The group members experience powerful forces to remain in the group.
* The group is guided by norms that defeat divergent thinking.

Time Pressures

A deadline can certainly concentrate the mind. A *real* deadline, such as meeting a Christmas market window, can focus a group's energies and compress the normal creative process. As such, it may serve as a vigorous, necessary spur for convergence (see Chapter 4). Too often, however, the deadline may be more apparent than real. An impatient manager imposing an *artificial* deadline can short circuit the process of developing options and kill originality.

Hazel, of course, sees the group dynamics through her own distinctive lens. In the tradeoff between the highest quality solution and timeliness, she chooses the latter. If the asteroid is going to hit earth tomorrow, the creative plan to knock it off collision course won't help if it can't be activated until next week. And, like most managers, she feels as if she's in a perpetual meteor shower. She knows she has to move quickly as well as creatively.

The tragic destruction of the U.S. space shuttle *Challenger* on January 28, 1986, hurling to their deaths six astronauts and the "teacher in space," may be partly attributable to time pressures on the decision-making process. The launch had been delayed once, and the window for another launch was fast closing. As researchers have reconstructed the fatal decision-making process, not a few have noted that the leaders of the decision team were concerned about public and congressional perceptions of the entire space shuttle program and its continued funding. Another delay might damage the chances for future funding. With hindsight, the decision makers wished they had taken time to heed the warnings by a few vocal dissenters.[1] As we will discuss later in this chapter, dissension can usefully keep options open.

Overly Directive Leadership Style

Who in Hazel's group would have the temerity to challenge her conclusion that the puppy ad is the way to go? Hazel has given the *illusion* that the group has a choice in the matter ("I *suggest* that we go with. . . . Any questions? No?"), but she has clearly signaled how she wants the group to converge. Perhaps the quickest way to close off the pursuit of options is for the leader to express a clear preference at the outset. ("Why should I jeopardize my standing with Hazel and the group by contradicting her?")

Such concerns are not without foundation in reality. When William Niskanen was chief economist at Ford Motor Co. in 1980, his free-trader views came into conflict with his superiors' new protectionism in the face of increasing Japanese competition. Niskanen was fired. CFO Will Caldwell explained to him, "In this company, Bill . . . , the people who do well wait until they hear their superiors express their views. Then they add something in support of those views."[2] Not exactly the kind of environment to foster divergent thinking! Perhaps you think: "That was the eighties! Today we empower people." We agree that the rhetoric has changed—but many leaders still would need their jaws wired shut in order to keep their preferences to themselves.

The urge to merge is reinforced in any organizational decision making because decisiveness is valued in management. Managers of creativity thus usually have to fight both external pressures to choose something quickly and act, and their own tendency to drive for closure. Hazel's personal thinking style biases her toward immediate action. When the group is considering option A or B, the person who suggests C gets freeze-dried by one of Hazel's famous baleful

OPEN AND CLOSED LEADERSHIP

Psychologist Matie Flowers composed four-person groups to discuss options on a difficult personnel issue. A financially troubled school district with a powerful teachers' union had a 62-year-old math teacher whose declining mental faculties were apparently preventing her from maintaining discipline in her classes. Each group member was assigned a role: superintendent of schools (the leader of the group, actually a trained confederate), the school principal, a school counselor, and a member of the school board. Each person was provided with a set of "facts" bearing on the case.

The *open* leader had been instructed not to state a suggested solution until the other three had; to ask for and encourage discussion of each option; and to state twice that the most important thing was to *air all viewpoints*. In contrast, the closed leader gave a preferred solution at the beginning, did not encourage discussion, and stated twice that the most important thing was for the group to *agree* on its decision.

- The groups led by an open leader resisted the urge to merge. They generated, on average, more solutions. They also presented more of the supporting facts than the "closed" leadership groups.[3]

---

stares. And her mental gearshift doesn't have "reverse" on it. "Never revisit a decision" is her motto. So even if she were not under such pressure to deliver the ad campaign ahead of competitors, she would still push for a quick decision so as to move on to implementation.

Well, Hazel, we never promised you *efficient* creativity! Just *effective*. And effective means a balance between exploration and speed. Between opening up options and closing them down. Between divergent thinking and convergent.

In Figure 3-1, the *A* diamond represents a group spending very

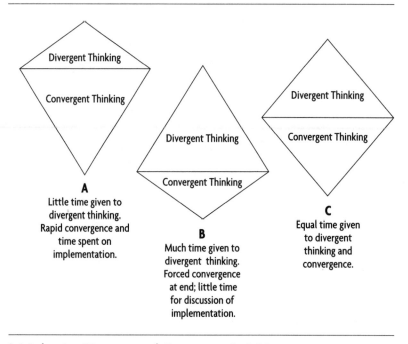

3-1 Balancing Divergent and Convergent Activities

little time on creating options and most of their effort on implementation issues. This may be appropriate when the problem to be solved or the issue to be resolved is narrowly defined, well understood, or fairly routine. The *B* diamond represents a meeting of a group of people who *love* to discuss, debate, think up options—but who leave very little relative time and resources for homing in on a solution. If time is no issue, this model may be appropriate. However, you see where we are headed—to the *C* diamond in Figure 3-1, which is especially appropriate for creative problem solving. If you don't spend the time and effort to create the requisite variety we spoke of in Chapter 2, you are unlikely to identify a novel solution. If Hazel's deadline is real (i.e., cross the line and the project is dead) then she probably acted appropriately. However, almost certainly she could have allowed more divergent thinking in order to get a more creative solution. Too much time spent on divergence leaves little time to consider implementation, but too much time spent on convergence shortchanges the divergent thinking process.

Insularity and Isolation

Birds that flock together become more of a feather. And the longer they flock together, the more of a feather they become. People who work together over time may not *look* more alike (as some say long-married couples do) but the deep knowledge possessed by individual members increasingly becomes collective. And we flock together mentally because it is comfortable. Even a talented heterogeneous group is unlikely to explore a full range of alternatives when it isolates itself from those outside the group who have know-how or know-why to contribute. For example, in their study of groups of scientists, Donald Pelz and Frank Andrews found that when membership in the groups turned over frequently, the groups were more creative than were those with stable membership, even when the stable groups were interdisciplinary. Within three years, even interdisciplinary groups had become homogeneous in how they approached problems.[4] Moreover, the more that group members share common information, the more likely that information will weigh heavily in group decisions. Just because we *all* know something doesn't make it important, useful knowledge. We need to figure out what we don't know we don't know—and that means looking outside the flock.

Group Cohesiveness

People have liked being in groups since our conference rooms were caves. We need to feel accepted and valued by others. In fact, a good part of our own identity is tied up with membership in some group or other. Most of us have belonged to groups in which we have felt good about ourselves, safe, and secure. We like our fellow members and look forward to meeting with them. We would suffer if the group were to disband or if we were somehow forced to leave.

THE COMMON KNOWLEDGE EFFECT

Daniel Gigone and Reid Hastie devised an experiment in which three-person groups were asked to make judgments about the likely performance of students in a course. Each group member was provided with a set of facts (e.g., the student's high school academic performance, number of classes skipped, standardized test scores). Some of these facts were given to all three members, some were given to two, and some to only one. So the group collectively had all of the information about the student, but some of it was more or less redundant. Gigone and Hastie found that the more *common* knowledge in the group (i.e., the more people who had the same information), the more weight was given to it and the more it influenced the final group judgment, even if it wasn't the most *salient* data. (Interestingly, group members were unaware of the influence of common knowledge on their judgments.) If one wishes a group to think broadly, this study suggests that special efforts will need to be made to encourage the group to consider all of the information at its disposal, not just that which members have in common.[5]

The glue that holds group members together has many origins. Initial liking has repeatedly been shown to foster cohesiveness. The more you like your fellow members, the more strongly you are motivated to remain in the group.[6] Second, merely being in extended contact over time can lead to mutual liking and cohesiveness.[7] Familiarity breeds . . . comfort. A third powerful force drawing people together is an external threat. Combining efforts to combat a rival or enemy unites the group in a common purpose. (As we shall see in Chapter 4, a common threat can sometimes stimulate creativity.)

So we like clans. However, high cohesiveness—the forces that draw people together and keep them together—is a primary determinant of "Groupthink."[8] Irving Janis came up with this Orwellian term to describe "a mode of thinking that people engage in when they are deeply involved in a cohesive in-group, when the members' strivings for unanimity override their motivation to realistically appraise alternative courses of action."[9] The Groupthink tendency is really troublesome for creativity. It results from illusions among members that everyone else is in agreement ("The naked emperor is really elegantly dressed today"); self-censorship of any doubts ("Who am I to question all these smart people?"); and pressure from group members on dissenters ("Mustn't be disloyal—I'm part of a team"). The result? The group aborts the divergent thinking process and seizes quickly on one or two options. It is wonderful to have esprit de corps. But when these groups are decision-making bodies, we can pay a steep price for group cohesiveness. Janis drew many of his observations about Groupthink from examining some critical decisions at the highest levels of U.S. foreign policy making— where creativity is often needed.

The invasion of Cuba by 1400 expatriates in 1961 has been called one of the "worst fiascoes ever perpetrated by a responsible government."[10] Within three days, all of the invaders had been killed or captured. All of the major assumptions held by President Kennedy and his National Security Council were completely misguided. They thought the Cuban population would spontaneously rise up to support the small brigade of invading ex-patriots. They underestimated the ability of Castro's large, well-trained army and airforce to respond. And the brigade landed in a swamp. A big one.

Kennedy's advisors were not stupid people. How could the "best and brightest," whose different backgrounds clearly positioned the group for creative abrasion, fail so miserably to generate alternatives to the CIA plan presented to them? At least part of the answer lies in the dynamics of cohesive groups. Pulitzer Prize–winning historian Arthur Schlesinger, Jr., a member of Kennedy's group, berated himself for his silence during the deliberations:

though my feelings of guilt were tempered by the knowledge that a course of objection would have accomplished little save to gain me a name as a nuisance. I can only explain my failure to do more than raise a few timid questions by reporting that one's impulse to blow the whistle on this nonsense was simply undone by the circumstances of the discussion.[11]

Cohesive groups present an interesting paradox. On the one hand, members of such groups feel accepted and should be free to say anything they want without fear of antagonizing their fellows. On the other, they don't want to appear ignorant, disruptive, or a spoil-sport. The lesson for managers of creative groups is clearly *not* to reduce the cohesiveness, but rather to harness that cohesiveness in the service of creativity. This can be accomplished by understanding the power of group norms and, if necessary, changing them.

Inappropriate Group Norms

Norms are the rules group members follow, even when no one is watching. They are usually unwritten, often unconscious, almost always powerful. And they can help or inhibit creativity. Consider, for example, these invisible powerful rules:

* Don't interfere with other peoples' jobs. (Mind your own business.)

* Try to keep everyone happy. (Be nice.)

* Don't contradict the boss. (Know your place—and accept it.)

* Conform to the group. (Don't upset the apple cart.)

* Don't presume to know more than your elders. (Defer to more senior members of the group.)

How likely is it that a junior colleague will challenge a fellow group member's plan with one of her own when doing so might make her look like she's not minding her own business, is not being very nice, does not know her place, is being disrespectful, and is trying to upset the apple cart? A group in which these norms are allowed to stand unchallenged is a group that is damned to eternal blandness. You can't expect creative options if group members have all been trained to sit up, roll over, and speak only on command. Creative options will simply not emerge unless the prevailing norms are replaced with those more conducive to creativity. People will either not speak up in the first place; or, doing so, will soon discover how groups treat norm breakers.

Resisting the Urge to Merge: Encouraging Dissent

When Robert Kennedy was asked by his brother to assume the role of devil's advocate in the Cuban Missile Crisis deliberations, he did so with such gusto that only his relationship to the president protected him from the open hostility of other group members. As Oscar Wilde quipped, "We dislike arguments of any kind; they are always vulgar and often convincing."[12]

The Group Reacts to Dissenters

Ever been in the following situation? Group members are closing in on the solution to a problem when someone speaks passionately in favor of some other option, maybe even one that has already been discussed and rejected. How do group members react? Eye-rolling? We crave agreement, not dissent. And dissent, even effective dissent, is often unpopular. A dissenter will, first, attract a lot of attention. Other members will attempt to bring him around. Failing that, the group will attempt to ignore or exclude him from group discussions. If that fails, he may be physically expelled from the group or "reassigned." Dissenters present a dilemma in group discussions. A person who challenges the emerging consensus may earn a certain grudging admiration for standing up for her principles in the face of group pressure. And she does bring new perspectives—perhaps valuable ones—to the table.

On the other hand, minority views prevent the group from reaching a quick decision and challenge the correctness of each majority member's judgment. "We all had a pretty good idea of where we should be going, and I was feeling pretty good about myself and the group. Now you're saying we were all wrong?" As a result, the dissenter is generally heartily resented and disliked by the majority.

Wise leaders—or even just competent ones—help a group develop norms that encourage divergent thinking and welcome dissent. At Intel, it is essential to get "knowledge power" into the organization, and employees learn early on that "you know more than your boss does" about many things. Open dissent is absolutely encouraged from top management on down, and is repeatedly taught at all levels.[13] Research shows that when the strength of an "originality norm" is increased, group members not only give more creative responses, but they tolerate and like minority respondents more than when the norm is weak.[14] Creativity flourishes when the unusual is expected and dissent is welcomed.

The Value of Dissent

How do dissenters manage to stimulate creativity if their opinions are so unpopular? It is not because the rest of us necessarily believe they know what they're talking about. Rather, they force us to examine our own positions, search for information on *both* sides of the issue, evaluate the arguments against them—in short, engage in the kind of divergent thinking that is at the heart of creativity.[15] Majorities, on the other hand, move the group in *one* direction—toward consensus and conformity. ("Why should I search for new options? We already have the answer.")

THE POWER OF MINORITY DISSENT

Charlan Jeanne Nemeth and Joel Wachtler devised a laboratory analog of majority and minority influence on creativity. College students were presented with the task of determining whether a standard geometric figure was or was not embedded in a more complex pattern. Experimental confederates were employed to simulate either a *majority influence* (four confederates) or a *minority influence* (two confederates). Nemeth and Wachtler found that majorities caused subjects to converge on their judgments, whether or not they were correct. Minorities, on the other hand, caused subjects to give novel, correct responses (i.e., to correctly identify the standard figure in other complex patterns) that had not previously been identified by the majorities. In short, majority influence served to promote conformity, or a mindless aping of the majority judgments. In the case of minority influence, "One can be influenced to reanalyze a problem and, in the process, perhaps function more creatively and accurately."[16]

Managing Divergence: Resisting the Urge to Merge and Creating Options

So it's not just a matter of *tolerating* dissent. We *need* it. If your group is going to be creative, beginning with the ability to generate lots of potentially useful options, members must resist the urge to merge. Dissent can be uncomfortable for everyone, certainly including the dissenter. So it's important to get it into everyone's head that dissent can be vital to the creative process and is normal behavior in your group—not just a hindrance to group consensus. But even if we start with a diverse group and deliberately augment the membership with aliens as suggested in Chapter 2, and even if we con-

sciously promote a group process encouraging dissent, the urge to
converge may seem overpowering. You will be glad to know that
resistance is not futile! Let's look at some mental tools and process
techniques that can help stave off *premature* convergence.

Techniques for Resisting the Urge to Merge

Harnessing Group Norms: Ground Rules Rules for creative groups? Sounds
stifling. However, one of the reasons that we need to develop conscious, explicit norms is that individuals come into any meeting
with a different set of expectations of behavior, born of their personal
backgrounds and experience. Some folks grew up in families where
lively debate over the dinner table encouraged both argumentation
and listening to others. Others grew up in families whose operative
rules were: don't ask—and don't tell. And some people continued
to be treated as children, with nothing useful to say, even when they
were adults. It is small wonder that when we all get together, we
often need to talk about how we are going to talk.

Granted, most of us feel a bit foolish creating rules about how
we will work together. Surely, we think, we are all adults and have
years of experience in dealing with group dynamics. That, of course,
is the problem. Many of us have long years of practicing the dysfunctional behaviors we learned from professional or personal experience.
If we have come from a very competitive company where information
is power, we may unconsciously hold back in order to look brilliant
at the right time (and end up missing the moment for our insight).
Or we may have worked in an organization where disagreement was
impolite. If we are the third or fourth sibling in a large family, we
may hesitate to suggest an idea for fear of looking foolish in front
of our "elders."

Arguments don't have to be personal. Statements like "That's a
ridiculous idea," or "The problem with you is . . ." are just plain
abrasive. People who don't understand *creative* abrasion may confuse
it with interpersonal conflict, and as a result avoid it. Yet abrasion,
as noted in Chapter 2, is essential for creativity. "Inspiration can

come from anyone on the team," points out Susan Schilling of Lucas Learning. "By disagreeing, we get the best . . . for the product—but it's not personal disagreement." So we need group norms—habits of behavior—that make certain kinds of conflict okay or even mandated. In the world of Education meets Entertainment, Schilling found, people from a background in education were more accustomed to collaboration, whereas in companies producing games, "Whoever yells the loudest wins!" In order to tap the group's creativity, "we needed to build a set of internal rules about how we would agree and disagree."[17]

Many groups take time to compose these ground rules—rules of behavior to which all members agree that encourage creative abrasion. One group we know opted for short but sweet: "Anyone can disagree with anyone else. No one can disagree without giving a reason. We will actively listen to each other. We will not use the words 'always' and 'never' in referring to each other's behavior." We know another group whose ground rules originally took up two walls of flip-chart sheets. Not surprisingly, such an abundance of rules is no longer remembered, much less invoked. While we favor pithiness, the important thing is to get agreement on the rules and to enforce them. If disagreement threatens to blossom into anger, team members can point to the principles and remind everyone to listen to each other. It feels a bit like elementary school to post those principles around the meeting room, but the process of agreeing on the principles and then putting them up on the wall where all team members can see them does help everyone keep group interaction in mind. And that's the point of the exercise. We get so caught up in content that we forget process.

Process rules can evolve in surprising ways. Reporter Hal Lancaster recalls "a dinner meeting where the liberal consumption of after-dinner drinks prompted surprising candor between middle and senior managers. Thereafter, it was understood that a meeting conducted under 'Armagnac Rules' meant that you could speak freely, without fear of reprisal."[18]

When "don't rock the boat" takes precedence over "generate

THE NASA MOON SURVIVAL PROBLEM

Your spaceship has crashed, stranding your group on the moon, hundreds of miles from base. Fortunately, no one is seriously injured and much of the cargo can be salvaged. Unfortunately, you can't bring everything, so you must decide which items are most vital for your survival as you make your way to base. Each group member must rank in order of importance all that has been salvaged, including such items as oxygen tanks, water, and food, as well as matches, parachute silk, and a compass. Then the group convenes to arrive at a consensus.

Normally, when compared to the objectively "correct" answers (as determined by NASA experts), groups are no better than individuals in their final rankings. Some groups, however, are given special norms to follow:

* "Avoid changing your mind only in order to avoid conflict and to reach agreement and harmony.

* "Withstand pressures to yield which have no objective or logically sound foundation.

* "View differences of opinion as both natural and helpful."[19]

Groups following these instructions were judged more creative and arrived at rankings that were superior to the group's best member 75 percent of the time.[20]

---

as many alternatives as possible and evaluate each one carefully," creativity is likely to suffer. Fewer than two years after the Cuban Bay of Pigs fiasco, when the nation and the world faced the Cuban Missile Crisis, John F. Kennedy proved even presidents can learn. Fidel Castro installed Russian missiles capable of converting major U.S. cities into major craters, and the United States had to decide how to react. This time, Kennedy instituted a new set of "ground rules" in the foreign policy discussions that included bringing in outside experts, appointing devil's advocates, and deliberately refraining from expressing his private opinion (which was that military action against Cuba would be necessary!). The result was that the initial assumption that the military would have to act against the missile silos was replaced by a decision to set up a blockade. Time was bought, egos were assuaged, and the crisis was resolved. When U.S. citizens realized later how close we had come to a devastating conflict, we were grateful the president had introduced his advisors to different group norms.

Challenging Unconscious Assumptions When is a paper clip not a paper clip? When you straighten it out to solve a problem requiring a piece of wire. When is an engineer not an engineer? When she is an anthropologist, visiting a customer's home to understand when, why, and how a product is being used. We think of tools and people in certain roles and have trouble reconceiving those roles. The human mind is extremely susceptible to routine thinking. It is efficient not to question the way we interact with our surroundings. If we stopped to think about it before we sat in a chair, if we did not assume that our medications were uncontaminated, if we did not expect an accountant to give us different information than the house painter—if we did not make hundreds of unconscious assumptions every hour, we would be virtually paralyzed. The trouble is, those assumptions can also keep us from thinking creatively, either individually or as a group. Shared assumptions are a form of convergent thinking. Yet if we can free just a few strands of the mental bonds in our minds connecting persons or objects with their function, we open up new possibilities. Why have you scoured the house for a screwdriver when a dime would do the trick? Well, because a dime is supposed to be used to buy a piece of "penny" candy—not as a tool. Sometimes simply alerting group members to their own susceptibility helps them develop the ability to question their own assumptions. Asking some basic questions can lead the discussion in new directions:

OBSTACLES TO CREATIVE THINKING

Consider the following three problems:

1. Given a candle, a box of matches, and some thumbtacks, attach a candle to a bulletin board so it won't drip wax on the floor.

2. Given six toothpicks of equal length, use all six to make exactly four equilateral triangles.

3. What is the rule we're using to develop the number series 5, 10, 15? The objective is to discover the rule by trial. Generate your own sets of three numbers and we'll tell you whether they conform to our rule or not. When you think you know our rule, tell us what it is.

Turn to the last page of this chapter for the answers.

---

* What are our assumptions here? Are they the only valid ones?

* Are there different ways of viewing this situation, for example, from someone else's perspective?

The examples in "Obstacles to Creative Thinking" illustrate three factors to which we are particularly vulnerable:

1. *Functional fixedness* refers to our inability to free ourselves from the expectations of how something (or someone) normally functions. Boxes are containers, not platforms, so we are slow to think of emptying a matchbox to attach to the wall. When we rely on our past experiences of how things are used, we often get stuck, unable to break out of old thinking habits.

2. *Fixation* is similar: our mental wheels are stuck in the mud of approaching a problem from the "obvious" direction. (When a

problem is presented in two dimensions, we naturally try to solve it in two.)

3. The *confirmation bias* refers to our tendency to seek support for our convictions, and reluctance to either look for or accept contrary evidence.[21] ("I'm such a good judge of character. Almost all the people I've promoted have worked out fine." Yes, but how about all the people you *didn't* promote? Maybe they worked out fine elsewhere within or outside the organization as well.)

Devil's Advocate In the Roman Catholic tradition, a devil's advocate is an official of the Congregation of Rites whose duty is to point out defects in the evidence upon which the case for beatification or canonization rests. While we favor instituting a group norm that encourages *everyone* to act as a critical thinker, challenging premature drives to consensus, sometimes a formal devil's advocate role should be assigned. We mentioned above how President John F. Kennedy used his brother Robert in that role to good purpose, although the vehemence with which he pursued his role alienated many group members. To be most effective,

* The devil's advocate must, first, have the absolute support of the group leader. When a designated dissenter becomes merely a token (as was the case in President Johnson's councils during the escalation of the Vietnam War) he will not be taken seriously.

* The devil's advocate should be a good role player. It should not be clear what her actual position is. She should be able to argue as though she believed the dissenting viewpoint implicitly.

* The role should rotate among group members from meeting to meeting. This precludes both the danger of "tokenism" and also the risk that over time group members will begin to confuse the advocate with the devil himself. (Without the support of the leader, this can lead to disaster for the dissenter's future in the organization.)

* The devil's advocate should focus on the issues and refrain from personal attacks.

A top manager who wanted his staff to think creatively about a dilemma, asked two of them to take contrary positions. The issue was how the company should respond to a distributor who both greatly expanded their market for the consumer product (a home appliance) and at the same time inhibited product innovation. One staffer presented the majority opinion that the distributor had the company in a stranglehold and should be challenged, even if the company lost money in the process. The appointed devil's advocate pointed out all the advantages and benefits to be derived from their relationship with the powerful distributor. Interestingly, the group converged on an innovative strategy that incorporated both viewpoints.

Reader's Theatre At Hewlett-Packard Laboratories, Manager of Worldwide Personnel Barbara Waugh has used "Reader's Theatres" both in the labs and in the company as a whole to present (and legitimize) divergent views. The "play" put on by employees takes its script from the actual experiences of the employees, who read their parts before an audience of colleagues. The resulting emotional and visceral experience has effected huge changes in the way the majority feels about an issue. For example, although a liberal company in many ways, Hewlett-Packard initially decided against offering benefits to long-term partners of gay and lesbian employees. Confronted with dramatized evidence of discrimination and hardship, senior management reversed its original decision. The drama placed viewers in the uncomfortable position of experiencing firsthand what their colleagues had told them about in general terms before. Reader's Theatres powerfully compel the audience to view life through the eyes of the minority. The vicarious experience challenges comfortable assumptions and forces attention to dissenting views.

Okay, so we have some techniques for preventing premature convergence. But the manager's job is also to help the group create

---

THE AVAILABILITY HEURISTIC, OR THE VIVIDNESS EFFECT

Are you more likely to be killed by a moose or a grizzly bear? Are there more words that begin with the letter *k* or that have *k* as their third letter? It is probably easier to visualize one alternative over the other: the deadly fangs of the world's largest carnivore; lots of words that start with *k*. The tendency to believe that something is more true or more likely to happen if we can vividly imagine it is called the "availability heuristic." In many cases, the availability heuristic gives us an accurate representation of reality; in others, however, we are led astray. Far more people are trampled or impaled by moose than are mauled by grizzlies; there are many more words with *k* as their third letter than their first. Yet many, if not most, people would probably overestimate the likelihood of each of these less plausible events. The lesson here? Make something vivid, such as the dramatizations in Reader's Theatre, and observers will be more likely to imagine them, hence find them plausible a powerful force for generating new, believable, options.[22]

---

requisite variety, that is, that big menu of options from which to select potential solutions, market, or service opportunities. The group members undoubtedly *want* to be creative. However one cannot order creativity like a pint of beer. You may need some tools and techniques to jump-start their imaginations. Some of these techniques are used within the group itself; for others, the group must look beyond its own boundaries.

Creating Options within the Group

Brainstorming

Probably the best-known technique for generating options is brainstorming. Brainstorming sessions range from the intelligent and

useful to the banal and unproductive—what one manager interviewed termed "intellectual masturbation." The difference, as in so
many techniques, is in process and purpose: how the brainstorming
session is conducted and what its intent is. Studies in psychological
laboratories consistently show that individuals working alone come
up with more and better ideas than they do when working in a
group and the larger the group, the greater the disparity.[23] Why?
Self-consciousness and anxiety about being evaluated by other group
members, and the inherent inability to listen simultaneously to
others while creating one's own ideas.

Although the experiments generally use college students brainstorming somewhat trivial subjects (e.g., "What if people had two
thumbs on each hand?"), we should not ignore the lessons of the
researcher's laboratory. People can believe others will think their
ideas are stupid. They can forget their own ideas while others are
talking. Unless skillfully managed, brainstorms can merely promote
the *illusion* that the group is being creative. For example, people tend
to prefer group brainstorming sessions to individual idea generation.
They believe they were more creative and prolific in groups, even
if there is evidence to the contrary. So—use brainstorms or not?

The lesson we draw is that brainstorming in groups is better
than not dedicating any time to generating options. In some cases,
nominal groups—members working on the same task in isolation—
may be the way to go.[24] But when skillfully facilitated and working
on substantive issues such as "How can we survive this crisis?" rather
than a superfluity of thumbs, a brainstorming group can often match
the nominal groups in number and creativity of ideas. Moreover,
proponents of brainstorming can take heart from a study showing
that when individuals and groups were instructed to produce a
best idea, rather than *lots* of ideas, groups performed better than
individuals.[25] It is also common to combine the nominal and brainstorming techniques by having individuals generate their ideas on
Post-it notes. The facilitator can then either collect the "yellow
stickies" and arrange them according to some category scheme or
can let the group develop the scheme. Once the stickies are arranged

by category, the group can then elaborate on them as a group, using the same brainstorming rules.

A variant on traditional brainstorming designed to eliminate the blocking of ideas is *electronic brainstorming*. Participants type in their ideas, while the ideas of other members appear in a separate window on the screen. The electronic brainstormers are encouraged to read the others' contributions and elaborate on them. Evidence suggests that because participants are free to focus on their own idea production, more ideas are generated compared to traditional brainstorming.

We find ourselves returning once again to the importance of thinking styles. There certainly are people who would prefer sitting before their computer screens and interacting with their fellow group members electronically. But how well would that work for highly verbal, image-oriented individuals in ad agencies or design firms? Or when an important part of the brainstorming session involves manipulating physical objects?

Take IDEO, one of the top design and engineering firms in the United States, as an example. Almost every project includes some brainstorming. An IDEO "brainstorm" gathers staff members with diverse skills—human factors, mechanical engineering, industrial design, and often a client—to generate product ideas. A staff member selected for facilitation skills runs the face-to-face meeting. Everyone knows the rules, but they are also stenciled around the top of the walls in the room usually used for this purpose: "defer judgment; build on the ideas of others; one conversation at a time; stay focused on the topic; encourage wild ideas." The folks at IDEO have an advantage over most of us in that they can draw. By the end of the session, in addition to the words on the white board, there are sketches on the board and on the paper covering the table around which the participants sit. Note that the rules encourage the kind of free association that people usually think of as brainstorming—but within bounds. A successful brainstorm has to have a clearly understood topic, an experienced facilitator, media for capturing ideas, and accepted rules of conduct.

Role Playing

Most of us gave up role playing when we reached adolescence. However, role playing, like brainstorming, can release floodgates of information. When MTV needed a new game show in 1996, staffers went off-site to "game-storm." They spent a day recalling childhood diversions like capture the flag, actually playing children's board games, and analyzing TV game shows. The big hit of 1997, *Figure It Out* came from the game-storm; executive Kevin Kay borrowed ideas from the game 20 Questions and from the TV shows *I've Got a Secret* and *The David Letterman Show.*[26]

One of the nice features of role playing is that it has a fast-forward button as well as reverse. You can try on the future. When Interval Research, a company researching prospects for new media products, wanted to consider how people would use a videophone, they put on an "informance," an informational performance by staff members acting out how friends trying to arrange a dinner party over the videophone might interact. In the process, they realized that who controls the video "eye" was very important. When one participant suggested that the caller wanted to be able to look around the room, an actor at the other end objected. "I might be sitting here in my skivvies or something," he said. "I don't want him to be able to look over here."[27] Role playing raises issues that might not occur in theoretical discussions.

At times, realistically playing the role of users requires significant adaptation. Imagine Interval Research's challenge in getting a group of twentyish researchers to design interfaces with electronic equipment for elderly people to use. How could Generation X, health club–addicted designers possibly understand the challenges of an aging body? Sure, you could get them to visit some nursing homes or talk with their grandparents. But their observations will still be distant from experience. Far better if the designers *feel* what it is like to inhabit an eighty-year-old body, so that their designs will be adequate. The answer? Give them gloves to reduce dexterity, glasses smeared with Vaseline to mimic blurred vision, and weights on their arms and legs to simulate time-worn muscles—and *then* let them role play interactions with the proposed technology.

Some groups even hire actors to simulate the future. At Intel, developers of the next-generation semiconductor chips wanted to peek into the future to see possible future communication appliances. After visiting families in their homes to understand how parents and children in frantic Western civilizations communicate, they hired actors to portray the "usual" morning rush in an upper-class suburban home, using a futuristic appliance that attached to the refrigerator. This imaginary device (portrayed in the video as a small handheld computer-cum-videophone) captured video messages among family members, such as Mom's reminders, recorded in the morning for the children to replay when they got home. ("Set the table; finish your homework before you turn on the television," etc.). It also recorded the grocery list and served as an interface to the Internet. What does Intel learn from such exercises? Employees who see the video have expanded views of the future—where and how their chips might be used. These views in turn lead to speculation about the power and capabilities that such chips would need to accommodate such a variety of communication tasks.

John Kao's Idea Factory in San Francisco keeps an improvisation troupe busy acting out scenarios of the future created by clients. On more than one occasion, an otherwise dignified vice president has suddenly leaped from his spectator seat to join in the improvisation to make a point. The process of role playing pulls the clients into the future through their own imaginations. They never expect themselves to join the players and would have felt silly if you told them they would. Once again, though, they open up options that might never have occurred through sober analytical reflection.

File-drawer Excursions

Picture this: you are sitting in a brainstorming session at award-winning design and engineering firm IDEO. The group has come up with a promising new product idea, but it would require drawing heat away from a surface very quickly —in fact, almost instantly. One of the engineers suddenly jumps up and without a word leaves the room to return with a cup of scalding water and some copper pipes the shape and length of drinking straws. She puts the cup down on the table and hands you the copper piping. "Stick it in the cup," she says. You do, and are amazed to find that the pipe is immediately hot. You almost drop it in your surprise. You had expected the pipe to heat up the way a spoon does in hot coffee— taking at least ten seconds. If you worked at IDEO, you would know where she got the pipes—from the "Technology Box," a six-drawered filing cabinet in which reside flotsam and jetsam from under the desks of artists and engineers as well as new "cool things" brought in by employees specifically to add to the collection. The two individuals who serve as "curators" of the collection decide whether something should be added. The six drawers holding the collection of physical objects and materials are labeled "Thermo Techologies; Amazing Materials; Cool Mechanisms; Electronic Technologies; Interesting Manufacturing Processes; and Light and Optics." The labels only hint at the multiplicity of contents: specialty foam that can be almost infinitely compressed and yet spring back into its original volume; strips of metal that retain memory of their original shape when reheated, no matter how distorted during use; superheavy materials; a supersaturated salt solution that discharges heat when it is transformed chemically into a solid; hollow beads smaller than the diameter of a human hair that can be filled with liquids or gases, and dissolve to deliver their contents. The box is like a menu, or artist's palette. During brainstorms, engineers and designers often dash out to retrieve a sample of some material or a component to support an idea or to suggest a possible solution to a problem. Or engineers and designers frequently pull out the drawers and finger the contents just to browse for inspiration. Why keep physical objects instead of pictures or text descriptions? One of the IDEO curators of the Technology Box, Dennis Boyle, explains that "some of these things are so unobvious, so nonintuitive, that you really have to experience them to believe them." Adds the other curator, Rickson Sun, "I think there is a mechanism in the brain that helps you recall experiences much more effectively than you recall data."[28]

Metaphors and Models from Nature

How about using Mother Nature as a supplier of innovative ideas? Interval Research director and cofounder David Liddle argues that nature is a good problem solver because of her "reckless and random" ways. Whereas humans rely on a narrow range of solutions based on logical processes, nature takes a trial-and-error approach that tests many more potential solutions. Sometimes she helps by giving us a direct functional model—solving the technical problems for us. What would we do if George de Mestral hadn't gotten his jacket covered with cockleburs? We wouldn't have that ubiquitous fastener of everything from shoe tops to teenagers upside down on walls—Velcro. (The name is derived from *vel*vet and *cro*chet). Of course, people have been removing burs since we were wearing saber-toothed tiger pelts, and no one else had thought to make a virtue (and millions of dollars) out of how tenaciously the burs cling.

Not that we can always figure out nature's recipes. If glue makers can ever fathom how the barnacle manufactures the world's stickiest underwater glue, they will have a winning innovation. Spiders— particularly Florida's golden orb spiders—still hold the world's record for ultrastrong materials. Humans need acids, high temperatures, and carefully controlled factories to make strong fiber, but these spiders spin silk stronger than steel in room-temperature aqueous solutions. Specialists in "biomimetics" at Cornell University are decoding the structure of the spider's silk, in order to synthesize genes that will yield fiber even stronger than the spiders'.[29]

Even computer nerds will steal from Mother Nature. "Our view of computer science is rational, mechanistic. But nature winds up doing things in a way we'd never think of," says David Liddle. The Interval Research creative team working on an antivirus program includes University of New Mexico computer science professor Stephanie Forrest and theoretical immunologist Alan S. Perelson at

Los Alamos National Laboratory. The software they designed to-gether attacks unrecognized computer viruses by imitating the body's immune system's ability to identify alien molecules. "I really believe that our computer systems are so complicated, we can't use them effectively till we make them look more like a biological system," says Forrest.[30]

Even when Mother Nature doesn't provide the functional recipe, she still offers "a huge library of design metaphors [and opens] up a wide range of possibilities."[31] The company Thinking Tools, working with Texas Instruments, took some hints from the navigational skills of salmon finding their way back to a spawning river to design a computerized distribution system. Shipping companies could more efficiently dispatch goods to far-flung areas, they reasoned, if each package could "seek" the best route.

Along the same lines, Paul Kantor, a professor at Rutgers University, observed that ants leave pheromone trails to help other ants find food. He has parlayed this observation into a $1 million grant from the Defense Advanced Research Projects Agency to develop Ant World Server to help Web browsers find information. Web users seeking particular information would create "digital phero-mone paths" that could be used by others looking for similar infor-mation. "Our metaphor asks, 'Why can't human beings be at least as smart as ants about searching for information?' "[32] Why not, indeed!

What these people have all done is to dissect their problem into the desired *functions* (e.g., adhesion or repulsion, aggregation or reflection, navigation or identification) and then ask how nature has already performed that task. Creative groups can use this technique to create options that might not otherwise occur to members.

Creating Options: Group Outreach

Managers of creative groups need to be physical as well as mental travel agents. Working within the group is not the only way to create new options. A number of techniques involve wearing out shoe leather.

Visits to Aliens

It is hard to generate creative abrasion when we are isolated or surrounded by people just like us. We can enrich the pool of ideas by visiting people and environments that are "alien"—outside our normal networks. These aliens may be found almost anywhere— outside our group but elsewhere in the organization, or outside the organization entirely. Visits to aliens can build new knowledge, expose us to approaches to a problem that we would never think of, or even inspire a different definition of a problem. Groups that insulate themselves from those outside the immediate team or from outside the organization run the risk of rapidly running out of new ideas. Research on new product teams in high-technology firms found that those teams with the least amount of contact with those outside the team were the least innovative and productive.[33]

Paul Horn of IBM Research suggests underdefining jobs, so that people will move outside of their specified roles. "We encourage scientists and researchers to venture far outside their realm as experts in semiconductors, physics, mathematics and computer science. Today, more than 25 percent of researchers' time is taken up by working outside the lab with customers on first-of-a-kind projects."[34] Such visits will be valuable if we are prepared to observe, absorb, and apply the experience back to the occasion triggering the need for creativity. Stanley Gryskiewicz, vice president of global resources at the Center for Creative Leadership in Greenboro, North Carolina, follows the "N + 1" plan when scheduling industry conferences. Besides the number of conferences he plans to attend each year, he goes to one on a subject outside his area of expertise.[35]

But you may not need to stray far to identify useful aliens and their ideas; they may lurk down the hall. In their study of innovation in computer industry firms, Brown and Eisenhardt found that innovative companies had extensive cross-project communication. One manager noted, " 'It used to be that it was a badge of honor not to use anybody else's ideas or to improve upon them . . . now everybody's borrowing everybody's stuff, the cycle is just so short and the pressure is so intense.' "[36] Raychem Corporation actually rewards thievery! Employees who successfully steal ideas from elsewhere in the company earn a "Not Invented Here" trophy and a certificate that states, "I stole somebody else's idea, and I'm using it." But shed no tears for the "victim," who also gets a certificate that states, "I had a great idea, and so and so is using it."[37]

Empathic Design

Customers, customers' customers, and noncustomers are all informative aliens—but not necessarily if you *ask* them anything. That probably sounds contradictory. How can you learn anything from clients if you don't do market research? You can. In fact, we argue that you will get more radical ideas from potential and actual clients if you *do not* conduct *traditional* market research. It's not that you can't learn from surveys, focus groups, and mall studies. Of course you can. The first impulse many people have when confronted with an opportunity or necessity to innovate is to send out a questionnaire to ask people what they need or to hold focus group meetings to discuss needs in the environment of the triggering occasion. There's nothing inherently wrong with these approaches (although questionnaire construction requires more sophistication than the uninitiated might suspect)—except that they limit the options that will be raised. People *can't* tell you about needs they don't know they have, *won't* tell you about ones that embarrass them for some reason, *will* say what they think you want to hear, and *will* blithely prophesy behaviors they will never undertake. In short, for the best of reasons, with the best of motives, and often totally unaware, people can be clueless.

Think of it this way: suppose you are traveling in a familiar country where you speak the language. You know (generally) where you want to go and have some decent although not detailed maps.

SEARCHING FOR REASONS: PEOPLE CAN BE CLUELESS

Psychologists Richard Nisbett and Timothy Wilson have analyzed a large number of studies, including some of their own, to determine just how insightful people are about the reasons for their own behavior. Nisbett and Wilson find that people make assertions that "may bear little resemblance to the actual events." (p. 247) In one of N. R. F. Maier's classic studies of creativity, two cords hung from the ceiling, too far apart for both to be reached simultaneously. Asked to tie the ends together, subjects were unlikely at first to think of the solution: to create a pendulum by tying a heavy object to the end of one rope and swinging it within grasp—until Maier "accidently" set one cord swinging by brushing up against it. However, few subjects accurately reported that this action stimulated their thought.

In a more dramatic illustration of people's inability to access their own reasoning, Nisbett and Wilson presented subjects with a video of a teacher who spoke English with a European accent. In one version of the video, he was warm and enthusiastic; in the second, he was cold and intolerant of his students. Subjects were asked to rate not only the teacher's likeability but three attributes—his physical appearance, mannerisms, and accent—all three of which were identical in both tapes. Not surprisingly, subjects who saw the warm version liked him better and also rated his attributes more favorably. However, subjects denied that their liking or disliking of the teacher influenced their ratings of his attributes. In fact, subjects who saw the cold version maintained that their reason for disliking him was *because of* their distaste for his appearance, mannerisms, and accent, the *opposite* of what really happened. They were unaware that the teacher's relative warmness or coldness was in fact influencing their assessment of his attributes.[38]

You can always start down the right road and stop and ask good questions and get sensible answers that will guide you. Similarly, if a product or service is familiar, you can ask customers about finely drawn preferences. Say you are in the market for a car. How would you like it to sound? Most people can answer that question: "quiet," or "like a purr," or "a throaty roar." And vehicle designers can oblige. They know how to design sound. Harley-Davidson motorcycle aficionados can distinguish the sound of their engines from that of others—and can even describe it. Harley-Davidson sued Honda over imitating the sound of their motorcycle engines! Here is another question people can answer: How would you like your new car to smell? Almost everyone (if you give them a theoretically fat wallet) says: "like leather." When Nissan Design International was researching preferences in leather smells for the Infiniti J-30, they stuck ninety pieces of leather under peoples' noses and isolated the three that would sell in the U.S. market. (Turns out, all three were U.S.–made leathers. Evidently even our noses are ethnocentric!) How can potential customers give such sophisticated guidance to the creative process? Think about your knowledge of cars. You have a long history of experience to draw on. You know what cars sound and smell and feel like.

In many cases, however, the group faced with a creativity opportunity wants to identify options that are *not* already well understood, or for which no current model exists. Instead of being in a familiar country where everyone speaks your language, you are a stranger in a strange land. How then can you *ask* people what they want? One of the most powerful sets of techniques to create options we have dubbed "empathic design." *Empathic design* is a set of techniques, a process of developing deep empathy for another's point of view and using that perspective to stimulate novel design concepts.[39] These techniques are most heavily used in new product development, but they are applicable any time you need to create options.

Here is the central premise underlying empathic design: people often cannot articulate what they want or need in an innovation. Groups undertaking empathic design are like anthropologists exploring a foreign culture. Their objective is to internalize a deep under-standing of the environment in which the target population lives, works, and plays—to "go native." They take with them their own deep knowledge about what their organization is capable of—the expertise they can bring to the foreign culture. The expertise may be technology or skills or processes. Then the explorers can identify needs that they could creatively meet, innovation options that clients will never request. At the foundation of empathic design, then, is *observation*. Sometimes you don't even have to observe the behavior, only the physical evidence left behind. Other times, however, you will need to watch people in their daily routines—observe the actual behavior as it occurs.

Why does observation stimulate options that wouldn't arise through questioning? One reason is that people's memories are necessarily selective. Ideas, needs, and desires occur to us while we are in the process of actually using a product or conducting an activity that we may not recall later in reflecting on that activity. You have undoubtedly had hundreds of ideas along the lines of "Why can't they make this thing . . ." as you drove your car or made a travel reservation, used a gardening tool or a computer—even tried to open a door the wrong way because the handle clearly signals "pull" when you have to push to get it open! Colgate-Palmolive researchers had family members videotape people doing chores in their homes to record their stream-of-consciousness observations on what they were doing. What did they see? People commenting on the smell of products, or lack of smell. People combining products in unusual ways—mixing laundry soaps together with dishwashing detergents to get curtains white, or filling the empty bottle of one glass cleaner with another product to take advantage of a superior spray mechanism.

We don't always know our own preferences. When you are reading a map, do you turn it so that up is north or orient it to the direction you are headed? Designers at IDEO working on a car navigational system discovered that people differ in how they read maps. This discovery—never mentioned in interviews—came about

---

UNOBTRUSIVE MEASURES

Psychologists and sociologists have long been aware of the difficulties in getting information from people by simply asking them. As we saw in the last sidebar, people sometimes think they know what caused their behavior, but are wrong. In other cases, they don't know and can't tell you; in still others, they know but either won't or can't tell you (perhaps because they lack insight into their own preferences or their answers are clouded by a desire to appear "normal" or otherwise good in the eyes of the interviewer). In a now-classic work, a group of psychologists cataloged various general techniques for extracting information from people without their awareness.[40]

* *"Erosion" measures.* The popularity of museum exhibits is determined by noting the frequency with which the tiles in front of the exhibit are replaced.
* *"Accretion" measures.* During the "Big Dig" in Boston in the late 1990s, archaeologists were granted prior access to excavation sites for the new highway. They found that privies, and what

---

because the designers observed pairs of people constantly turning the map as they discussed directions.

Moreover, we develop routines for coping with problems—workarounds. Do it long enough and eventually we become unaware of any need for improvements. Most inexpert computer users (and a surprising number of experts) have primitive rituals to assuage the devils that lurk under the keyboard. ("Turn the machine off twice in a row and the mouse works; count to three before clicking from one application to another or the computer might freeze up.") However, if computer software designers were watching us, assuming they could avoid collapsing in hysterical laughter, they would learn

our ancestors tossed down them, long buried over the centuries, were a treasure trove of old colonial quotidian life.

* *Archival measures.* A sociologist in Philadelphia cataloged the marriage licenses recorded and found that the probability of two people getting married varied directly with how close the two people's families' houses were to one another. Sir Francis Galton even used archives in the nineteenth century to determine the efficacy of prayer! Reasoning that royal families were prayed for most often, he suggested they should therefore be long-lived—if prayer helped. Instead, he found the average life span of royalty to be only 64.04 years, writers and scientists 67.55 years, and gentry 70.22 years.

* *Observational measures.* To determine the popularity of various radio stations, auto mechanics have been instructed to check the radio push-button settings and report them to the investigator. More contrived measures include arming research subjects with pagers, beeping them at random intervals, and asking them what they are doing at that moment.

how their programs fail us. We might think to tell them of all the keyboard rain dances we perform, but the likelihood is that we would not remember them all.

When the Sundberg-Ferar product development firm was helping Rubbermaid develop a new walker for adults with limited mobility, they convened in nursing homes focus groups of people using walkers. "What could we do to improve your walkers?" they asked. "What don't you like about them?" The participants shook their heads. They liked their walkers as they were. Nope, they couldn't suggest any improvements if the walker could be redesigned from scratch. The researchers gave up and excused the group members.

Only as the respondents got up and retrieved their walkers to exit the room did the researchers find that one woman had tied a bicycle basket to her walker with shoe strings; a man had fashioned a holder for his cordless phone out of duct tape; another had hung an aftermarket automotive cupholder on his walker! They had not thought to mention to the researchers these little home-made additions. These observations led Sundberg-Ferar to design a built-in, flexible mesh pouch for walkers, providing what Rubbermaid called a CCA, a compelling competitive advantage.[41]

Activities often have an emotional or psychological content that remains untapped by questionnaires or surveys.[42] Kimberly-Clark launched a very successful new diaper line after in-home visits by design firm GVO. The designers recognized that both toddlers and their parents were embarrassed by diapers—yet small children still needed them. As a step toward "grown-up" clothes, the design team developed Huggies Pull-Ups which satisfied the ego requirements of customers—and kept the children dry.[43] MTV sends researchers into the field to dig through the dormitory rooms, closets, and CD collections of eighteen- to twenty-four–year olds, because younger teenagers aspire to be like these older role models. The younger consumers often won't admit or don't understand themselves the psychological impact of the others on their tastes, but MTV can foresee what users are going to want.[44]

People also fail to identify options in interviews simply because they don't know what is possible—what your group can do. You may have a technical solution to a problem that would not occur to anyone with less expertise. The lumber products company Weyerhaeuser was in danger of losing a lot of business because one of their customers, a major furniture maker, was laminating together thin boards produced by Weyerhaeuser competitors to create inexpensive table legs. Weyerhaeuser was unable either to match the competitors' prices or to convince the customer to pay more for superior quality. After a visit to the customer's plant, Weyerhaeuser engineers came up with a whole new way to make table legs—a new, much thicker particleboard that did not have to be laminated.

The consequent savings to customers in tooling and labor costs put Weyerhaeuser back in the competitive running.

Cool-Hunting

Related to empathic design is the hunt for what is "cool"—the bizarre, the different, the norm breaking. The term cool-hunting comes from the fashion industry—locating what people are doing individually that may be adopted by a larger segment of the market. The underlying concept is to stretch the boundaries of your options by seeking nontraditional, possibly idiosyncratic and extreme examples of solutions before they become popular. So, for instance, when cool-hunters saw kids wearing baggy pants or dressed all in black or painting their nails green, they thought, Hey! such outlandish garb could become a trend if supported and promoted by the industry. When Converse's cool-hunter DeeDee Gordon was in Los Angeles, she saw white teenage girls dressing like *cholos*, or Mexican gangsters, wearing tight white tank tops known as "wife beaters," a bra strap hanging out, long shorts, tube socks, and shower sandals. As she recalls, she came back to tell fellow cool-hunter Baysie Wightman, "I'm telling you, Baysie, this is going to hit. There are just too many people wearing it. We have to make a shower sandal."[45] They did, retrofitting the hugely popular Converse One Star by cutting off the back and putting a thick outsole on it. The sandal was an immediate and long-lasting hit. On the advice of cool-hunters, Sony designed their Walkman for athletic users, the Freq, with heavy-duty clips, like chains, since they had noticed the emergence of chains as decoration among the ultracool. When Youth Intelligence, a New York firm, suggested to telecommunications giant Sprint that tattoos would become popular, Sprint used temporary tattoos as part of a calling-card promotion targeting students. The program produced twice as many sign-ups as expected.[46]

Cool-hunters, like empathic design teams, use up a lot of film, and go where the knowledge is—where cool kids hang out. Gordon spent hours in the then-cool area of New York, SoHo, snapping pictures of everyone walking by. Wightman watches the skateboarders or snowboarders for ideas. It is definitely difficult to pin down how cool-hunters get their ideas, but after following some around for a while, one writer concluded that

> the key to coolhunting . . . is to look for cool people first and cool things later, and not the other way around. Since cool things are always changing, you can't look for them, because the very fact they are cool means you have no idea what to look for. What you would be doing is thinking back on what was cool before and extrapolating, which is about as useful as presuming that because the Dow rose ten points yesterday it will rise another ten points today. Cool people, on the other hand, are a constant.[47]

Most cool-hunting is done among the young and uninhibited as well as possibly inexperienced. So, for instance, if you were designing a new magazine, what could you learn from visiting some of the tiny Web sites set up by start-up publications? Although cool-hunting trips are mostly conducted by fashion-driven organizations in search of new product ideas, the process of generating options by seeking the far-out behaviors of possible trendsetters applies more broadly.

Attribute Benchmarking

Almost everyone knows about benchmarking—at least the usual kind. You send out a task force to compare your performance or process with that of other organizations. It is a win-win activity. If the other group does it better than yours, you can imitate. If they do it worse, you can crow (once you are back home). There are whole books on how to benchmark—but we are suggesting a somewhat different kind here. First, you don't want to go to performers within your own industry. Oh, sure, you can learn a lot, but you are likely to get more creative ideas if you: (1) go outside your known competitors and (2) isolate attributes, characteristics, or functions that are especially critical to the innovation opportunity you are addressing. When 3M was designing hearing aids, the engineers pondered how to make the instrument as invisible as possible. Expert in electronics, miniaturization, and the function of the auditory nerve, they nevertheless had little knowledge about aesthetics. The options they could generate were limited. Who knows the most about matching skin tones with various materials? Cosmetic dentistry, they decided—and they found a wealth of information by visiting firms in that business.

Solutions to one problem can be transferred to another, but if you don't stretch to think in terms of functionality instead of product or service category, you are unlikely to identify them. After World War II, Heathkit came up with a novel idea for commercializing sonar technology. What use could the technology be put to besides locating submarines? Consider its function: Sonar identifies under-water objects and allows a visual display of their shape. Hmm, what might Sonar reveal underwater that would be useful to consumers, consumers such as . . . fishermen! Hence was born the predecessor to today's fish-locators, purchased by many sportsmen for their boats. The fish-locator's performance is limited, of course, to the functions provided by sonar technology. As one purchaser ruefully noted of his new equipment, "It doesn't really work. It shows me where the fish are—but it doesn't make them bite!"

When Ceramics Process Systems Corporation was founded, the MIT professors who started the company understood from the beginning that, internationally known experts though they were, they were unlikely to possess all the knowledge they needed to apply their technological breakthrough to various problem arenas. Counteracting the temptation to build on only the scientific foundations the founders were most familiar with, the first president had a framed statement on his wall: "Our most important technical breakthroughs will come from disciplines and literature outside our industry and scientific field."[48] When they subsequently experienced difficulties in separating ceramics pieces from the mold and realized that temperature differentials could help, they sought the best expertise on fast freezing they could—the frozen foods industry. When they needed to figure out options for producing a smooth, thin layer of an emulsion, they brought in a Sherwin Williams paint expert.

A government postal service trying to improve the customer experience had a major breakthrough in their thinking when the members of the task force began visiting retailers known for personalized, friendly service. An option that they had never considered was to have postal clerks come out from behind their counters to ask "may I help you?" just as a salesperson at the Nordstrom clothing store would. When this approach was implemented in the Washington, D.C. area, customers were initially puzzled both because the context was so different for this kind of service and because they did not expect innovation from a quasi-government agency.

We've now considered a pretty wide range of techniques designed to avoid the urge to merge and to promote a wider exploration of options. While these techniques all help generate options, they don't help select one. All those possibilities! Now to narrow down to the one that will work in your context. Chapter 4 addresses the next stage of the creative process, namely convergence.

Back to Hazel...

Friday arrived, and Hazel was disappointed. The troops were uninspired—the storyboards were bland, devoid of the humor and the spark she had hoped for. She decided to gather the group members for another round of brainstorming. "Any suggestions?" she asked, with faint hope. "At this point I'm really open to suggestions." Despite Hazel's apparent new openness, Geraldine was clearly skeptical about Hazel's willingness to revisit the original decision to go with the puppies. "I was thinking," she said hesitantly. "My brother was a Peace Corps volunteer in West Africa. Maybe we could invite him in if we are going to talk about picturing children in a developing nation." A quick glance at Hazel. She was nodding! Geraldine was encouraged enough to continue. "We don't know that we couldn't do something inoffensive. I think he could give us some perspective."

Jose wanted to start even further back in the process. "I think we should go visit some distance learning centers," he said. "Frankly, I don't have the slightest idea how it all works. The trainers from the center didn't give me a real feel for what message we should be putting across. I'll bet we would come back with all sorts of ideas."

"I know it sounds weird," Hank offered. "But we could sort of try out what it would be like to do distance learning, you know—role play the teacher and the students—if it's too expensive for us all to go to the center. Linda knows a lot about Greek mythology, for instance. She could be the instructor and some of us could be the students over the company closed TV network. And the rest of us could observe. Just a few minutes worth, Linda," he added, seeing her start to object. "Just to get an idea of what it might feel like and how it's different from regular school."

"Why not have the center include us in their next regular session tomorrow evening instead?" Linda said. "Then we'd have real instructors and real topics—see what it is like as a consumer. We might see a way to do the university professor lampoon. And I'd much rather give up my dinner time than try to simulate it ourselves."

David chimed in: "Then we could get together tomorrow morning and brainstorm the messages again. I get some of my best ideas at night."

"Any chance we could get your brother in to talk with us tomorrow morning, Geraldine?" Jose asked. "Then we could brainstorm in the afternoon."

Hazel sat back in amazement. There was so much more energy in the room than when they had come in. Given this level of enthusiasm, the group would surely come up with more options. Then, could she get them to agree on one in time to make the deadline?

Key Points

Generating lots of options, while only part of the overall creative process, is often equated with "creativity." Particular care must be taken to maximize the group's ability to think divergently:

* Give the group the maximum allowable time to generate options; use brainstorming, but be aware of its limitations.

* Group leaders should frame the problem as clearly as possible, but refrain from indicating a preferred solution.

* Except when strict security is required, keep the group's boundaries as permeable as possible. Encourage members to discuss options—and solicit new ones—from spouses, friends, and colleagues. Visit aliens whose expertise may be tangential to your primary concerns.

* Recognize that a group can sometimes be a little too cozy. Rotate membership and bring in "new blood" as projects change.

* Develop a simple set of ground rules designed to promote divergent thinking, welcome dissent, and depersonalize conflict.

* Protect dissenters by publicly supporting them.

* Be alert to implicit norms (e.g., "don't rock the boat") that inhibit creativity.

* As the group approaches a consensus, appoint a member as devil's advocate, instructed to challenge the group forcefully and persuasively.

* Seemingly implausible or impractical options are often the most creative. Help make them more plausible by having members vividly imagine their success or through role-playing techniques.

* Tap the natural and social world for ideas. Encourage the use of metaphors from nature and other worlds of knowledge.

* Empathic design can help identify the unarticulated needs of customers, customers' customers, and noncustomers.

Answers and interpretation

1. A matchbox is supposed to hold matches, right? Not be emptied of its contents and tacked to the wall to support a candle. When people

are presented with this problem with the contents of the matchbox already emptied, they are much better at solving it.

2. 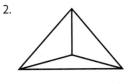 Hey, who said the solution was limited to two dimensions? Yet most people who approach this problem *assume* that they are so limited. We must stretch our thinking to encompass a third dimension if we are to avoid being fix-ated on our false assumptions.

3. What did you try? 15, 20, 25? 100, 105, 110? For each of these, we would answer yes, they fit our rule. You might then conclude from this feedback that our rule is to count by 5. If so, you would be wrong. The rule is simply to name three ascending numbers. If you're like most folks, you will only give number sequences that you think *confirm* the rule, not those you think might *disconfirm* it (say, 15, 20, 30 or 1, 2, 3, both of which, you would be told, fit the rule).

4

Converging on the Best Options

Larry was feeling very pleased with the group's progress. The walls were a kaleidoscope of various hues of Post-its and flip-chart sheets. Clearly, the three afternoons of concentrated effort by his team had produced a set of creative options, many of them fleshed out and elaborated. Good thing, too. It was essential that the revenue agency radically reshape how it did business with state taxpayers or that legislative committee would be on him before he could say "next year's appropriation."

"Well, it's 4:30 and I think we're all about talked out, but we should be able to wrap this up in the next hour or so. I'm really impressed with all the creativity that's gone into coming up with these options. Now let's spend the remaining time narrowing them down to the one we can go with. I'd still like a draft action plan I can take to Chuck tomorrow."

But the chorus of protests soon put an end to Larry's warm glow.

"Hey, this is too important to stop now. I have some more ideas I wanted to try out," began Patricia.

"I don't think we need any more ideas—the walls won't hold them. But I don't feel I've done a very effective job arguing for my plan. First of all . . ." continued Ming, before he was interrupted by Boris.

"As I've tried to explain, obviously not forcefully enough, I think

we're on the wrong track completely. The issue shouldn't be how to make the public happy—there always will be jerks out there—it should be image! There's a lot we can do to look good without necessarily changing the way we do things. We're doing fine as it is."

"Larry, I'm with you," said Ellen. "I think the plan that combines retraining everyone in how to deal with the public along with your ideas on using information technology is the way to go. Let's fish or cut bait."

Nguyen was the last to enter the fray. "Listen, guys, I know we all have to get back to our jobs, but I really feel that I need to think about this some more. Let's adjourn, have some drinks, and get back together in the morning."

In the silence that followed Nguyen's last suggestion, the only sound, Larry realized, was that of his fingers drumming on the table.

What a disappointment! Larry's belief that creativity means just generating lots of novel options has resulted in a stalled, fractious group—even though they have given him just what he asked for. We saw in Chapter 3 the dangers of rushing to premature consensus, and Larry has been studious in allowing a full exploration of divergent ideas. Any manager knows that there comes a time when the process of creativity must move from the divergent to the convergent stage. But when Larry allotted "an hour or so" for convergence after almost three full afternoons of divergent thinking it was a little like planning a fishing trip for three days, then spending an hour in the boat. At the risk of repeating ourselves: Creativity is a process, and each stage of the process must be given substantial, serious attention.

Incubation, or "Sleep on It"

Why do we tell people to "sleep on it"? In ancient Rome, a rite of incubation (from *incubare*, "to lie down upon") involved lying on a mat to communicate with underworld deities through dreams. In the five-step creative process, incubation occupies the step between divergence and convergence. During this fermentation period—a time when the various options occupy the brains of the individual members but without group discussion—those brains continue to work on the problem, but freed from the constraints of conscious, rational, logical thinking—the kind of thinking that can impede creativity. During incubation, new options may emerge, as well as sudden insights of convergence. This transitional stage, bridging divergence and convergence, has been likened to "mental meandering" by psychologist Donald Campbell, who finds it

> one of the values in walking to work. . . . Or if driving, not to have the car radio on. . . . [C]reativity has to be a profoundly wasteful process. And that mental meandering, mind wandering and so on, is an essential process. If you are allowing that mentation to be driven by the radio or the television or other people's conversations, you are just cutting down on your . . . intellectual exploratory time.[1]

Of the people in Larry's group, Nguyen seems to have one of the better ideas. Even though Larry is trying his best to hustle everybody along to a final solution, Nguyen realizes that some reflection time, some mental meandering, is needed. After a bit of relaxation—and sleep—everyone will be in better shape the next morning to reevaluate the options and begin the convergence process.

In fact, there are many examples from the research on individual creativity that suggest the power of tapping into the unconscious during sleep or a relaxed state. Elias Howe beat Singer to the patent for the sewing machine when he dreamed he was in a jungle surrounded by natives holding spears, with holes near their tips. He awoke with the realization that putting a thread hole near the tip of the needle (instead of at its head, as for hand sewing) would work. Some inventors have tied in even more directly to their unconscious problem solving. Sir Frederick Banting, searching for the cause of diabetes, had a dream that suggested tying up the pancreas of a dog and monitoring the insulin produced. He tried it and learned about the balance between sugar and insulin and the relationship of this imbalance to diabetes. Otto Loewi dreamed of an experiment with frogs to demonstrate the chemical, rather than electrical, nature of nervous impulse transmission. Awakening in the middle of the night, he scribbled down the idea—but couldn't read his note in the morning! The next night he had the same dream and this time, happily, his note was legible. Like Banting, he became a Nobel laureate.[2]

However, apparently creative solutions do not occur just to geniuses during their nightly incubation. Floyd Ragsdale, an employee of Du Pont, was having trouble with a machine that manufactured Kevlar fiber, used in bulletproof vests. Downtime on the machine cost $700 a minute, so Du Pont's best engineers tried unsuccessfully to fix the problem. Ragsdale, an engineer with no college education, had a dream in which he saw the tubes of a machine and springs. He came to work the next day and told his boss, whose reaction was to scoff. After Ragsdale's shift ended, he went ahead anyway on his own time, inserted springs into the tubes and the machine worked, saving the company more than $3 million.[3]

So do we suggest encouraging employees to sleep on the job? No, but neither do we advocate keeping everyone in a state of unrelenting mental alertness. The point is that dreaming, meditation, showering, driving to work, may all provide opportunities for subconscious thought—but only if sufficient time is provided for this reflection to bear fruit. And as we shall see in Chapter 5, much can be done to create conditions at work to foster reflection and incubation of creative ideas. Managers are often reluctant to allow this time for reflection—especially if they themselves usually drive to immediate action. Randy Komisar, a "virtual CEO" who advises start-ups in California's Silicon Valley, believes that "a lot of people are stuck with the inability to shed distractions and therefore cannot use their intuition. They have anxiety around not having the answers. To use intuition, you have to relax, let the answer come to you.

THE DYNAMICS OF INCUBATION

There have been many attempts to understand the mysterious, unobservable nature of incubation. The traditional Freudian take is that people unconsciously work through repressed childhood sexual conflicts, *sublimating* them into creative products. Few people find this view particularly useful—that innovative Windows application actually represents the resolution of some childhood incestuous yearnings? Instead, most psychologists adopt some type of *information-processing* approach. Removed from conscious attention, cognitive work does not stop, but ideas begin to associate randomly. They become unshackled from the forces—logic, convention, habit—that normally prevent the uninhibited linking of thoughts and information. Most of the resulting unconscious associations are worthless—unusual, perhaps, but not useful. But those associations that "work" may subsequently pop back into consciousness, where they may be recognized as a creative insight. There is some disagreement about whether the mere passage of time is sufficient to produce a creative insight, or whether there has to be some additional information that triggers the insight,[4] but it's clear that time away from the task is crucial for the creative process.

People are uncomfortable with that; they believe they have got to be able to think it through. Analysis can be highly overrated."[5]

Some individuals, perhaps like Nguyen in the opening vignette, have a preference for introversion in processing data. They want time to think by themselves before commenting on the options. Writer Harriet Doerr, who amazed the world by producing her first (best-selling) novel at age 73, explains, "Other people don't need to be alone with their thoughts so much. I sort of starve if I don't have time alone. I feel like I'm not caught up. There's unthought thoughts waiting to be thought. That's why I like gardening so much. I do my best writing with the sun and the plants. Some of it floats away, but not all of it."[6] For such individuals, incubation is an important part of their thinking style and critical to their ability to contribute. However, regardless of individual thinking-style preferences, incubation is important to creativity because of the opportunity it allows for our subconscious to work on a problem.

In today's "I-need-it-yesterday" world, incubation may seem an unnatural act. But when a group is running in place, rather than making progress toward convergence, some managers have found it useful to allow, or even insist on, recess. When Nissan Design International employees were bogged down in the midst of designing the Pathfinder, then vice president Jerry Hirshberg decided to have everyone play hooky. In the middle of the day, he took the entire company (including modeling shop technicians, secretaries, and the maintenance crew) to see the opening of the thriller *The Silence of the Lambs.* His decision was not easy to explain. A writer from *AutoWeek* magazine who had called while the entire company was closed, only to be informed by the temporary receptionist that everyone was at the movies, tested Hirshberg's own inventive capacity when he asked what the connection was between serial murder and car design! And Kengo Ishida, NDI's new president at the time, asked why everyone was leaving then, when the company was so far behind in the project. Hirshberg's explanation? "We're going now, Kengo-san *because* we're behind." And did it have the desired effect? Hirshberg reports that "The tension in the building began to dissipate. Within days, the ideas started flowing, knotty problem areas unraveled, and the design began to lead the designers, a sure sign that a strong concept was emerging."[7]

"Rather than 'amping up' the pressure when a staff is struggling," Hirshberg writes, "the *creative priority* often suggests a releasing of tension and a *stepping back* from the immediate problems as a far more effective managerial strategy."[8] Jerry Hirshberg explains his sensitivity to the need for "stepping back" from the canvas to his training as an artist, when he learned that merely working harder didn't always solve the problem he was wrestling with. However, like all managers, he is still tempted to drive for solutions. He tells the story on himself that when his group was wrestling with the design of the Sentra, the designers met with the Design Context Lab (a nontraditional market research group within the company) and came up with what seemed to be a strong consensus about the direction the development should take. The "phrase *destination product,* resonated with the group and stuck as a rallying cry throughout the project. It immediately prompted multiple images and new options. Feeling relief and considerable eagerness to get moving, I suggested we now zero in on some specific design directions.

" 'Wrrong!' intoned Nick Backlund, the Design Context Lab manager. 'Let's *not* focus yet. Let's adjourn.' He was one hundred percent right, and we did just that. In my rush for an answer, I was about to close a window that had just been opened."[9]

Convergence

Once the group stops emphasizing *novel* and starts concentrating on *useful,* some members may want to bail out. The fun is over, they think, once hard decisions have to be made. True, it can be a giddy experience to work where the rubber meets the air instead of where it meets the road, but innovative groups get satisfaction out of progress toward a goal. The challenges to managers in accomplishing that progress are numerous and include the following:

* working within reasonable boundaries;

* coming to a common, shared concept of the innovation;

* ensuring that the process doesn't end up so strongly identifying winners and losers that the "losers" leave;

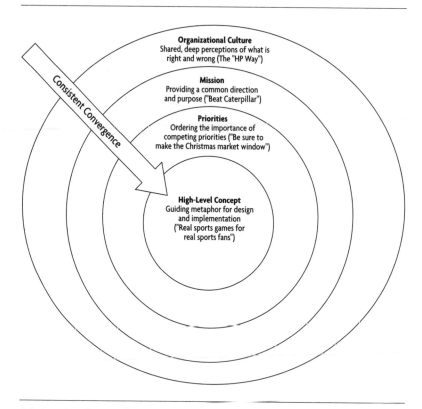

4-1 Levels of Boundaries

* helping the group define the goal clearly and keeping members focused on that goal. (It *is* possible for members to become so immersed in the details that the objective is lost sight of—what a manager we know calls losing sight of the forest and getting "lost in the bark.")

As in prior chapters, let us first discuss the managerial issues and then suggest some specific techniques for encouraging convergence. We suggest a hierarchy of boundaries that guide the selection of one option from many, starting from the broadest and least confining guidelines (organizational culture) and becoming ever more project-specific (Figure 4-1).

ORGANIZATIONAL CULTURE AND INNOVATION

Using the Department of Labor's taxonomy of the characteristics of U.S. organizations, Sharon Arad, Mary Ann Hanson, and Robert Schneider analyzed those characteristics that affect innovation. The analysis of organizational *values* related to innovation identified four factors: (1) people orientation (e.g., collaboration, supportiveness, team orientation); (2) risk taking (willingness to experiment, aggressiveness); (3) attention to detail (precision, results orientation); and (4) stability (security of employment). An organizational culture that supports risk taking, collaboration, quality, and security, these results suggest, is likely to be innovative and "high performance." They further found that these organizational values correlate positively with use of teams and information sharing, both of which suggest a high level of group interaction.[10]

Organizational Culture

How would you describe a strong organizational culture? One in which members share perceptions about the criteria for making decisions: what is right and wrong, acceptable and not, encouraged and discouraged. Could be the National Rifle Association or the Garden Club, the 127,000 employees of the huge Hewlett-Packard corporation or the 25 worldwide at tiny start-up CoWare. Obviously, culture in general can abet or inhibit creativity, and in Chapter 6, we discuss how leaders can design the culture of their organizations to promote creativity. Here our interest is more specific: How can the cultural values of an organization help members of a group within it converge on the best solution when many are offered?

Even quite high-level organizational values about what is "right" and "wrong" can influence decisions and hence convergence. In Los Angeles, a city sometimes more noted for deal-making angles than angels, Castle Rock Entertainment has a reputation for open, honest, fair dealing. Alan Horn, chairman and CEO, believes that the values he and his founding partners shared permeate the company "stem to stern." Anyone who does not share the passion for honesty, for dealing fairly with people, is soon out of a job. "We go out of our way not to give people a run-around," Horn declares. Having a reputation among talent agents for giving honest responses— quickly—means that the agents view Castle Rock as a good company to work with. And agents often hold the key to attracting top actors and directors to creative projects.[11]

At CoWare, a Santa Clara, California–based company that provides comprehensive software/hardware codesign tools for developers of "systems on a chip," cofounder, president, and CEO Guido Arnout is similarly passionate about corporate values. Some early stands in support of the values of community and respect are already legendary in the young company. For example, a prime CoWare customer was almost "fired" because of an ethnic slur directed toward an employee. Only after the customer representative apologized did business (critical to the survival of CoWare) proceed. This incident demonstrated the founders' commitment to the value of "respect for the individual" beyond any doubt.[12] As Rosabeth Moss Kanter notes, "values must reflect enduring commitments, not ephemeral notions."[13]

Such values aid convergence because if any suggested solutions to a problem violate the community norms, they are clearly out of bounds and can be rejected on that basis. There are other, intangible benefits to a strong culture if the group members share common values: a sense of belonging and trust that encourages open communication and risk taking, an enthusiasm for the organization. These we will discuss in Chapter 6. But let's think about those times when you have to make choices among some specific design options in creating a new product. Can you put your money not just where your mouth is, but where your heart is?

Consider the following dilemma at Mattel's Fisher-Price division. The action figure market for little boys is a *big* one—and Fisher-

Price is in the toy business (among others). But the company values, reflecting a dedication to pleasing primary purchaser Mom as well as child, include a strong prohibition against violent toys. So how could they pursue this important market segment without producing shoot-'em-up Rambo figures? Marilyn Wilson-Hadid, vice president of marketing (the dominant function at Fisher-Price), and Peter Pook, vice president of product development, argued long and hard. Pook insisted that the action figure market segment was critical. Wilson-Hadid steadfastly maintained that no Fisher-Price toy could present violence in a favorable light. Every product concept Pook offered, Wilson-Hadid countered with: "How are we going to talk to the mothers about this?"

Options included ideas such as "equip-men" with super power tools that were a kind of "un-gun," but would appeal to the same desire for combat as action figures, with their oversized weapons. The final positioning? Rescue Heroes—"cool guys that are good guys": Billy Blazes, Fire Fighter; Rocky Canyon, Mountain Ranger; Gil Gripper, Scuba Diver; and Jack Hammer, "Construction Expert." Each figure is equipped with a special tool that does something dramatic when a trigger is pulled, pushed, or released. The policeman has a noisy bullhorn and siren, the (female) Fire Fighter has a chopping axe, the Scuba Diver has a clamp, the Construction Expert has a jackhammer. The toys have been a huge success because they please both little boys' desire for action and Mom's preference that it be more positive than violence against others. In fact (somewhat to the surprise of the designers), children are observed to engage in "helpful behavior," such as using the toys to "rescue" other figures in imaginary straits. The product thus protects what Fisher-Price teams value as a distinctive advantage: the "Mom benefit."[14]

The Mission Thing

First the bad news about the ubiquitous Mission Statement. Even though the great majority of organizations have one, it has earned a bad name. Some are superficial or inconsistently applied; others are so general and nondistinctive as to be next to worthless. ("At our university, we will give our students the best possible education to prepare them for life and work." Well, yes, but what university wouldn't do that?) A mission statement will not rescue a company or group in trouble, nor will a wish list disguised as a mission statement generate employee enthusiasm. But the good news is that a thoughtful, common mission does serve to unite people. The purpose of the group does not have to be formalized into a gold-framed statement on every office wall. It just has to be clear and shared, so that group members have criteria by which to make hourly decisions. What is important and what isn't? What kinds of innovation serve the purpose of the group and what kinds don't?

Notes British Petroleum CEO John Browne,

> A business has to have a clear purpose. If the purpose is not crystal clear, people in the business will not understand what kind of knowledge is critical and what they have to learn in order to improve performance. . . . Our purpose is who we are and what makes us distinctive. It's what we as a company exist to achieve, and what we're willing and not willing to do to achieve it.[15]

The mission or purpose of a group, then, exists within the value system or culture of an organization. (Some authors draw a tight distinction between mission and objectives; here we are concerned with alignment and convergence on a common direction. We leave it to others to tease out the distinctions.) The point is that a common goal unites team members and gives them a sense of purpose. A group or corporate mission can serve as such a uniting force.

Groups may converge around a battle flag. Earth-moving equipment giant Komatsu's slogan was for a time "Beat Caterpillar." Common rivals, enemies, or threats can spur creativity by uniting people who otherwise avoid working together. During World War II, the British produced radar, faster airplanes, and computers in an unprecedented collaboration born of the common mission to defeat Hitler. "Strong links were forged between scientists and engineers, between labs and the plants that were to produce their inventions, between designers and the military users of the new devices."[16] Once the war was won, British science, government, and labor returned to internal squabbling, and both innovation and the economy sagged.

The "enemy" need not be a rival country or company. At Northwestern Medical Hospital outside of Chicago, patients were dying of a hospital-borne infection. A task force was formed to combat the strain identified as bacterium *enterococcus*. Begun by two infectious disease specialists, the task force was soon widened to include a pharmacist, who discovered that the germ actually thrived on antibiotics; computer technicians and admissions personnel, who found a link to outpatients bringing in the pathogen; and even maintenance personnel, who identified a shortage of sinks, resulting in retrofitting drinking fountains to encourage frequent hand washing.[17]

For many people, fighting *for* an objective is more inspiring than fighting *against*. At office supply giant Staples, Inc., founder Thomas G. Sternberg stated the company's mission as "Slashing the cost and hassle of running your office!" and every employee receives a wallet-sized card with that mission inscribed on it.[18] The informal mission of Intuit (maker of financial-planning software Quicken) is equally simple: "to make customers feel so good about the product they'll go and tell five friends to buy it." When Steve Jobs and Steve Wozniak started Apple Computer, their goal was to design and build affordable personal computers.[19]

WebTV Networks, Inc., has a somewhat similar mission. Founded in 1995 by Bruce Leak, Phil Goldman, and current CEO Steve Perlman to provide an enhanced television service integrated with Internet access, WebTV's corporate vision is "to connect average people through their television sets." This vision has been a powerful force for convergence: Compromises can be made in time to market, costs, and features, but the vision is never violated. This does not mean that the vision can never be changed. Evolution happens. "It may be modified later, but for now we'll all march to the same drummer," says Perlman.[20]

So missions can aid convergence and choice by providing boundaries for decision making. If we are Komatsu, how do the new product concepts we are considering stack up against Caterpillar's product line? If we are Intuit, which suggested improvements will really make the customer feel good—about paying bills? If we are WebTV, which options are low enough in cost and easy enough to use with the television that Dad and the twelve-year-old will *both* want to use it (and even Dad will be able to figure out *how*)?

Priorities

Creativity can coexist—in fact, some would say, must coexist—with priorities and boundaries. When Louis Gerstner came from running credit card and consumer goods companies to take over the leadership of IBM, he cut and refocused research at IBM's Nobel Prize–winning Research Division. His priority? Stop letting other companies commercialize IBM's research first. That decision meant that researchers started focusing on potential for real-world applications in their projects. Clear overall priorities provide much guidance for convergence within individual projects. What is more important: making the trade show or having a more visually exciting introduction to a particular product? Pleasing the political constituency or keeping costs down?

WebTV CEO Perlman gives his teams a list to guide their design decisions. In descending order of importance, the priorities are:

1. Vision ("Connect average people together through their televisions.")

2. Schedule ("Market windows don't move.")

3. Cost ("There's serious buyer resistance above $199.")

4. Features ("Bells and whistles are fun—and make engineers happy.")[21]

Creative groups are always tempted to emphasize Features over the others because developing new features exercises the developers' expertise and imagination. However, in many businesses, a wonderful solution a few weeks late is all but valueless. Miss the Christmas/Hanukkah season in the toys, games, or computer businesses, and you have lost half your profit. Easter bunnies don't deliver the same kinds of presents. And there are known price points above which certain products become infeasible, making cost paramount. For WebTV in 1998, $199 and $299 for their two levels of hardware interface with the television were the critical price points, above which the equipment was too much of an investment for the average U.S. family. At electronic games company Electronic Arts, the artists who build the fantasy environments in which the characters act would delight in creating simulations of reality that would rival film. However, details cost money, and the games have to remain affordable. Therefore, the artists are compelled to build images with the minimum possible number of polygons so as to stay within budgetary bounds.

Randy Komisar tells the story of setting some tough priorities when he was leading Lucas Arts in 1995. He felt certain that the company really needed a sequel to Rebel Assault (a popular 1993 game). The game developers argued that a sequel was not creative enough and wouldn't live up to the expectations set by the first very successful game. Sequels, they noted, average only 70 percent of the original business and while there was less risk of failure, there was less chance of a windfall. A big debate ensued internally over the priorities: innovation versus schedule and plan. Komisar decided that the sequel was too good to pass up. "The reward versus risk was a no-brainer—but the timeline was key. A *day* older can mean a *year* older when the game hits the store shelf, if you miss Christmas." Therefore, resources had to be allocated to this project, and other projects would be delayed. "Left to their own devices," Komisar says, "the teams would never have made the same tradeoff. Instead they would have insisted on making the Christmas deadline for all the projects—and would have missed on them all."[22]

As these examples demonstrate, priorities are often *not* consensus decisions by group members, but conditions imposed by group leaders in order to drive convergence.

High-Level Concepts

How about this for a product concept of a new sports car: "Schwartz-enegger—rugged but cultured"? In 1994, Ford's "Team Mustang" used it to guide design decisions about the sound of the engine, the upholstery, the lights.[23] Even working within the guidelines of culture and mission, group members still need guidance for specific, often minute decisions about the design and implementation of the innovation they are attempting. The whole has to be a harmonious aggregation of the parts. Product concepts or high-level specifications are powerful convergence mechanisms. For example, Fisher-Price designers working on a play kitchen for little girls found it helpful to keep in mind, "*realistic* kitchen play through water play."[24]

At Electronic Arts, the vision for their electronic sports games evolved over time. "The original high concept was sports simulations—an action game with strategy and statistical accuracy. Up until then the sports games had been action games with player numbers on the backs of the figures. We tried to create games with more real sports action, more verisimilitude. Then we said: 'OK, what does this mean?' And we came up with: Real Sports Games for Real Sports Fans."[25] And this concept has some real teeth! In the old Apple II days, Electronic Arts signed a contract with former Oakland Raider coach, John Madden, to use his name in a football game. However, when the product, "John Madden Football," was presented to Madden, he wouldn't allow the game to be shipped, since available memory on the old Apple limited the game to seven players on a side! It was two years more on the drawing board before John Madden Football, true to "Real Sports Games for Real Sports Fans," could be sold.[26]

The advantage of vivid high-level concepts is that group members are herded in the same direction, but with considerable autonomy. They know where they need to go—and they can decide for themselves how to get there. One of the ironies of management is that the more you wish (or need) to delegate, the clearer must be the objective. Suppose we agreed to meet in New York City on the corner of Fifth Avenue and 48th Street exactly one year from this date, at 4:00 in the afternoon. Assuming that we had the resources to get there, it is not necessary for us to specify the exact mode of transportation nor the exact route. We can decide that for ourselves. This is obviously an oversimplified example, since creative teams operate within multiple constraints. However, the principle is sound. The clearer the destination and schedule, the more decisions about how to get there can be delegated. Because they are bounded but still subject to some individual interpretation, high-level concepts leave room for group creativity and interpretation. Rather than constraining group members, such clarity empowers them to act on their own.[27]

Consistent Convergence

Convergence at one level is incomplete if the solution violates the assumptions of a higher level. That is, if the high-level product concept assigned to a project does not fit the priorities or the organizational mission, or if it violates community culture, any convergence is likely to be temporary—unless you intend to revisit one of the higher-order guiding boundaries. Fisher-Price's Rescue Heroes originated because the product concept of an action figure as usually personified violated an organizational value of delivering "Mom benefits" as well as value to the child—so the product concept had to be altered. Of course whole new businesses sometimes grow out of violating boundary guidelines, but managers need to make such moves deliberately.

Prototyping

"If you have a choice between planning and prototyping, choose the latter," says Paul Horn, senior vice president and director of IBM Research.[28] The prototype is a compelling mechanism to aid

VALUE CONSISTENCY

Organizations sometimes mirror individuals in terms of their priorities and how they deal with challenges to those priorities. The work of social psychologist Milton Rokeach examined the role of *centrality* (akin to importance) in predicting attitude and behavior change. For individuals, their *sense of self*, conceptions of who they are (comparable to organizational *culture*), is most central. Next most central are *values*—those beliefs, such as freedom, equality, and wisdom, that people consider essential as guiding principles in their lives (akin to organizational *mission*). Our *attitudes*—likes and dislikes—toward policies, people, foods, whatever, are least central (like organizational *priorities, product concepts, and specifications*).

Rokeach was particularly interested in situations where people experienced inconsistencies among the self, values, attitudes, and behavior. For example, if Joe considers himself a caring, humane person (self-image) who considers equality a prime social virtue (value), but realizes he has voted against a candidate (behavior) because he didn't think a woman could handle the job (attitude), then he is likely to experience some serious inconsistency. According to Rokeach, since self-concept and values are more central than attitudes, Joe is likely to change his attitude and behaviors to bring them into line. Just so, an executive who realizes that a company policy (e.g., withholding benefits to same-sex partners) is in conflict with its culture (the "HP Way") will be motivated to change the policy.

---

convergence because it is a preliminary vision of an innovation, embodied in some shape or form that can be shared. It can be handled, viewed, experienced, or discussed. Prototypes come in all sizes and shapes, from two-dimensional drawings to full scale, fully functional objects.

We tend to think of prototypes as hardware. Many are. Wander into any product development studio and you encounter a visual history of invention, in the form of numerous trial designs—objects that look strangely familiar and at the same time different because the actual finished product evolved beyond the particular prototype you see. At California-based design and engineering firm IDEO, you see various sized and configured computer mice and video/television remote controls that fit the hand differently, pieces of medical equipment made out of foam core and tubing, children's toys. Each prototype embodies an idea, and like coral skeletons, is a mute but potent reminder of a past organic process.

But simulations and videos can also function as prototypes, as can behaviors that are presented in informal dramatic presentations. Perhaps your innovation opportunity is an organizational change that is needed, or a behavior shift, or a new service. All of these can be prototyped. The role playing described in Chapter 3 as a divergence technique to flush out different viewpoints can be used as well to present a nascent innovation for convergence. Interval Research employees spent days observing a beautician in order to figure out how such an individual, who regarded a computer as an automated abacus for billing, might use computers and media for other tasks more directly relevant to hair care. After coming up with a number of ideas, they rigged up a prototype system that would allow a mirror to be transformed into a television screen, an enlarged view of an appointments book, or a video telephone—all positioned right in front of the seated customer and the beautician behind the chair. They then role-played and simulated the interactions of beautician and clients with the system, using gestural interfaces so that no one had to interrupt normal routines to touch anything. The simulation synthesized all that they had learned in their observations about operations in a beauty shop with all the technological solutions on which the team had converged. It also communicated graphically the concept to others.

Prototyping as Communication

Prototypes are invaluable communication tools because they provide a focus for discussion among people with different perspectives. No matter what their thinking-style preference or professional background, all the individuals address the same concrete embodiment of an innovation concept. The fact that they will *view* the prototype differently does not detract from its usefulness. In fact, being able to express those different views with respect to the same artifact greatly aids communication. The reason that the blind men describing an elephant differently is such a powerful metaphor for conflicting perspectives is that they are all describing the same animal. Good prototypes embody the whole animal, albeit in primitive form.

Thus the engineer working on a new television, let us say, focuses on its performance, whereas the industrial designer will also consider how user-friendly are the controls. They can evaluate the linkage between function and form by pointing to various parts of the equipment as they talk. One product manager with a very new and somewhat inexperienced team charged with creating a highly interactive Internet-based product, found it useful to set up a single computer in a conference room *daily* and gather his team around the single screen for discussion. "This way," he explained, "we all see exactly how far we are along in our progress. The prototype changes daily in small and subtle ways, and each of us needs to understand what the others are doing."

Prototypes are useful not only for communication among developers to aid in convergence but between the creating team and the target users. When the innovation is one the public at large understands, anyone's observation can lead to change. Jerry Hirshberg of Nissan Design International tells the story of how an executive secretary's opinion altered the design of the Cocoon. Everyone in the company was in the courtyard admiring the prototype of a new vehicle when Cathy Woo wandered out a bit late, having paused to pick up her cup of tea. Thus unaffected by the cozy warmth of everyone's adulation, she was the first and only to note the emperor was naked. "Well, it just looks fat, dumb, and ugly to me!" she said, with uncharacteristic bluntness. In the silence that followed, the designers recognized the truth of the observation that they had been hiding from themselves—and "now felt free to get out the scalpels and perform the major surgery [on the design] required."[29]

A word of caution about showing prototypes to potential users: Many people do not understand what a prototype is and will think you are closer to a solution than you may be if you show your progress prematurely. Notes Larry Shubert of the IDEO design company: "Often, once we've developed a prototype or model, clients without a lot of product development experience will want to start shipping the product the next day. They don't understand the amount of time, effort, and energy that goes into all the detailed engineering required to turn the concept into a real product."[30] Software engineers working on a new sales tool at a major computer company solicited the support of the vice president of sales by demonstrating their prototype just before Thanksgiving (the third week of November). To their delight, he loved the concept; to their dismay, he announced that they should have a finished version on every sales person's desk by Christmas—a month later! The project leader's reluctant acquiescence to this unrealistic schedule led to a new nickname for the project: The Christmas Goose. They were certain that their "goose would be cooked" for missing the deadline.

Moreover, your prototype needs to embody those aspects of the innovation that are really critical to users. When a creative group came up with a new service concept for home banking, they couldn't figure out how to explain clearly to their current and potential customers how the customer experience would change. They could show the software that the customer would use, but not how easily a customer could also reach a knowledgeable service representative at the bank. So they made a video of their new concept in action and showed it to customers. The video portrayed a customer first accessing information through the software, then encountering a problem, then telephoning the bank and using a touch-tone phone to work through the (at the time) novel menu of "push one for . . ." and reaching the person best equipped to aid them. The prototype was well received; users made minor suggestions and helped the convergence process immensely. However, users were very unhappy when the actual service turned out to differ in a few but significant ways from the prototype. Users calling the bank were put on hold to listen to "awful" music while a recorded message assured them that the "next available customer service representative" would help them if they just stayed on the line. Meanwhile, the message handcuffed them to the phone by telling them that their call would be answered in the order in which it was received! What these developers forgot was that, in order to get accurate information from users about a prototype, one has to portray those characteristics most important to the users—in this case, time spent on hold as well as the rest of the service concept. However, when potential users understand the process of creation and can be trusted to distinguish a prototype from a near-finished product, they provide extremely important input into the process.

Prototyping as Experimentation

What if you don't know what you need to know? Prototypes are also useful for experimentation, to discover what works before going to full scale. Organizational innovations especially can benefit from experimentation with prototypes, since the rollout of an organizational change can affect so many other aspects of work life besides the ones directly targeted. In the 1980s, managers at a manufacturing company shifting from drafting on paper to drafting on computers believed they had two choices: train their engineers to do their own computer-aided drafting or train some draftsmen to serve as technical helpers and continue to translate the engineers' scribbles into highly specified blueprints. There were a lot of variables to be considered, from cost to the willingness of the engineers to learn Computer-aided engineering (CAE). Today the answer seems obvious, since engineers are trained to use computers in school, but at the time the answer was far from clear. The organization therefore decided to try it both ways, in two different divisions. They soon found that individuals varied tremendously in their willingness and ability to use the computers, but that the idea of a pool of trained technicians to do the work was not satisfactory either. Too many mistakes continued to occur in the translation process. Moreover, questions of compensation arose that challenged the current job classifications. Unions became involved. It soon became clear that having a central pool of technicians only *appeared* to be easier than persuading the engineers to learn CAE. It actually would be cheaper to construct attractive incentives for the engineers to learn CAE than to create a new class of employee.

Whether the prototype is social, behavioral, or physical, "quick and dirty" approximations can often yield enough information to be extremely useful. Highly innovative minimill Chaparral Steel is famous for its ability to gain lots of information at low cost. When employees decided that metal splashboards along the path of the white-hot steel would be a good idea, they first used water-logged plywood prototypes to determine the best height and angle of the boards. They went through a lot of plywood, but it was a lot cheaper than working with special alloys! Such experiments provide so much information to the group that members can converge rapidly on the ultimate design.

Convergence Techniques

The culture, mission, priorities, and high-level concept all set the limits within which creativity can flourish. Within those limits, there are many techniques besides prototyping for helping groups achieve convergence. Here is a sampling of some of the most important of these techniques.

Core Capabilities and Driving Forces

Crystal balls and Ouija boards may be outdated technologies, but we'd still like to see the future. How can an existing group converge on changes in its mission required by an altered environment or by a new group on a guiding purpose? Or how can a creative group converge on a new venture, a new product line—anything that involves a hard look at strategy? One technique is a combination of two exercises: establishing the organization's core capabilities and identifying the key driving forces affecting the environment in which the organization operates. These exercises can take a few hours or a few years, depending on how superficial or deep you wish to be. The following description gives you some idea of how such an exercise works. However, "don't try this at home" is a reasonable warning. You may need experienced facilitators to help you through to a strategic plan based on the exercises.

The *core capabilities* of an organization are a system of interdependent knowledge assets that provide competitive advantage.[31] In short, what we are better at than anyone else. Identifying your organization's core capabilities may sound easy, but in fact it is devilishly difficult. If you come up with more than five, chances are they are not core! Working at the *operating* unit (or business unit) level, and involving a vertical slice of individuals (i.e., some representatives from all organizational levels), you can determine your core capabilities by asking key questions:

* What knowledge do we possess that has *built up over time*, is *not readily imitated*, and is *highly valued* by our clients or customers?

* Is this knowledge *superior* (not just equivalent) to that of other organizations in our field?

* Can we *base many products or services* on this knowledge system? And the toughest question of all to answer:

* Is this knowledge likely to *remain valuable* in the future? (The driving forces exercise helps you answer this question.)

Core capabilities may be technologically based (e.g., knowledge of abrasives and coatings at 3M). Or they can be unusual operational abilities (e.g., distribution at Dell or Gateway Computers, or the World Bank's ability to work with multiple constituencies, worldwide).

Here is one way to conduct the exercise: Each individual group member writes down several suggestions for core capabilities—one per index card or "sticky." People then take turns posting their ideas on a wall and clustering them with other ideas already there. (This may be done silently or with discussion.) Next, each cluster of suggestions is labeled with a statement of the core capability, and the group members decide on the top three to five to be used in the exercise. The core capabilities are then set to one side as the group turns its attention to identifying driving forces.

Driving forces are changes in the environment—social, political, physical, technical—that may affect your organizational purpose and direction. The advent of the Internet, for example, influences the operations of almost every organization in the developed world, from schools to banks to florists. The objective of this part of the exercise is to identify three to five driving forces that you think are most likely to affect your organizational operations. The process of convergence is the same as that outlined for core capabilities, starting with individual suggestions written down on cards or stickies and clustering those ideas until there is some consensus around the three to five most important driving forces.

Now for the real fun. Combine the two exercises, with driving forces noted down the vertical axis on the left, and core capabilities listed across the top, so that the intersection of the two forms a matrix of cells (Figure 4-2). Each cell represents the interaction of a core capability with a driving force. As you discuss the cell, you may discover that your organization is poised to take advantage of the driving force (opportunity) or the force may represent a threat that needs to be addressed. More typically, however, analysis of a given cell will reveal both opportunities and threats (see Figure 4-2).

You may also find that a particular core capability looks more like a core rigidity[32] when you consider a driving force. For example, a faculty committed to individualized attention, which you viewed as a core capability, may not be an advantage if you are going to be promoting more distance learning. Or, consider a medical diagnostics company with a core capability of rapidly and accurately testing for certain diseases in patients who have contracted the disease. But now the company anticipates a powerful driving force—

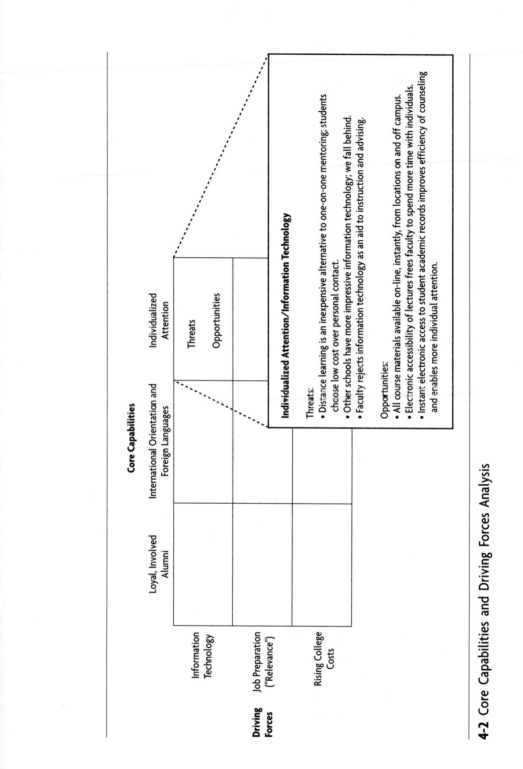

Core Capabilities

	Loyal, Involved Alumni	International Orientation and Foreign Languages	Individualized Attention
Driving Forces			Threats
Information Technology			Opportunities
Job Preparation ("Relevance")			
Rising College Costs			

Individualized Attention/Information Technology

Threats:
• Distance learning is an inexpensive alternative to one-on-one mentoring; students choose low cost over personal contact.
• Other schools have more impressive information technology; we fall behind.
• Faculty rejects information technology as an aid to instruction and advising.

Opportunities:
• All course materials available on-line, instantly, from locations on and off campus.
• Electronic accessibility of lectures frees faculty to spend more time with individuals.
• Instant electronic access to student academic records improves efficiency of counseling and enables more individual attention.

4-2 Core Capabilities and Driving Forces Analysis

the completion of the Human Genome Project. Their capability may, as a result, become outdated as the capacity for identifying individuals at high risk for certain diseases becomes possible.

What if you have the rather unsettling experience of finding that your mission or other guiding boundaries are challenged by the analysis? Our hypothetical college whose strength lies in direct education may have to rethink and redirect that mission in the face of likely developments in technology. And what about that driving force of increased globalization of markets? Perhaps current services need to be rethought, for example, by providing students with practical training in cultural sensitivity.

Future Scenarios and Backcasting

We have just gone forward to the future. Let's now try backing up *from* the future, using a technique called backcasting. Imagine, if you will, two future (let's say five years out) scenarios for the environment in which your organization will be operating. One of these scenarios might be very advantageous, the other disastrous. Working backward, what is a likely chain of events leading up to each scenario? Which events can be anticipated, altered, ignored, and responded to?

Consider a group of administrators at Cozy College, convening to develop a set of strategic plans. The school is in good shape, with a healthy endowment and five applicants for every spot in the freshman class. Cozy has a set of core values and competencies: individualized attention, a strong foreign language and international orientation, and loyal, involved alumni. There is also concern about some perceived trends in higher education: distance learning via the Internet, rising college costs, and the need to prepare students for work immediately after graduation. The group has just concluded a core capabilities–driving forces exercise (see Figure 4-2) in which they have extrapolated from the present to some point in the future. They have concluded that as long as the economy stays strong, Cozy will be able to parlay its core capabilities into a strategic advantage over competitor schools. The threat of distance learning must be considered, of course, and appropriate steps taken to ensure that future students appreciate the advantages of personalized instruction.

Now the group decides to adopt the backcasting technique. They attempt to envision the world five to seven years out: Distance learning has evolved to the extent that "virtual classrooms" have become commonplace, with interactive capabilities and Internet "office hours" with professors. The skills required for high-level jobs have changed dramatically. English has increasingly become the lingua franca throughout much of the world. And the costs of technology, financial aid, and salaries have continued to rise at twice the rate of average family incomes. Where does Cozy want to be in this environment? What does it want to avoid or escape?

Imagine two scenarios: The positive future is one where wise investments, strategic use of resources, and grateful alumni have made it possible for certain departments, notably those emphasizing international studies, to expand. Satellite campuses have been set up in Latin America, South Asia, and East Africa. The admissions office is in the pleasant position of enrolling one student for every ten applicants.

In the negative future, many students have chosen to transfer to a virtual campus, where their diploma will cost a fraction of one earned at Cozy. Faculty and administrators are being laid off and, due to serious declines in foreign language enrollments, those departments are being reorganized into a single, smaller department. Two students now apply for every available slot. The college must rethink its most cherished values.

How could such radically different outcomes be anticipated? Well, that's not really the point of the exercise. Rather, backcasting enables the group to reverse-engineer the steps by which each outcome might have evolved, which steps are controllable, and how these could be effected to realize the positive scenario and changed to avoid the negative scenario. For example, in the negative scenario, students are transferring in large numbers. How could this bleeding be stanched? Are they leaving for purely financial reasons, finding that the value-added provided by Cozy is outweighed by the financial savings? If so, can technology be better incorporated into the instruction, with benefits for students and the institution? Can a case be made that "virtual diplomas" are not worth the pixels that comprise them? Can the personalized instruction that Cozy values be more strongly promoted to prospective students, perhaps through a public relations firm?

What actions are likely to lead to Cozy's enhanced international presence in the positive scenario? Can satellite campuses be viewed as an educational strength and a financial asset even in (or perhaps especially in) a down economy? What assets would have to be generated or diverted in order to create these campuses? What will be the impact on other, perhaps equally needy, programs? Each of these questions takes the group further back from the future toward the present.

Creating scenarios and backcasting take considerable time and effort. But when combined with the driving forces–core capabilities exercise, the group can gain both a highly focused view of the strengths, weaknesses, opportunities, and challenges to the organization, as well as a big-picture perspective of how it is poised to meet the future. The danger is that the exercise will focus only on the positive and the members will leave with a convergence rooted in unreality. Because of these complexities, it may be wise to bring in a skilled facilitator.

Facilitation

Picture this. It is an important meeting and creative abrasion is likely. We've got flip charts and white boards and sixteen colors of pens. We have stacks of cards and enough masking tape for attaching flip chart sheets on the wall to encircle the building. Our pencils and minds are sharpened. We are *ready!* Now, who is going to write up our ideas and help us converge on a solution? One of the senior managers in the room? Let's consider what makes a good facilitator:

ability to structure a discussion, synthesize comments, capture ideas in text and informal graphics. The managers may be okay so far, although it's unlikely that we have a Picasso in our midst to create good graphics. But how about the rest of the qualifications? Objectivity, patience, extraordinary listening ability, ability to probe and question assumptions? Maybe—but some of the very qualities that helped those individuals become top managers, such as decisiveness, make it difficult for them to be expert in facilitating group creativity. Moreover, they may find it difficult to be utterly objective, compared to someone who is not invested in a certain outcome, but only in reaching agreement.

There are interesting cultural differences among organizations on this issue. In some, groups take for granted that they will have a facilitator to speed things along and keep issues impersonal. In others, involving an expert facilitator is regarded as wimping out.

Suppose the decision has been made. This meeting needs a facilitator. The next decision is whether to bring in someone from the outside or use in-house talent. You probably have experts, perhaps in human resources, but if not, you may have to bring in an outside pro and perhaps invest time in educating that individual about your business. Is it worth the effort? Many corporate managers think so. For example, Quantum Corporation, maker of disk drives, has used such individuals routinely to help new product development teams reach consensus.

But you may certainly want to consider a member of the organization, one who is intimately familiar with its workings, to facilitate. In fact, discussions about whether or not to "bring in an outsider" often revolve around this very issue: Should we bring in a pro who doesn't know anything about us, but who knows how to run a meeting? Or do we lose too much not having someone from within the organization? And if she's from within, can she remain more or less neutral? Can everyone trust her? These are important questions that clearly need to be addressed. But organizations are likely to have home-grown talent with two particularly valuable skills.

First, you may have people with T-shaped skills.[33] Such individuals have deep expertise in a function or profession (the shaft of the T) and an ability to apply their expertise across a wide variety of situations in your operations (the crossbar on the T). They are able to articulate how your different customer segments, or geographic locations, or industrial partnerships, interact with their particular knowledge base. Thus, a financial officer with T-shaped skills can show how financial concerns would affect certain customer groups or product lines. An engineer with T-shaped skills can explain how a given technology might be used in many products or market segments. Experience in a number of multifunctional teams builds T-shaped skills. However, serving exclusively on such teams, without the opportunity to renew functional expertise, can greatly reduce the usefulness of a T-shaped skill. (That is, the shaft of the T is diminished, leaving only a shallow base of specialized knowledge.) An individual is a valuable translator so long as he or she has a reasonably current knowledge base. For this reason, some organizations deliberately rotate multiskilled individuals between teamwork and function-based assignments.

Another type of natural facilitator is the boundary spanner who speaks multiple disciplinary languages—perhaps both finance and marketing, or technical support and design. They are the ones helping the discussion forward by translating among the different professions or thinking styles, saying, "I think what Joe means is . . ." They often have served in more than one function in the organization or have a mixture of formal education that allows them to see any problem from more than one perspective. Such individuals are invaluable in helping groups move to consensus. One manager called them "the glue" that holds his teams together. A manager who had fulfilled this function referred to herself as "the fence." "When I was in [software] development, I was the only person who could talk to marketing people, and when I was in marketing I was the only one who could talk to development people."[34] However, in most U.S.–based companies, the route to the boardroom is through specialization, and few companies encourage a career path that passes through more than one discipline.

BOUNDARY SPANNERS

Tom Corddry, who at the time was manager of family reference multimedia products at Microsoft, was particularly impressed with people with multiple talents.

> *I'm really fascinated when I find that somebody has made a conscious [career] change already once. That they have crossed over the line. That they began as an artist and ended up as a computer scientist or began as a musician and then ended up as a computer scientist, or began as a computer scientist and then ended up as a painter. I know enough such people. I know they exist. And you really look for them because they may not do your ultimate best work but if you have enough of them, they kind of glue things together. They explain people to each other.*[35]

A Common Vocabulary

As every traveler in a foreign country knows, communicating through translators is less desirable than sharing a common language. Groups comprised of intellectually diverse members may find it worthwhile to spend time developing a shared vocabulary. Lucas Learning's Susan Schilling knew she needed to help her diverse group members develop a common vocabulary, as they came from various games and entertainment companies as well as from education. She held a series of four, two-hour meetings in which she asked members to describe their most recent product development experience— what were the milestones, how they made design decisions, what constituted an "alpha" test and a "beta" test. "We were articulating a model of how to work together," she explains. She also set up seminars on learning theory so that everyone could understand

and talk about the psychological underpinnings of their educational products. "An artist is welcome to come to these sessions to learn about learning theory," she notes. "It is not a diversion, but an essential part of their work."[36]

Normalizing the Bumps

Betsy Pace, CEO of fledgling Internet company OnLive!, discovered that projects in her highly unpredictable environment went through several predictable phases. Until she realized that the process was inherently cyclical, she was startled when her apparently cohesive and compatible group suddenly fell apart after the product was nearly finished and members started "reviewing resumes." That is, the functions started blaming each other for product inadequacies. All of a sudden, the marketing folks began questioning the competence of their engineering colleagues, and the engineers began wondering (out loud) about the reliability of the marketing intelligence guiding the design. With more acrimony than creative abrasion filling the halls, she wondered what to do. Her solution was remarkably simple and effective. She "normalized" (as psychologists would term it) the bumpy spots in the process by laying out the process for the group to see—but in highly unengineering terms (Figure 4-3). The "Bug Phase" was, well, bugging everyone. It was "as if there was this crazy aunt in the basement, pounding on the ceiling above her with a broomstick" and throwing the occupants of the house above into total disarray with the noise, the confusion, the anger. (No, we aren't sure just why it was an *aunt* either—just one of the little pieces of idiosyncratic organizational humor.) Happily, making the process visible helped a lot. Recognizing that tensions and stress were *always* high at this point in the process depersonalized conflict. Moreover, group members recognized that this, too, would pass—like a toddler's discovery of the word "no," it was just a phase.[37]

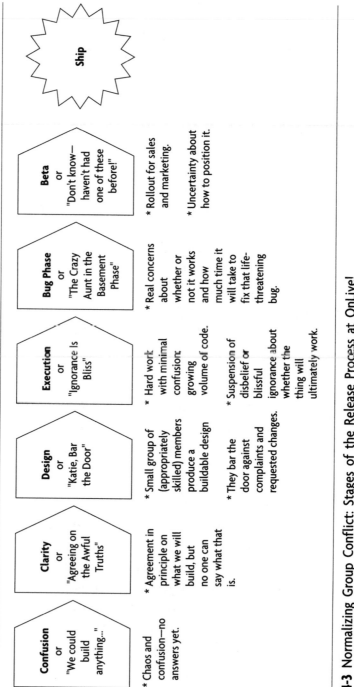

Confusion or "We could build anything..."	Clarity or "Agreeing on the Awful Truths"	Design or "Katie, Bar the Door"	Execution or "Ignorance Is Bliss"	Bug Phase or "The Crazy Aunt in the Basement Phase"	Beta or "Don't know— haven't had one of these before!"
* Chaos and confusion—no answers yet.	* Agreement in principle on what we will build, but no one can say what that is.	* Small group of (appropriately skilled) members produce a buildable design * They bar the door against complaints and requested changes.	* Hard work with minimal confusion; growing volume of code. * Suspension of disbelief or blissful ignorance about whether the thing will ultimately work.	* Real concerns about whether or not it works and how much time it will take to fix that life-threatening bug.	* Rollout for sales and marketing. * Uncertainty about how to position it.

4-3 Normalizing Group Conflict: Stages of the Release Process at OnLive!

Source: Adapted from Betsy Pace, OnLive! Technologies, 1997.

Use the Ladder of Inference[38]

Because our ability to absorb everything around us is necessarily limited, we learn early in life (as every parent knows) to focus selectively on some things and ignore others. One of our peculiarly human traits is to leap to conclusions with the agility of a Ninja. Such leaps are efficient and often essential; we can't stop and plod through every step of thought that led to a decision. However, because we draw conclusions automatically, we often confuse inference with fact. Watch what happens in the following conversation among three of the participants in our opening vignette, as they make their way to the bar.

"This dealing with the public stuff is important, I know," said Patricia. "But I'm impressed with the fact that while 83 percent of people file their state tax returns, 17 percent of the people who are supposed to don't. I wonder what we can do about that?"

"Oh, that's a no-brainer," snorted Boris. "We need stricter enforcement of the laws, and if that doesn't do the trick, we should make tougher laws. I think a special collection agency might be the way to go, kind of a SWAT team for scofflaws."

"That seems a bit harsh," Ming responded. "It seems to me that if the legislature made simpler tax laws and we made simpler tax forms, we'd get a lot more compliance. Maybe if we just assessed people 3 percent or 4 percent or whatever of their federal taxes, they'd be more inclined to pay."

Let's examine these two suggestions in a bit more detail, following each one from the raw "data"—Patricia's observation about taxpayers' compliance—to the two very different conclusions they reached (Figure 4-4).

First, Boris: What he focused on was the 17 percent of people who did not comply with the law. His automatic inference is that people are scofflaws, that they are willfully avoiding paying their taxes. That being the case, they should be subject to the full range of penalties for breaking the law. And into his head pops the option

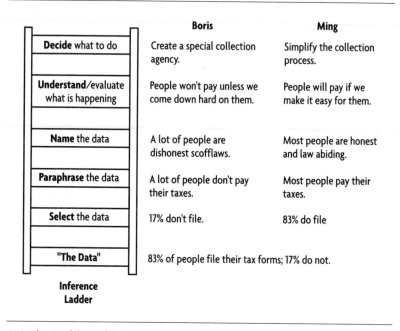

	Boris	Ming
Decide what to do	Create a special collection agency.	Simplify the collection process.
Understand/evaluate what is happening	People won't pay unless we come down hard on them.	People will pay if we make it easy for them.
Name the data	A lot of people are dishonest scofflaws.	Most people are honest and law abiding.
Paraphrase the data	A lot of people don't pay their taxes.	Most people pay their taxes.
Select the data	17% don't file.	83% do file
"The Data"	83% of people file their tax forms; 17% do not.	

Inference Ladder

4-4 The Ladder of Inference

Based on the work of Chris Argyris in Reasoning, Learning, and Action: Individual and Organizational *(San Francisco: Jossey Bass, 1982).*

of having some sort of "special" collection agency to root out the offenders.

Ming has a different take. What he heard was that *some* people might be deliberately evading the tax collector, but that the great majority of people are law abiding. He assumes that a lot of those folks who are not paying their fair share are simply befuddled by the complexities of the tax code, don't understand the forms, and maybe can't afford a tax preparer. People are basically good, want to do the right thing, but don't know how. Therefore, make it easier to pay their taxes—perhaps by indexing state taxes to federal taxes—and the taxes will get paid.

The conclusions these two have reached seem obvious to them; they don't realize that they have *interpreted* reality, climbing the ladder rapidly from data to final inference. From their perspectives, what each has interpreted *is* reality. There are two ways to use the ladder of inference to help a group converge.

Constructing Ladders A group can agree to climb ladders of inference openly and self-consciously. If everyone understands that such ladders exist and that we climb them within seconds, usually suppressing all but the final step to a decision, then the group can agree to be more explicit about how they reach conclusions. They can discuss whether others have different data or interpret data differently, and ask each other to illustrate conclusions. Susan Schilling at Lucas Learning has used the ladder of inference to help her group members understand that external conversations with others on the team are always accompanied by internal mental dialogues—and that it is important to bring those two conversations "into sync" so that convergence is real.

Reconstructing Ladders Group members can reverse-engineer the ladder, retracing the logic when they have ended up at loggerheads over some decision, starting with the data held in common:

* In the most objective terms possible, *what* was said, or done, or observed?
* What did each person *hear* (or see, or observe), in his/her own words? (What data did each select as important?)
* What *generalizations* were made from the selected data?
* How did each person *name* the data (i.e., categorize or label what happened)?
* What kind of *evaluation* or *conclusion* was drawn?
* Finally, how did each person decide to *act* based on the evaluation or conclusion?

When the parties have gone through these steps, it becomes clear why each reached the decision he or she did. However, more important, when the rationale underlying the decision is laid bare, people often see where their inferences differ—and can debate on the basis of those interpretations and logic rather than just on the basis of a final decision.

The ladder of inference is not just a conflict-reducing tool. In the above example, the conclusions reached by Boris and by Ming suggest two very different innovations—one focused on better enforcement, the other on altering the agency's internal processes. Should the group consider both approaches—"law and order" and "make it simple"—then they will want to follow the full range of inferences leading to and following from each approach.

In this and the previous two chapters, we have considered how to compose a group for creativity, how to encourage divergence, and how to manage convergence. This creative process takes place in a context, an environment—both physical and psychological. In the next two chapters, we consider how to design physical surroundings and the culture of the whole organization so as to build a *creative ecology*—an interdependent system that supports the creative process over time.

Ten days have gone by, and Larry is feeling a lot better:

Arranging to get the group back together for another day the following week to work out a final proposal was a good idea. Chuck wasn't real happy about the delay, but he did agree when I told him the team would rather give him a silk purse a little late than an on-time sow's ear. And I wouldn't have believed it, but that facilitator HR brought in was pretty helpful. I was skeptical about the exercises we went through, but they really helped move us—amazing, too, how a little drawing talent can help everyone see how everything fits together— treating taxpayers as customers, revising the forms, electronic filing. I'll bet we've made it so easy that we'll be left with only the hard-core scofflaws. Then we'll sic Boris on them! The important thing is that the team really feels some ownership for the proposal, and they know they can work on the changes we've targeted in their own way. I don't think Boris really believes we can pull it off yet, but even he commented on how good the process was. So I think he'll give it his best shot. Now we have to help Chuck sell the plan throughout the agency.

Key Points

* After a group has generated options, members need time for incubation, to allow connections and elaborations to be made subconsciously.

* Creative solutions are guided by a hierarchy of organizational and group boundaries:

  * Organizational culture sets the broadest constraints. Any solution must be consistent with the core values of the organization.

  * Thoughtful missions focus the group on convergence, either through uniting them against a common threat or through working toward a common objective.

  * Options are further bounded by the group's ordered priorities.

  * High-level concepts provide a sharp, vivid focus to the convergence task, while still providing considerable autonomy in how it will be accomplished.

* However, there are still opportunities for creativity in innovation. Within this hierarchy of boundaries, managers should use various techniques to aid convergence:

  * *Prototypes* are preliminary versions of an innovation. They provide a concrete focus for discussing the product or service by people from different backgrounds. They also provide information about how—or whether—the innovation will actually work.

  * Core capabilities and driving forces exercises can be combined to reveal opportunities, threats, and core rigidities.

* Backcasting enables a group to work backward from a projected future and to reverse-engineer the steps that got the group there.

* Strong facilitation skills may be essential in bringing a group to convergence. Facilitators may come from outside the organization or inside. In-house facilitators are particularly valuable if they possess *T-shaped skills* (deep expertise with the ability to apply that expertise across situations) or if they are *boundary spanners*, able to speak multiple disciplinary languages.

* Conflicts that hinder convergence can be handled by demonstrating to members that the standard bumps in the road are expected, predictable, and normal.

* Taking members up the "ladder of inference" can also normalize the conflict that comes from differences in how people leap from data to final solution, and aid convergence.

5

Designing the Physical Environment

No sooner had the product development groups moved into the new building than Vice President of Product Development Amanda Sturbridge started getting complaints. It looked like a bank, some said. There were too many walls and too few open spaces. The restrooms were located along the periphery and only the officers of the company had windows. The kitchen was too small and there was no way to carry on a conversation in it. "I thought this place was supposed to be for 'teamwork,' an engineer declared—"why else do we call it the Team Center?" At the same time that some people were complaining about the barriers to conversations, others were griping about the lack of privacy. "I can't think in these blasted cubicles," one designer declared. "I can hear every single word the guy in the next office says." A marketer, newly arrived from a start-up in California's Silicon Valley said, "How can you expect creativity if you don't have any room for games? At my old company, we had fooze-ball in the halls, a Ping-Pong table, a video room . . . nothing cool is going to happen here! Who the heck designed this building, anyway? Some bureaucrat?"

Stan, the bureaucrat in question, sat at his desk in Facilities Management and mused about all the disgruntled e-mails and voice mails Amanda had so thoughtfully forwarded to him. "Where the hell were all these suggestions and ideas when we were building?" he asked himself. "I asked Amanda to review all the plans for the Team Center, and she didn't mention any of this stuff. Was too darned busy to spend any time with me, as I recall. So I had it built just like the last building we put up—and this one was even cheaper. Oh well, they'll pipe down after a few weeks and settle in."

What does the physical environment have to do with creativity? Very little directly—but a lot indirectly. Organizations need a *creativity ecology*—an interdependent, interactive, self-sustaining, and reinforcing system that includes not only people and processes but also settings. Architecture, use of internal space, acoustics, even furniture by themselves won't make groups more creative—but all of these features surely can and do *support* or *inhibit* creativity. The wrong kinds of surroundings drain off energy as groups fight physical barriers to critical group and individual activities. The right kinds enable the creative process—open communication channels among group members, well-designed places for brainstorming and noisy divergence, spaces devoted to incubation and reflection, easily accessible and well-equipped meeting places for convergence, flexible areas that invite reconfiguration by group members for creative activities, and accessible information technology that links people and ideas.

The office environment also makes a powerful statement about the value the organization places on creativity. When the symbolism inherent in space captures the organizational mission and values, that concordance can increase employee motivation and translate into greater creativity. Metaphors such as "highly centered medieval village," or "nineteenth-century American town square," or "campus think tank" suggest a community-based culture and, when the organization lives up to the promise, creates a sense of wholeness for all who work there.[1] On the other hand, a mission statement that ballyhoos the importance of communication and equality is effectively nullified by the "thud" of heavy oak doors when everyone works closeted in private offices. In this chapter, we explore the *physical* environment that nurtures a creativity ecology; in the next, we discuss the *cultural and psychological* environment that nourishes creativity, and how that environment can be most effectively managed.

Unlike our other chapters, this one builds more heavily on experiments being conducted by practitioners than on scientific research. Moreover, we do not attempt to cover some strong practice-based philosophies about the connection between physical environment and energy flows, such as *feng shui*. The direct link between the design of physical space and creativity is unproven, hence the *caveat lector*. Such reliable research as exists tends to focus on facilitating communication rather than directly on enhancing creativity. However, any configuration of the physical environment that eliminates the barriers to divergence, incubation, and convergence is likely to be helpful. Therefore we introduce you to some practices in organizations that managers believe (or hope) will aid creativity.

Physical objects (including buildings) speak to us—loudly, if nonverbally. Both regular occupants' and visitors' initial, and perhaps lasting, impressions are based on the arrangement of space and people. Architecture expresses both ego and identity. If you have been in an investment bank or an unreformed insurance company recently, you know this. Offices say more about the organizational culture than articles, Web pages, and announcements. The boss gets the corner office with the view, right? Peons in the center of the floor need not apply for a window. Wait twenty years and you may get one when you get promoted to vice president. Not as big an office as an *executive* vice president, mind you. The rigid hierarchy embodied in such physical symbols costs creativity three ways (at least). First, it is hard to change offices with fixed walls. Suppose someone gets hired in at a senior level—this sets off a game of office dominoes as each individual in the hierarchy bumps the one below to make room. Or there is need for meeting rooms—what department gives up private office space? Change is expensive. Second, the corner-office syndrome signals the importance of inequality— and hints at the dangers of thinking otherwise. Third, the offices constitute a kind of hazard course for communications, which have to flow in often unnatural paths around physical obstacles such as walls, stairs, doors. To the extent that communication is the mother of creativity, such spaces create innovational orphans.

On the other hand, those annoying rabbit warrens of identical, doorless cubicles symbolize uninspired, egalitarian boredom. And sometimes unbearable levels of noise. Where can an individual escape for reflection? Where can a team meet for noisy interaction without bothering others? And does equality promote creativity? CEO Andy Grove works out of a cubicle in the middle of Intel's particular rabbit warren; so does Alcoa CEO Paul H. O'Neill; and CEO Gordon Forward's office at endlessly inventive Chaparral Steel is next door to the lockers where employees gather their hard hats before heading off to the mills. In such organizations, hierarchies are broken down and communication flows much more easily—but is that enough to accelerate creativity?

Physical surroundings communicate presumed management attitudes. Which do you believe—what the *building* says or what the *boss* says? In the vignette at the chapter opening, Amanda certainly wanted a team-based, creative environment (and holds the teams accountable for their innovation), but she was "too busy" to get involved in the design of the new building and now it screams "conformity." She will have to live with a building that inhibits rather than encourages creativity because she delegated design to the corporate Facilities Management office, whose priority was cost—not creativity. Too often, organizations turn the designers' notion that "form follows function" on its head: form dictates function—because people are all but forced to behave as the architecture mandates.

Creativity is a process that harnesses energy, allows knowledge to flow. We want physical environments that enable those flows. Knowledge, like water, flows along lines of least resistance. However, as we have noted in the prior chapters, creativity involves different types of interaction, different types of knowledge flows. Therefore, it is desirable to architect physical environments that not only accommodate but aid the various activities in the creative process: divergent thinking, incubation, and convergence. Before we suggest the generic, relatively easy ways that you can enhance your environment for creativity, let's take a look at some industrial-strength approaches used by some pretty far-out organizations. Extreme examples help stretch our notion of where the boundaries lie.

Ways of Promoting the Creative Process

Walk into the Idea Factory in San Francisco and you aren't sure if you're in a warehouse, a renovated airplane hanger, a movie set, or a playground. Arranged below the ceiling in a single cavernous room is a variety of areas: a small theatre comprised of lighting equipment and a semicircle of modular wooden bleachers with built-in handles for convenient moving; a screened-off corner cubicle in which a software programmer sits intent on his screen; metal racks of books and magazines with the feel of a browsing library and a few racks hosting an inventory of small plastic figures and what looks like dollhouse furniture or equipment. To your right is a meeting room without walls—a three-quarter crescent of slightly slanted designers' tables, covered with paper for sketching and designed to be set at standing or sitting height or raised up out of the way entirely. This curve of drawing space is arrayed in front of two huge white boards mounted on pulleys for raising and lowering; in the center of this circle is an amoeba-shaped table on wheels, surrounded by stools and positioned under a sound-deadening fabric and wire construction reminiscent of a white top hat that someone has sat on. CEO John Kao's "office" is a corner of the room demarcated by screens, a couple of large couches, and a table. Every piece of equipment or furniture in the entire huge space seems a temporary squatter in its current position, ready to be moved at a moment's notice.

The objective is to be able to transform this space into whatever setting will help Idea Factory clients creatively *experience* the past, present, or future of their own organizations—through directing and/or participating in improvisational "plays"; through visiting microcosm worlds made of plywood and paint, enlivened with video; through group exercises of creating sand tray images with the miniature figures and props. Within the generous bounds of the large room, almost no architectural or structural characteristics limit the flow of ideas, communication, and action. It is a Hollywood set, to be broken down, moved, and re-created weekly, if not daily, to suit the needs of the moment.

On the opposite coast of the United States, and with much less conscious intent, the Massachusetts Institute of Technology in Boston once boasted a building that was almost as malleable. "Building 20" was a "temporary" structure built during World War II as a laboratory for radar research, and demolished in 1998! Much sadness accompanied its demise, as it was heralded as having "spawned, by unanimous consent, more creative science—far more—than any other building of its size in the history of the United States. Because it was made completely of wood, it was easy to personalize and customize—just knock a hole in a wall or the floor to accommodate a new piece of apparatus."[2] And was there ever apparatus! Researchers reveled in the piles of junk left lying around from previous experiments and pirated them for their own research. There were no turf battles, because the "turf" itself was so pitiful. As a result, a great spirit of collaboration prevailed, often between graduate students and Nobel laureates, joined by a common ownership of superficially worthless space.[3]

Okay, so moving into a deserted warehouse or locating a decrepit building to hand over to employees isn't exactly practical unless you are a corporate start-up. How about cordoning off some section of a building that can be shaped by the group inhabiting it? A new product development team at design and engineering firm IDEO took unusual advantage of their mandate to arrange the space they were allocated. They decided that the wing of an old airplane would make an ideal backbone for all the wires connecting their local computer networks, and they managed not only to locate one, half buried in the sands of southern California, but to transport it up

DISTANCE AND COMMUNICATION

Thomas Allen studied the effects of physical layout on the probability of interaction in seven research laboratories. Over a period of several months, 512 respondents were periodically asked which colleagues in the organization they had interacted with on technical and scientific matters. The relationship between the likelihood of two people interacting and the physical distance between them was strongly negative ($r = -.84$). Most striking, however, was Allen's finding that the probability of interaction approached zero at about 25 meters. Although this study was conducted prior to the advent of e-mail, the importance of proximity in facilitating that richest, multichannel communication called "face-to-face" is unlikely to have changed.[4] These findings heavily influenced the design of the Decker Engineering Building for Corning Glass Works: optimum visibility on every floor; strategically placed ramps, stairs, and escalators to encourage vertical movement; and open architecture with informal gathering places.

north to their Palo Alto offices. Once installed, the wing constituted a relatively inflexible part of the environment, but the team enjoyed the freedom to shape their own surroundings.

The Danish hearing aid company, Oticon, has another approach to flexibility. They kept control of the architecture and office building blocks in the hands of the organization—but allowed groups working together on projects to configure their workspace with those generic elements. When CEO Lars Kolind took over the organization, it was complacently drifting into ever-shallower shoals of market share. The vigorous shaking he gave the organization involved a lot more than changing the physical infrastructure, but one of the many radical moves he made was to take away all the cozy offices that individuals hid away in and design a moveable office arrangement.

Each individual was given a two-drawer filing cabinet on wheels, in which to store personal files. All other paperwork was routed to the top floor of the building, where it was scanned into a computer for sharing—and shredded. (A potent symbol of the dedication to a paperless existence is a large transparent tube that reaches from top floor down to the dumpster in the basement. All day, a highly visible snowstorm of shredded paper cascades through the tube in full view of employees in the cafeteria.) Employees working on a given project together roll their files to one of any of the tables throughout the building and set up temporary shop around the computer work-station on the table containing all the information they might need from any database.[5]

The design concept that most explicitly mirrors the steps in the creative process is that of *zones*. In the early 1990s, the sixth floor of Arthur Andersen Consulting's head office in London was gutted and completely redesigned. Gone were the private offices ringing the exterior and the cubicles filling the middle spaces. Out went the boardrooms. No more desktop computers—only laptops. Interactive, electronic white boards abound, permitting downloading to laptops. The floor was fitted out with a structure designed to facilitate creative interaction. The "Chaos" zone, separated from the rest of the floor by partitions decorated with bright red pictures of connecting wires and cables, is designed to facilitate divergent thinking. Everything is portable, so desks and equipment can be wheeled around when people need to meet. A red brainstorming room is intended to perk up lagging creativity, while calmer blue and green rooms can be used for more contemplative activities. At the other end of the floor, the "Zen" zone is for incubation. The panels separating this area have scenes from nature. A sign reads, "No meetings. No phones. No interruptions." Between Chaos and Zen stretches a corridor called the "Touchdown Bar," which houses workspaces where workers can sit, plug in phones and computers, and work for awhile.[6]

Sun Microsystems in Menlo Park, California, has also made

COLOR AND STIMULATION

What little scientific research that has been conducted on the effects of color on physiological and psychological reactions conforms more or less to conventional wisdom. Some experiments have used colored light projected directly into subjects' eyes, while in others the subjects have been placed in rooms painted in a particular color. In both types of studies, red was found to be arousing, with increases in blood pressure, pulse, visual cortical activity, and reported headaches. Some subjects reported feeling overstimulated and had difficulty working in the red room. Blue is associated with opposite effects: lowered arousal levels, decreased blood pressure and pulse rate, and a general calming.[7] Of course, few people would paint rooms entirely in screaming fire engine red, and predominantly blue motifs have been found to produce boredom. Therefore, it is difficult to generalize these results. Perhaps it is safest to conclude that the extremes should be avoided, while judicious uses of color may promote a range of arousal levels that may be conducive to either interaction or incubation.

significant modifications in its space to enhance collaboration and informal interaction. Consultants had noticed that engineers tended to gather briefly in office doorways and kitchens, then disperse. This observation suggested that spaces should be designed that encourage the informal conversations, but discourage the dispersing. Now "Forum" spaces radiate out from the kitchens (where many of us seem to be most comfortable conversing) as open areas designed to encourage informal, serendipitous gatherings. Nearby conference rooms are available for unscheduled meetings. Outside, Sun has arranged fifty wooden benches, tables, and chairs for reflection and quiet work. "Sun rooms" are more self-consciously designed for

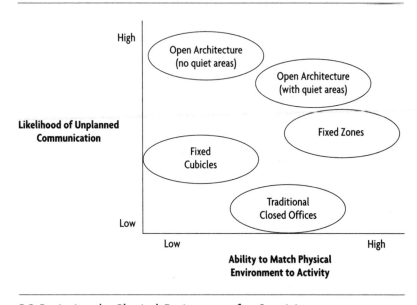

5-1 Designing the Physical Environment for Creativity

incubation. All have exterior views; some have Ping-Pong tables, others stereo equipment. All are intended for relaxation (although each has white boards—just in case).[8]

What these examples (extreme as some of them are) have in common is an attempt by management to provide support for creative activities along two dimensions: (1) unplanned communications among group members and (2) the ability of those members to configure or control their physical surroundings to match the desired cognitive activities (Figure 5-1). The objective is to make the form (of the architecture and ambiance) fit the function (the mental activity).

Space—The Final Frontier

In most organizations, free space is a contradiction in terms. Space is almost as precious and rare as time. However, if our aim is creativity, we need to find and protect some of both. How can

---

A SCIENTIST CONFIGURES HIS SPACE

Nobel physicist Freeman Dyson has a clear concept of how space needs to be configured differently for divergence and convergence: "Science is a very gregarious business. It is essentially the difference between having this door open and having it shut. When I am doing science I have the door open. . . .You want to be, all the time, talking with people. Up to a point you welcome being interrupted because it is only by interacting with other people that you get anything interesting done. . . . But, of course, writing is different. When I am writing I have the door shut."[9]

---

your group members experiment, prototype, and play with physical surroundings unless there is some nonterritorial space that can be temporarily preempted for a creative purpose? The very presence of open space is likely to inspire some experimentation. Expansive space can translate into expansive thought. An instructor of sculpture was surprised at the change in student work when he moved from the cramped, low-ceilinged quarters in which he had taught for years, to a new, much larger studio with high ceilings. The sculptures turned out by the class members were two to three times as large in the new studio![10] In a similar fashion, flexible, creative space can translate to creative activity. When workers have ready access to spaces that promote divergence, incubation, and convergence and when they largely control the ability to move from one to the other, they will experience the sense of freedom and autonomy that is at the heart of the creative process. The creative environment is indeed an ecological system in which space, people, and creative behavior are interwoven.

Let us now take a more systematic look at each of the three stages in the creative process described in the prior chapters—divergence, incubation, and convergence—and consider ways you might en-

CREATIVE PEOPLE, CREATIVE SPACE

In the 1960s, Professor of Architecture Leonard Eaton studied the personality characteristics of individuals who had commissioned houses by Frank Lloyd Wright early in his career in Chicago—at a time when Wright was seen as a revolutionary and before he had become fully accepted. How would these individuals differ from those who became clients of a conservative architect (Howard Van Doren Shaw) at the same time and place? Based on interviews and archives, Eaton found two primary differences between the two groups of male clients. First, the Wright clients were far more artistic, particularly as musicians. Second, almost 30 percent of the Wright clients were inventors, compared to 2 percent of the Shaw clients. Wright's innovative use of space resonated with creative male clients who wished to live surrounded by that space. Many of them had basement workshops where they would design and prototype their inventions. Thus, the space also facilitated the creative process.[11]

hance the physical infrastructure to support each. Again, we draw more on practice than on theory.

Enhancing Divergent Thinking

General Stimuli

Despite the fact that we humans were designed with five senses and multiple capabilities in our brains, we generally use only two senses and a small portion of our brains while we are at work. Most of us are gainfully employed in a black and white, text-based world where sound means noise and smells are generally odors. We have *lots* of stimuli around us—but they tend to be all one kind. It is perhaps unsurprising, then, that managers focused on creativity design in different stimuli—sights, sounds, even smells in some extreme exam-

MULTISENSORY STIMULATION AND CREATIVITY

A group of extremely bright (average I.Q. of 158) young adults participated in a study to determine the effects of multiple types of sensory stimulation on creativity. Over a period of five weeks, experimental subjects were seated in a darkened room and stimulated with high-frequency signals from an oscillator, a rotating spiral wheel, incense, a floor vibrator, and loud music. Each week, both before and after being stimulated, they were given five minutes to draw a picture of a vase of flowers, using pencil and crayons. A panel of artists judged the drawings made following stimulation to be more creative than those made before. Of course, it would be risky to generalize too much from this one study, particularly since the subjects were unusually intelligent (and young), but it does suggest that sensory stimulation may have beneficial effects on creativity.[14]

ples—to increase the likelihood that their employees will tap into different parts of the brain or make unusual linkages between action and what their senses identify.

Even the average text-sodden office climate can be enriched—relatively inexpensively. Most offices have some visual stimuli. The artwork on the walls, sculptures, aquaria, can all be designed to stimulate, to calm, or to inspire. Loraine Waller, human resources services director at Bupa, spent several months selecting more than 150 works of modern art for their London headquarters. The result? "A more creatively stimulated, satisfied and motivated workforce," she believes.[12] Some organizations invite the budding artists from local elementary or high schools to display their work on a rotating basis. Visual art is actually quite easy to obtain.

One way to increase the general level of stimuli around your group members is to broaden the range of publications left lying around on tables where people congregate. If your reception areas are like most, the publications reflect the dominant perspective of the organization. Mostly economists? You have *The Economist* for sure. Work at a university? Then you subscribe to *The Chronicle of Higher Education.* How about some far-out journals that no one in your organization brings to work. Think dentist office meets national laboratory, or Mensa meets Hollywood. *Modern Drumming* and *Southern Living.* Or *Arizona Highways* and *Asimov's Magazine of Science Fiction.* The *Times Literary Supplement* and *Dirt Wheels?* Why not? The audiences to whom these magazines appeal are not people with whom your employees ordinarily converse, but their view of the world is likely to be entirely different—somewhat "weird," and, well, stimulating! One of us has a colleague who never says no to a four-week trial subscription, "no obligation" offer. As a result, the office reception area affords an ever-changing panoply of some most unusual reading.

In Skandia's Future Center north of Stockholm, the second floor is infused with the smell of baking bread. Why? Because Vice President for Intellectual Capital Leif Edvinsson believes the aroma is associated in peoples' minds with comfort, home, and delicious food. Just as many intellectuals have found coffee houses congenial to creative thinking, so too a sense of comfort through smells and other "icons" can "nourish innovative rulebreaking" in the office.[13] Of course, these are highly ethnocentric assumptions. Walk a beach in Thailand, and your nose will be assailed with the scent of sun-dried squid, roasting over charcoal. Such an aroma titillates the taste buds of the Southeast Asian but usually leaves the Western nose unimpressed if not offended. Smells have not only ethnic or national implications, but may have highly individual ones. Someone raised by a wonderful cook but in a strict, unimaginative family might not associate baking bread with creative opportunity!

However, the purpose Edvinsson intends is achieved if his European hires are motivated to enjoy work and to set their minds on relaxation mode. Practitioners of "aromatherapy" argue that mind-smell connections are more vivid than we usually acknowledge, perhaps because aromas, unlike other sensations, go straight to the bloodstream rather than being filtered by the brain. For example, at the Kajima Corporation in Tokyo, various smells are transmitted through the air-conditioning system in strict accordance with theories of how odors can stimulate the brain. The cycle begins with citrus to refresh, then fragrances to promote concentration, with a finish of pine forests for relaxation before the cycle begins again. The utility of smells in stimulating creative activity is conjecture rather than certainty at this point. However, it is at least a reasonable hypothesis that if other forms of stimuli feed creative thought, so may a variety of aromas and sounds.[15]

How about the sense of touch? Some organizations even enrich the creative potential of the office environment through kinesthetic stimulation. The NMB Bank south of Amsterdam in the Netherlands is a building influenced by the philosophy of Rudolf Steiner, who advocated the development of emotions as a foundation for intellect. Instead of the normal solid handrails, there are copper channels through which water flows, so you can dangle your fingers in water as you walk through the building.[16]

At the Skandia Center, Edvinsson also believes that the classical music inside and the sounds of the ocean waves outside contribute to a sense of rhythm—and rhythm is associated with many forms of creative expression besides music. Poetry and paintings, for example. However, again individual tastes differ. "Rap" music is very rhythmic, but given the haste with which we observe people over twenty-five rolling up their car windows when a utility vehicle pulsating with rap drives up alongside, we don't think everyone finds it appealing, much less conducive to creative thinking. It seems unlikely—and probably undesirable—that group members converge on a single taste in music. Moreover, once again, different phases of the creative process call for different types of musical stimulation. The issues are access and control. Do group members have some access to musical stimulus when and where they desire it? If the physical space is divided up into zones, each of which is designated for a particular type of activity, then the musical background for each can be designed just as the furnishings, wall and floor coverings are.

NOISE AND PERSONAL CONTROL

Environmental psychologists have long known about the harmful physical and cognitive effects of unpredictable, high-volume noise. Continued exposure may lead to elevated blood pressure, ulcers, and heart disease.[17] In laboratory experiments, people exposed to 110-decibel bursts of white noise were subsequently impaired in their ability to solve problems. However, when subjects either could predict when the bursts of noise would occur or had the ability to terminate the noise with a "panic button" (even though they did not use it), the negative effects vanished.[18] Of course much, if not most, of the noise we endure is neither predictable nor controllable, but when we feel that we have the ability to escape or avoid it, noise loses its power to affect us.

But when does stimulation become an assault? We are not always fortunate enough to enjoy a work environment free of noise pollution, noxious fumes, or stale air. Having to fight the environment, whether it be hot, crowded, or noisy, drains off the energy that could be devoted to creative activities. And when we feel we are losing control over our environments, we are most vulnerable to anxiety and poor performance. Creativity thrives when people feel that they are in control, when they have the ability to move from a noisy space to a more contemplative one, where they can personalize their "incubation" spaces, or where they know that the air they are breathing is healthy.

Aiding Interaction among Diverse Individuals and Groups: Water Holes and Safari Trails

The best stimulus for divergent thinking is direct, interactive communication among diverse individuals. Face-to-face if possible. Mediated if not. Of course, as described in Chapter 2, people differ in their thinking-style preferences and therefore some souls would rather "converse" by e-mail or in Internet chat rooms, whatever the task. However, research suggests that most people would rather communicate face-to-face for complex tasks, and the divergent stages in the creative process certainly qualify as complex.[19]

Moreover, as discussed in greater detail in Chapter 6, one of the (many) jobs you didn't know you signed up for when you became a manager is to enable serendipity. By definition, *serendipity* involves unexpected connections—between people, between events, between ideas. To enable more unexpected connections among people, we need to have more *unplanned communication*. Such communication depends on (1) *who* is around (hence the need for the careful composition of groups and exposure to aliens as described in Chapters 2 and 3) and (2) *how easy* it is for that communication to take place (hence the need for the attention to enabling rather than hindering unplanned communication).

At a water hole in Africa, one sees groups of animals that would have no other reason for proximity—gazelles with giraffes, zebras with elephants. If the drought that drives them together is severe enough, the wildebeest may even chance a drink when the lions are across the pond. Organizational water holes are kitchens and coffee pots, mailrooms—any centrally located facility that will draw people on an ad hoc, informal, and inherently unpredictable basis. In the ground floor of the main Harvard Business School faculty office building, one often finds informal discussions in the hall outside the centrally located restrooms!

Since we have mentally displaced to Africa, let us stay there a bit and think about safari trails—routes that optimize the chance of experiencing lots of different animals and animal activities. In our workplaces, we can also enhance the probability of serendipitous connections by paying attention to the pathways that people routinely follow. At Oticon, the stairways are much wider than essential, so that people can stop and chat without interrupting traffic. At Procter & Gamble, escalators have replaced that great anesthetic of open communication, the elevator. Chats can continue in relative privacy while moving from floor to floor. Passageways that wend their way through various work areas serve much the same purpose (although hopefully less annoyingly so) as the circuitous routes constructed through department stores in the United States. If you have to detour through men's shirts to reach the down escalator, perhaps you will remember that Father's Day is coming up and will pause to purchase. Safari trails at work serve similar mind-jogging objectives. At IDEO, there is no straight shot from street to a designer's desk, but employees see small meetings and colleagues working as they walk. The resulting overview of colleagues' activities serves several simultaneous purposes. Many new office designs include a "Main Street," a wide thoroughfare, often with sofas and white boards along one side, to encourage interaction while permitting traffic to flow. Not that such designs are all that new. When Steelcase built a corporate development center in 1989, the interior architecture included "neighborhoods" and "town squares" designed to encourage people to connect. "We're trying to maximize the serendipitous," explained an organizational psychologist at Steelcase.[20]

Seeing work-in-process, especially in the form of prototypes and sketches, stimulates thought and offers the possibility of that magical "aha" when some unforeseen connection clicks in the mind—what Fisher-Price designer Peter Pook calls "drive-by idea snatching."[21] That connector on the medical equipment Joe is designing just might work for the bicycle rack you are laboring over. The stroll to the kitchen may offer an opportunity to talk with someone you have been trying to catch for a couple of days now, and the electronic white boards installed there will ensure that any creative ideas can be instantly downloaded. And finally, seeing all the activities going on presents one with a kind of visual overview of the organization's activities. One reason that colocating multifunctional new product development teams has gained so much popularity in recent years is that seeing (and often hearing) the issues that colleagues in other functions deal with is an education in the entire new product development process.

Being able to see your colleagues depends on at least open doors, of course. When Internal Revenue Service Commissioner Charles Rossotti first took over the position, he discovered that open doors were not exactly an organizational norm. So, guess what infrastructure he decided was so crucial that he invested his own money in providing it? No—not some high-tech computerized communication devices. He bought . . . doorstops!

Aiding Incubation

Before, during, and after periods of divergent thinking comes the eye in the storm—moments of reflection and periods devoted to incubation. Not only is the incubation stage an integral part of the creative process but quiet time is essential for a couple of other reasons. As we noted in our discussion of thinking styles, individuals who strongly prefer an Introversion approach to information gathering and evaluation want to think about a problem before committing to a solution or even proposing an idea. Such people will contribute most if they are given the opportunity to quietly consult with themselves. And finally, even exuberant Extroverts occasionally need a respite from constant interaction—especially if the creative process has been abrasive.

So we all need sanctuaries at times. In their zeal to provide the free flow of communication (and, let us be honest, to save money), organizations have invested in "moveable" cubicles that are actually reconfigured about as frequently as the Great Wall of China. Managers responsive to the needs of their employees often find themselves re-creating the walled office. At Fisher-Price, an employee can request a screenlike door for an otherwise open cubicle, to provide a modicum of protection against invasion at unwanted times. At one of the IDEO offices, the cubicles are fashioned much like stalls, with a "barn door" that can be slid aside to open one wall to the corridor or closed for privacy. The Institute for Research on Learning in Menlo Park, California, has collaborated with Steelcase to experiment with enclosed private cubicles faintly reminiscent of space capsules, with areas for a computer, some files, and quiet workspace. The door slides back along the curved side of the round enclosure to allow as much or as little outside exposure as desired. As described above, Arthur Andersen in London has an entire "Zen" area set aside for meditation and quiet work. And, of course, many employers unwittingly (or at least without concern for stages in the creative process) provide incubation time by encouraging their employees to work while strapped into tiny seats, encapsulated at 35,000 feet in an office that relies on absolute faith in the Bernoulli principle to stay aloft. Most planes hardly provide ideal conditions for incubation, given their zoolike atmosphere, but at least people are disassociated for a few hours from interaction with their fellow employees. So they can relax into the comforting knowledge that no one on the ground can reach them for a few hours and they can allow their thoughts to incubate.

Incubation requires a change of pace from the intense work needed for creativity. But surroundings built for that change of pace don't have to be just for quiet, Zen-like reflection. Creative environments often include playgrounds—for refreshment, exercise, and socializing as aids to incubation. In mild climates, such playgrounds can include year-round volleyball or badminton courts. Nickelodeon's animation studio in Burbank, California, sports a miniature golf course with a "hole in Walt" (Disney).[22] But where sunshine or pleasant temperatures are scarce (or outdoor space nonexistent), deliberate attention to playgrounds is even more critical. Not only do groups need a break now and then, but the sense of play is linked in peoples' minds with informality, energy, risk taking, excitement, work that is play.

Enhancing Convergent Thinking

Convergent thinking, like divergent thinking, can occur anywhere in a building. Two or three people talking in the kitchen are about as likely to reach agreement on action as they are to come up with new options. Therefore, the same architectural features that enable divergent thinking can also encourage convergence. And given information technology, group members need not confer in person to converge on a solution. However, once again, poor design of physical space can create barriers to the creative process. If there is no convenient space adequate to hold all group members simultaneously, convergence is more arduous.

The space need not be the traditional conference room, although it is always helpful to have a room appropriate to the size of the group and with something besides wallpapered walls to write on. Sound obvious? Then why are some important convergence meetings scheduled in rooms that are designed to discourage any capture of consensus? A library is great for reading, but book-lined walls provide no space for writing. The disadvantages of small, oxygen-starved quarters are obvious, but a huge auditorium only encourages a wrong-end-of-the-telescope perspective, facilitating isolation rather than creative engagement. We tend to consider the physical surroundings of a meeting to be less important than the quality of the available coffee. Of course, some managers have concluded that convergence is much more likely to be swift if the meeting place is highly uncomfortable. Hold a meeting in a room without chairs, so attendees must stand, the reasoning goes, and decisions will be made quickly. That design will aid efficiency, perhaps—but not creativity. As noted before, premature convergence is an enemy of innovation.

In designing physical space, managers of cross-functional teams confront a basic, irreconcilable dilemma. Members of the team desire and need colocation in order to access the divergent points of view so critical to option creation. But at the same time, they need access to their functional colleagues to reinforce or challenge their representation of their disciplines. "I want to be able to bounce ideas off my fellow designers," explained a designer at Fisher-Price. "And the engineers and marketers feel the same way." The functions are the source of deep disciplinary knowledge. In fact, if members of a cross-functional team lose their connections back into that community, they become less valuable to the team. At the same time, as we noted in Chapter 4, colocation greatly aids fast decision making and convergence.

In relatively compact organizations, one solution is to array the disciplines around some common areas created at their intersection. These areas aid both divergent and convergent thinking—but especially the latter, since it is convenient to hold deliberate gatherings at the organizational crossroads and the junctions symbolize the willingness of all parties to listen to each other's perspectives. At Fisher-Price, a development group working on toys for girls decided to create an open area at the juncture of their design, engineering, and marketing groups—and to furnish it with couches instead of chairs and a conference room table. The informal ambiance of a living room (albeit one with flip charts) symbolized the team and family feeling they wanted to encourage. Nissan Design International is small enough that the disciplines are interwoven, but no one is further than a few minutes walk from the other engineers or designers or modelers. At IDEO, the offices scattered around Palo Alto are small enough that the disciplines are intermingled. However, some functions have only one or two representatives in a given office and colleagues are in other buildings; therefore, human factors experts, for example, have biweekly (face-to-face) meetings to share their disciplinary knowledge.

In companies as large as Nortel, design engineering, manufacturing, and sales tend to be located in different cities, miles apart. Colocation is not easily achieved. In such cases, managers have to spend much time and thought on how to design information technology and media (including videoconferencing) for virtual teaming. If the project is important enough, companies will go to enormous expense to reap the benefits from colocation. Chrysler proved that car development could shrink from the industry average of five years when they brought out the Neon in a mere thirty-one months. Of course there were many changes responsible for that reduced time to market, but one helpful factor was the fact that the cross-functional team (which involves hundreds of people in the case of car development) was housed under one roof in a state-of-the-art Tech Center. At the time, it was the only such concentrated facility in the world.[23]

Physical Icons

Physical objects, old and new, embody knowledge. They are the fossils left behind for our analysis when the creating organism has long since departed. They are often emotion-laden, evoking personal memories, the sense of an era, or the feel of a culture. Or they symbolize who we are—our beliefs, our aspirations. Physical objects thus create an atmosphere that affects those working in it. Creative groups tend to surround themselves with interesting *things*—collections of objects, sometimes funny, sometimes serious, but always thought provoking. For convenience, we think of these objects as divisible into Knowledge Icons, Cultural Icons, and Playful Objects.

Knowledge Icons Knowledge icons are pieces of thought, frozen in time. Walk around almost any area dominated by designers—IDEO, GVO, the Nissan Design Center—and you will have to thread your way among a wild variety of objects, many of them prototypes— early designs rejected on the way to the final product. You see a dozen different-style telephone receivers mounted on a wall, a piece of equipment for diagnosing medical samples, a child's electric guitar or an eight-inch track ball for preschool prospective computer nerds with as yet undeveloped small muscle skills. As discussed in Chapter 4, prototypes trace the evolution of the successful product. Why do designers keep these premature expressions? They are both history and stimuli, reminding the designers of dilemmas resolved and intriguing ideas that did not work—for that particular problem. They are a visual library, a menu of possibilities, reminders of a certain market. Designers use these visual suggestions much as they do the IDEO Technology Box described in Chapter 3—to stimulate both the conscious and unconscious mind. When a designer is working on the development of an office chair, for instance, she will browse through the prototypes of an earlier version to recall why certain features were rejected. However, if she is at IDEO, she might also borrow ideas from something as far afield from her immediate application as the complex mechanics embodied in the robotic whale developed for the movie *Free Willy*. A valve originally designed for an artificial heart, for example, turned out to be a terrific mechanism for the top of a drinking bottle for bicyclists!

Competitors' products serve a similar purpose. At Fisher-Price, shelves around a common meeting area are lined with toys from other manufacturers. Not only will designers borrow and reject ideas on the basis of examining the competition, but being surrounded by embodiments of competitive intelligence lends a certain healthy motivation to avoid Custer's fate when he was similarly encircled—and therefore to keep moving.

Cultural Icons Organizational lobbies are often like people's homes. They tell us a lot about the culture and values of the inhabitants. At IDEO, the lobby of one of the primary design shops in Palo Alto proudly displays the bright orange soapbox car that won the local, hotly contested Sandhill Derby, an annual event that pits venture capitalist and entrepreneurial firms against each other. The visitor also sees in the lobby other products reflecting the eclectic design talents in the firm: fishing reels and tackle, a fountain beverage container, computers. Of course, objects are also spread around throughout the building—some of them directly tied to organizational history, and others reflecting attitudes toward the world. At the Skandia Center, such objects as a ship's steering wheel and old typewriters are placed around as reminders of past exploration and invention. These displays are the corporate equivalent of the family refrigerator door; they help instill pride in the organization and its accomplishments, and they reinforce the kind of psychological environment (discussed in the next chapter) that is so important for creativity. What does your lobby or group area say about your culture?

Playful Objects Joke decorations symbolize play, not taking one's self too seriously, room for enjoyment. In a vice president's office at Chaparral Steel, an alligator appears to be emerging from the green rug at one side of the room. It's realistic enough to inspire a second hasty glance at the half-submerged head and beady eyes. At Electronic Arts (or for that matter, any company working on games or entertainment), cubicles look like the morning after a particularly inventive and raucous Halloween party: pictures of space creatures, four-foot inflated sports cars, grotesque puppets, plastic brains, stuffed gorillas. Some areas mimic the customer's world; for instance, a realistic Sports Bar at Electronic Arts, complete with bar stools and a mirror with decals, for the John Madden Football product team. Researchers studying the ability of various management teams to manage conflict found pink plastic flamingos given to a company by a customer gracing the corporation's "otherwise impeccably decorated headquarters."[24]

Information Technology Infrastructure

Why all this emphasis on physical togetherness for creativity, you ask? Wait a minute! This is the information age, the electronics age, the age of seven-day, twenty-four-hour operations around the globe. Architect the software in the United States, program the code in India, manufacture the chips in Korea. Who needs colocation? We've got Lotus Notes and videoconferencing and electronically shared white boards and T3 lines capable of carrying more bits and bytes than the seashore has sand *and* sand fleas. We have inference machines and powerful search engines to roam through databases for critical information. We have expert systems that teach and genetic algorithms that learn. We have simulations that can reproduce sensations as well as sights and sounds. We have Web sites using Virtual Reality Modeling Language to help us present ourselves to each other as avatars in three dimensions and in endless variations of color.

Yes. True. But we would need another book to explore all the ways that computers and information technology potentially affect the creative process. Information technology infrastructure is tremendously important. Most of the creative environments we have described rely heavily on electronic linkages and computer storage. And, as we noted before, many organizations have no alternative to relying on electronic networks to connect their far-flung operations.

However, we find that all the technology in the world does not—at least yet, and maybe never—replace face-to-face contact when it comes to brainstorming, inspiring passion, or enabling many kinds of serendipitous discovery. A study of geographically dispersed new product development teams found that team members conducting complex tasks *always* would have preferred to have a "richer" medium (that is, one supporting more channels and more interactive) than they actually had to use.[25] Fax is fine for one-way communication; e-mail for two-way, asynchronous, and relatively emotionless communication (where capital letters are "shouting," and therefore taboo); telephone for communications that require no visual aids; and videoconferencing if no subtlety in body language is necessary. But face-to-face communication is the richest, multichannel medium because it enables use of all the senses, is interactive and immediate.

Enhancing the creative process depends on supplying the richest medium that you can. If you have a physically dispersed group, you want to get members together whenever possible, not only so that they will become well enough acquainted to survive the inevitable (and desirable) intellectual disagreements inherent in the process but also so that they can build the kind of enthusiasm and energy around their project engendered by being a member of a cohesive group. When physical proximity is impossible, you may be able to use videoconferencing. We know of groups that not only brainstorm together but have parties and celebrate milestones together—by video. If video would blow the budget, then you may have to fall back on telephones and shared electronic white boards. One thing is for sure: communication is too important to be left to technical specialists. The manager needs to plan the communication structure of the group as carefully as he or she does the composition of the group.

To return to Stan and Amanda...

Amanda was stuck with the overall building. And the griping didn't stop. She hadn't realized how important her design input could have been. In desperation, she imported some arcade games, but there was no room for them—until she turned radical and took possession of one of the conference rooms. Out with the long polished table and in with the games, plus "scribble boards" as the teams began to call the white boards, all over the walls. Some pretty amazing graffiti appeared. Next, she was able to carve out an informal sitting room in the middle of the sea of cubicles. Beanbag chairs and more white boards! Her biggest coup was persuading management to outsource the property office function, so that she could take over two large storerooms formerly filled with inventory of desks, chairs, and computers. This move saved the corporation money and freed up precious space for creative activities. Fortunately, one was attached to the kitchen, so that it could be converted into an "Idea Café" for informal meetings over snacks. The second was available for group "informances" or other experimental exercises. "Not bad for a retrofit," she thought. "But if I ever have the chance again to help design a building for creative work, I'll find the time to get involved!"

Key Points

* Well-designed space encourages creativity by facilitating divergent thinking, incubation, and convergence. Poorly designed space can inhibit creativity by blocking communication and preventing incubation.

* Workspace design reflects the organization's mission and values, including the importance of creativity, more eloquently than does a formal mission statement.

* Organizations having the luxury of designing for creativity can build in spaces for encouraging creative abrasion, enabling incubation, and promoting effective convergence.

* Even when space is at a premium, retrofitting existing areas for creativity may still be possible. Keeping some open, unstructured space available for experimental activities is particularly desirable.

* Unexpected, serendipitous connections can be promoted by facilitating unplanned communication.

* Creativity may be enhanced through stimulation of the senses. However, individuals should feel in control over the stimuli, able to access and terminate them.

* Designing space for cross-functional teams to interact is highly desirable. However, members also need to be in close proximity to people from their own disciplines.

* Creative groups tend to surround themselves with interesting objects—physical icons—that symbolize play, culture, and old projects. Such icons can help create a stimulating, fun, creative environment.

* For complex tasks, face-to-face interaction is most desirable. When face-to-face is impossible, design information technology links to be as "rich" as possible.

* There is no substitute for face-to-face interaction.

6

Designing the Psychological Environment

Despite the fact that more champagne was trickling down his cheeks than had gone down his throat, Ted was feeling euphoric. As he looked around at the raucously celebrating group that had just poured a bottle of the expensive stuff over his head, he reflected back on the many trials and triumphs of the Fox Team. Their motto, "Over the Top," waving on a banner overhead, captured the spirit that had gone into producing the company's first lightweight, all-terrain hiking boot. Not only was the sales force reporting an enthusiastic response to the first batch into the market, but the team had just won the coveted corporate "First, Best" award.

"I never thought of myself as a leader," Ted mused. But this project had demanded more than the usual management skills, as important as they were. For one thing, everyone on the team already had stock options and a reasonable salary. So Ted couldn't count on money to get them really charged up. Taking them out to visit hiking clubs had been a good idea—visiting customers had engendered a lot of enthusiasm and suggested some pretty radical ideas. The big one, of course, was the thin, shock-absorbing sole that the engineers had initially said was far too risky to manufacture, but which protected the foot while giving hikers a real "feel" for the terrain. And the team members he had selected certainly had a good time together, both working and

playing—despite an initial rough start. But what made Ted most proud was the way the team had rallied after they got the bad news that their initial design of the boot tongue abraded the foot—so they had to go back to the drawing boards. He hoped that he had contributed to their positive attitude by presenting the bad news as a challenge he was confident they could meet and learn from. Good thing he had been right. Working on the tongue redesign had suggested a number of changes for the heel as well.

The project had been lucky, too. If Joe hadn't gone camping just the weekend that he did, and if he hadn't told the rest of the team about the way the tent lines seized up so he couldn't get the tent down, the group might never have thought of the now-patented grommets that kept the boot laces from slipping. "But just maybe I helped that happen too," thought Ted. "The group would never realize it, of course, but if I hadn't had the Monday morning 'show and tell' meetings . . . or if I hadn't insisted that particular Friday that we all leave the darned grommet problem until Monday to solve. . . In fact, . . ." Ted thought, with the sly grin that had inspired the team's name, "I'm getting a pretty big head over my part in this project. But they'll whittle it down to size at tonight's 'roast,' I'm sure."

Leading a Creative Group– What's Different?

"*Creative groups* are made, not born." Asked how his responsibility for creativity had changed after his entrepreneurial venture grew into a software giant, Oracle CEO Larry Ellison replied that his job now was to build an environment conducive to creativity.[1] A group of "ordinary," intelligent people in a creative environment is more likely to innovate than a group of "creative" people in a stifling environment. Leadership makes the difference. Ted has earned his "big head."

Managing by the numbers (e.g., the financial reports of the organization) is easy compared to leading people through norms and communication—especially if your preferred thinking style moves you to curl up with some nice reports, analyses, and detailed data. Moreover, in the management of creativity, you are responsible for inspiring passion and enabling serendipity. Not in your job description? Almost nothing *important* is! The really crucial stuff is hard to describe. In Chapter 5, we emphasized the effect of the *physical* environment on creativity. In this chapter, we discuss the importance of the *psychological* or *social* environment. We invite you to think about how you can make it safe, desirable, and even easy for your group members to express creativity.

Risk Taking and Failing Forward

Recall our discussion of norms in Chapters 3 and 4. The acceptable "way we do things here" has a profound effect—both positive and destructive—on group process. Creative groups require guiding values and norms that channel individual energy without thwarting. Sound tricky? Or worse, vague? There are literally dozens of values and norms espoused by groups. Members absorb them, often unconsciously. (Fish don't scrutinize the water they swim in.) Here we focus on two norms of behavior that differentiate creative from noncreative ecologies: risk taking and the ability to fail forward.

Risk Taking

Dick Liebhaber, executive vice president of MCI, has observed: "We do not shoot people who make mistakes. We shoot people who do not take risks."[2] To suggest that there is a connection between risk taking and creativity is not to suggest that all skydivers are creative or that all creative individuals like living on the edge of danger. Individual thrill-seekers apparently have an innate, probably chemistry-based propensity for personal risk—and there is no reason to expect them to express more or less creativity than the norm. Taking group members bungee jumping as a way to stimulate the creative juices, therefore, is unlikely to help. Innovativeness does require a certain tolerance for risk, however, because by definition, doing something creative means breaking away from the usual. Every creative idea replaces something—some concept, method, or technique—that was probably doing a pretty good job. To replace this with something "new and improved" necessarily entails risk. Therefore, creative individuals and groups must stick their necks out, go out on a limb, break eggs, *and* leap tall buildings in order to accomplish creative goals. Organizational norms about risk taking (embodied in the actions of top management) can either encourage radical ideas and guide them into useful channels—or dam the stream entirely.[3] At Massachusetts biotechnology firm Genzyme Corporation, Vice President of Regulatory Affairs Alison Lawton says she learned new norms of behavior when she came to Genzyme. "Unless you challenge the system and try to innovate, you don't know what you can achieve."[4]

We've all heard stories about managers discouraging risk taking, but the following CEO may win in the "Luddite response to new technology" category. He encouraged his top management to originate ideas to enhance the corporate image. Thinking to pleasantly surprise his boss, one enterprising vice president launched directly into action and created a Web site on the Internet for the corporation. To the astonishment of the vice president, the CEO opened the next board meeting by thundering "Who the hell put our company on the Internet? Don't you know that isn't used by anyone except sex-craved druggies?" The offending vice president reported feeling ready to "slide under the table and crawl for the door." After confessing his culpability and defending the Web site as a legitimate bulletin board to the world, the vice president was rewarded by an assignment to a site in a foreign country—an assignment he perceived as punishment for taking a risk. Obviously, this is an extreme, if true, example. You would never behave like this CEO. But even a mild-mannered rebuke, such as "We shouldn't be spending money on this kind of untried channel," could have much the same dampening effect.

In contrast, consider the following situation. Dave Fournie was mill superintendent for the Medium Section Mill at Chaparral Steel when he championed a $1.5 million arc saw for trimming finished steel beams (a huge investment for this relatively small minimill). Originally prototyped at the vendor's site, the saw was brought back to the Chaparral site in Texas in order to conduct realistic tests under production conditions. The arc saw failed spectacularly.

> The magnetic fields attracted small, unattached pieces of metal (including watches and pens), transforming them into projectiles, and the engineers were never able to refine the equipment to the point of effective operation. After a year of unsuccessful tinkering, the saw was replaced. Subsequently promoted to vice president of operations, Fournie is somewhat amused to find that outsiders "can't believe you can make a mistake like that and not get crucified."[5]

He had been allowed to take a recognized risk. He had other successes to his credit, and had the saw worked, it would have been very valuable to the company.

Imagine how different you would feel about risk taking, depending on which of those two organizations you worked in.

Managers who encourage risk taking are also careful about how negative feedback is delivered. "You are on a downward spiral" fails to inspire (or instruct!). However, even negative feedback can motivate, if it is given carefully and constructively. People embarked on an intellectual journey do in fact need to know how they are doing. Honest feedback need not be brutal. Alan Horn, chairman and CEO of Castle Rock Entertainment, is constantly presented with creative ideas: screenplays, first cuts of a movie, ideas for marketing. It is critical, he says, to have "a heartfelt, internalized respect for what these people do." When they come in to present an innovative idea, "I want to remember that they are *completely* vulnerable at that moment. My job is not to kill them but to find the bright, creative, special parts of their proposal and focus on those first, to ease their anxiety, make them feel less vulnerable. Then I have to

---

PSYCHOLOGICAL SAFETY

Amy Edmondson studied the effects of "psychological safety" in a large number of teams in an office furniture manufacturing company. Psychological safety "is characterized by a shared belief that well-intentioned action will not lead to punishment or rejection." It was measured with a survey instrument that included items such as: "It is safe to take a risk on this team." Edmondson determined that psychological safety felt by team members influenced learning behavior (that is, the extent to which the team proactively communicates within and outside the group to enhance its learning), which in turn affected team performance. Equally important, Edmondson found that team leadership is crucial in creating the climate for risk taking that leads to enhanced performance.[6]

---

find a graceful way into the parts of what they've brought that need improving."[7] Delivered like this, the bad news is as important to furthering the creative process as is the good.

Failing Forward

Whenever one of his thousands of experiments failed, Thomas Edison would ask what the failure revealed and enthusiastically record what he had learned. He filled endless notebooks, including results of his abortive experiments on psychokinesis. Once asked by an assistant why he continued trying to discover a long-lasting filament after so many failures, Edison reportedly said he didn't understand the question. By his standards, he hadn't failed at all. Rather, he had discovered thousands of things that didn't work. His persistence was rewarded with patent number 251,539 for the lightbulb.

Modern managers need to take a similar stance. Stanley Gault, when he was chairman of Rubbermaid, said, "In today's world, you just can't afford to be overly conservative."[8] By *conservative*, he meant having a 100 percent success rate in new products. An innovative company or group will inevitably experience some failure, or it isn't being innovative enough, it is not taking sufficient risks. A climate that supports risk must view failures as opportunities for growth. However, there are intelligent failures and there are stupid mistakes. Failing forward involves recognizing the difference.

Sure, we all have made stupid mistakes—risky, negligent, ill-thought-out ideas with predictable consequences. We fallible humans do indeed err. If we have sufficient standing in the group we may even have been taken aside and given a divinely forgiving pat on the back. Unless the back-pat encouraged us simply to repeat the mistake, we learned. But it was still stupid, and there are limits to how many such errors a group can absorb.

Failing forward does not mean congratulating people for stupid mistakes. This just leads to more failure.

Intelligent Failures Failing forward implies intelligent failures. *Intelligent failures* result from taking known (or anticipated) risks—not from making repeated mistakes. Hopefully, the risks are acknowledged by upper management and have some potential for an innovative payoff. The most intelligent failures are honest and well-resourced attempts, including funding to bring in specialized talent if necessary. Individuals who fail intelligently also have contingency plans in place for the possibility of falling short of the stated goals. If the product or service doesn't warrant commercialization, perhaps there is knowledge that can be licensed, sold, given away for tax benefits—or reused in a different product. For example, in the 1980s, IBM research scientist, Bernard Meyerson, helped develop semiconductors that combined germanium with the usual silicon to yield a chip that could conduct electricity much more efficiently. His plan to incorporate the new product into mainframe computers was quashed when a superior chip technology was introduced. But rather than following some advice to move on to something else,

he formed a team to redesign his product for cellular phones and
other wireless devices, where the germanium technology was advan-
taged. In 1998, IBM projected billion dollar earnings within five
years for the new business.[9]

Learning from the Experience In failing forward, the organization (not
just the individuals involved in the failed attempt)—learns from
the experience. Most organizations bury their failures quickly before
anyone can call for an autopsy. Learning from failure requires honest
examination of what went well and what didn't. While project debriefs should be conducted for *all* projects, they are essential for
"failed" ones. Good project debriefs are not easy. First, you need
all the relevant parties present, not just those who happen to be in
the office that day. Of course, most members have moved on to the
next challenge. One company takes these meetings so seriously that
a member of the U.S.–based team flew back from his new project
in Japan to be present. Second, the same rules apply here as for any
group meeting: honesty, impersonal evaluations, a focus on learning
instead of on blame. Focusing on *what occurred* rather than on *who
did what* helps avoid finger pointing. Organizations that require the
employees who took the risk to commit suttee on the pyre of the
failure will not see a lot of volunteers for the next unusual project.
Taking team members down the ladder of inference mentioned in
Chapter 4, so as to track the origins of decisions is useful.

However, project debriefs, especially of failed undertakings, tend
to result in an arm-long list of desired changes. The team members,
viewing this litany of woe, often decide that there is too much to
be altered and, ostrichlike, plunge their heads resolutely into the
sand. A group of employees at an instrumentation company worked
for two days on a review of two recent new product development
projects, both of which had fallen short of desired objectives. At the
end of the two days, the narrow room in which they had held their
deliberations was wallpapered with flip-chart sheets, each containing
a number of implied or specified problems. The team members sat
back in their chairs, stunned by the magnitude of change needed.

For ten minutes no one said anything. Finally, the facilitator suggested finding a "top twenty" list. From there, the team went to a "top ten," and ultimately fleshed out in some detail five changes to be made. Most critically, each change was given a time frame and accountable people for implementation. The group moved from paralysis to action. Their selection of changes to pursue included those intended to improve performance (colocation of team members to encourage better and earlier communication among the professional disciplines involved), and those to prevent problems (including a technical representative as a member of the design group, to provide some insurance against designing in installation problems). The organization had learned, and their next innovation projects were improved. Intelligent failure includes this kind of active path for avoiding the same kinds of mistakes in the future.

Communication

Interactive communication is the lifeblood of creativity. Leaders who want to encourage communication flows are constantly clearing the channels of debris, breaking down dams, even installing pumps to pull information out of the depths of the organization. They need four skills: listening, presenting, connecting with others for ideas, and honest communication. Of the four, only presentation skill is *taught* (usually poorly).

Listening Skills

At MTV, the music video cable network, a couple of 25-year-old production assistants both named Melissa wrote a memo that startled the organization: "Screw the maudlin death images and relearn what it means to laugh. We want a cleaner, brighter, more fun MTV." Fortunately for them, MTV president Judy McGrath and CEO of MTV Networks Tom Freston regarded the memo as helpful.[10]

Members of creative organizations and groups need to feel free to express their ideas —even if they are not always acted on. Welcoming dissent and listening to peoples' news, good and bad—especially bad!—is part of an ecology of encouraging risk and failing forward that nourishes creativity. You know what it is like to try to communicate with someone whose glazed eyes are contemplating the answer to the riddle of life apparently displayed over your left shoulder. Most of us have mental Walkman earphones on a lot of the time. And active listening means more than just taking them off—although that is a start. "I don't want to hear about it" should be high on the list of taboo statements for a creative group, replaced with "What do you think—*really?*" Leaders must model the fact that listening is not a passive sport, that creativity thrives in a climate of full disclosure and thorough exploration of options. Observes Jeffrey Beir, vice president at Lotus Development Corporation, about creative groups: "you have to involve the whole team. Now, I don't mean democracy—you don't need to take a vote, but you do need to listen."[11]

Listening also involves creating a forum for open expression. At Hewlett-Packard's research laboratories, Head of Corporate Laboratories Joel Birnbaum used to hold "coffee talks"—broadcasts that, like President Roosevelt's fireside chats, were one-way communications, if informal ones. In recent years, Birnbaum moved to a much more participative mode. His "town meetings" still contained some broadcast information, but most of his time in these interactive meetings was spent listening.[12]

Presenting Skills

Forget the Golden Rule; it doesn't apply in communication with group members. You do *not* want to communicate unto others as you would have them communicate unto you, but rather as they wish to be communicated unto! Remember the explanation of different thinking-style preferences in Chapter 2? You may have a strong preference for data—lots of it. Facts, figures, percentages carried out to three decimal places. But some of your colleagues would rather hear about previous experiences—case studies, histories, proven solutions with logical progression from detail to detail. Still others want personal stories, experiences, complete with the impact on lives and family. And there are those who would prefer pictures to words.

So, suppose you want to set out a challenge to your group—perhaps the innovation opportunity is that you are consultants being asked to help redesign operational processes for a firm. How can you best present the problem so that each individual in your group will both grasp its essence and be motivated to think about it before you all get together? The typical presentation of the problem would probably include data and text descriptions of the client company, their current operations, their financials. That's fine for the left-brainers. But if you wish to engage everyone, you might think to add a specific story illustrating the problems the client faces. How about some photos of the crowding or the confusion in the office or factory to visually acquaint your group with the company? Perhaps you could share some excerpts from the interviews given by client company representatives. As suggested in Chapter 2, if your group has so little diversity of thinking styles that such disparate approaches are unnecessary, it may also lack enough intellectual variety to support creativity! Part of your job is to inspire group members' passion for the project, and it helps if you can connect with the individual mental maps of experience that they carry in their heads rather than try to get them to understand the map in yours. Adjusting your own communication style is an important exemplar for the group. Creativity will be enabled even more as you encourage an environment in which *all* members of the group understand and respect the subtle interaction of media and individual minds' preferred thinking styles.

Connectivity

Louis XI was "the spider king," not because of any arachnid appendages, but because he was so well connected—everywhere. His spy network was the Internet of the day, with nodes in every important country. While we do not recommend Louis' methods, we do admire his connectivity, his ability to scan the environment for ideas and options. Connecting people and ideas is critical to creativity. Barbara Waugh, Manager, Worldwide Personnel, uses the engineering language that surrounds her to explain a connecting mechanism at Hewlett-Packard Laboratories. Senior researchers, dubbed "Friends of Joel" Birnbaum, wander the halls of the labs on his behalf to identify potential research projects or small pockets of passion in a particular technology or potential product that can be connected and "amplified" to create a possible new business direction for the company. If the product ideas thus reinforced turn out to be good HP products, fine—if not, they may be spun out into a start-up into which HP can put capital.[13]

At Boston-based Teradyne, founder and Chairman Alex d'Arbeloff's widespread connections were often important to corporate innovativeness. For example, when Teradyne needed to move from purely UNIX-based software to run their semiconductor testing equipment products, d'Arbeloff personally introduced his experts to off-the-shelf software. He took them to a small local company on whose board he served. At this company, the Teradyne engineers were astonished to discover the power and flexibility available to them—out of a software catalog for products that ran on a personal computer. Instead of spending thousands of dollars to write new code, the engineers discovered they could choose from thousands of programs priced at only $200 or $300.[14]

The importance of connectivity is not confined to top managers, of course. Creativity flourishes at intersections throughout the communication web. However, top managers provide the resources and support for connectivity. At Unilever, whose food processing plants are scattered around the world, "knowledge networks" are connected electronically and their members periodically brought together physically so that they can share problems, ideas, and, most important, creative solutions. For example, the corporation's experts about the tomatoes that go into so many Unilever culinary products constitute a community of practice around that particular fruit, whether they work in Brazil or England. As of this writing, 24 five-day workshops had been held throughout the world to create a complete knowledge map of what Unilever knows about tomatoes—from seeds to consumer sauce preferences.

Honest Communication: Identifying the Moose on the Table

Picture yourself seated at a large dining-room table, sharing a formal meal with colleagues. On the table, covering most of the surface is a huge, dead moose. Despite the occasional interference of a hoof that has to be pushed aside so you can eat, no one speaks about the moose or acknowledges its presence. The topic is taboo. Sound ridiculous? Let's consider a parallel situation.

The top management of a billion-dollar manufacturer of filtration equipment is meeting to discuss how the company may restructure and innovate for the future. Present in the room as well is a consultant, who has had separate conversations with the top managers and the CEO. The CEO at dinner last night expressed his frustration to the consultant with the lack of initiative shown by his direct hires. Pressed to give an example, he explains. "Knowing that we were going to be working with you on what capabilities we need to develop for the future, I sent out a memo suggesting what our current five core capabilities are, and asked for comments. Not one individual responded to that memo. But if I complain, I know I'll *never* get any suggestions."

Yesterday, the consultant heard from top managers. As a group, they expressed concern about leadership of the company. "He isn't a real leader," one said of the CEO. "He tries to control everything at arm's length, through financial figures or very directive e-mails— but he never really inspires anyone about anything."

See the Moose? Pretty difficult for the CEO to express his frustration directly with those reporting to him, because he believes they will only retreat further from innovative ideas if he criticizes them. They, on the other hand, are unable to tell him that they feel he is both too distant and too directive. The Moose is the perceived lack of leadership, both from the top managers and the CEO. So the group members skirt an issue that is undermining all their discussion and lending a dysfunctional undertone to the meeting as both the CEO and his direct reports try to engage the consultant through meaningful glances. "See?" the glances seem to say, as behavior by either the CEO or the other managers appears to confirm their secret opinions of each other.

When taboo issues obstruct discussion and keep group members from dealing honestly with each other and the issues, any convergence is likely to be spurious. Oh, there may be agreement, all right. But it will be shallow and members will be unlikely to take any ownership for the agreement or its consequences. With the assumptions and agendas still hidden, they will retreat to more familiar preagreement territory. For true convergence to be reached, the Moose on the Table has to be acknowledged—and openly discussed.

In the case of this company, the consultant was able in separate conversations to raise the Moose and get all concerned to acknowledge that the taboo subject had to be addressed. The next step was a facilitated meeting in which all members openly discussed the nature of leadership and what they expected of each other. To his credit, the CEO was not defensive about his behavior, in part because everyone came to realize that his background as a financial officer and his personal thinking-style preferences had led him to communicate in a way that he found comfortable, but which others did not. Recognizing that those preferences and skills had influenced his behavior, rather than an autocratic love of authority, helped depersonalize the situation. For their part, the top managers realized that they *hadn't* shown the kind of initiative that would have been helpful—namely, insisting on some face-to-face meetings to discuss issues about which they had opinions. Instead of taking the e-mails and memos as directives, they saw they could regard them as opinion pieces, prototypes for them to shape and influence. Recognizing the Moose left room for discussing options, including considerable restructuring of responsibilities. The CEO was pleasantly dumbfounded at the depth and breadth of creative suggestions for the future. Leaving the discussion, he commented that the group had "taken a giant step forward."

Calling such taboo topics "Moose on the Table" takes advantage of the benefits of humor: easing of tensions, elevation of mood and optimism, and creation of a spirit of collaboration. One group has grasped the importance of clearing away such obstructive norms with such enthusiasm that its members feel free to call out during meetings, "Moose! Moose!" In another company introduced to the concept, the meeting room is inhabited by several small stuffed toy moose and it is not unknown for one team member to hurl a moose at another when an issue appears to be in the process of being swept aside. In both these organizations, the notion of a Moose on the Table is so well understood that its invocation provokes laughter, although addressing the taboo is a serious subject. "Speakers can say in jest things that might otherwise give offense because the message is simultaneously serious and not serious. The recipient is allowed to save face by receiving the serious message while appearing not to do so. The result is communication of difficult information in a more tactful and less personally threatening way."[15]

Promoting Passion

In the early days of management as a profession (and when we were enamored of the idea that it could be a science), Taylorism promoted standardization and division of work into tasks so small that each was essentially mindless. Efficiency was king, and we hired people for their muscles. Then came the quality movement, knowledge work, and the epiphany that hiring people for their *brains* was not only efficient but often effective. From brawn to brain. What is next? Passion. Hiring people for their hand, their head, *and* their heart. Hiring the whole person does not necessarily mean owning their lives, twenty-four hours a day. It means that when they are at work, they are also at play. If that sounds too idealistic to be real, you need to visit outstanding creative groups and feel the energy that flows from group members who have dedicated both head and heart to their work. It may be a passion for the organization, for the product or brand, or for the consumer experience. It's what gets them up in the morning.

What engages people's hearts? It *isn't* the urge to increase the stock price or ensure 15 percent returns to shareholders (although this may well be the *outcome* of fully engaging people's hearts). Consider the following newspaper headline: "Oldest U.S. worker at 102, says his job still a pleasure." 102? Milton Garland has worked for the Frick Company of Waynesboro, Pennsylvania, for seventy-eight years! " 'I love the work I am doing," he said, leaning forward in his vested, dark pinstripe suit. "My advice is to go into something and stay with it until you like it. You can't like it until you obtain expertise in that work. And once you are an expert, it's a pleasure.' "[16] His current duties include coordinating international patents and giving training classes. There was another class coming up first thing the morning he was interviewed. Work for seventy-eight years, you say? Get a life! But that's the point—he has. Listen to a 30-year-old at nearly the opposite end of the generations. Richard Barton, head of Microsoft's Expedia, a Web site for booking your travel online says: "Work is not work. It's a hobby that you happen to get paid for."[17] These are highly motivated people with passion for their work—and passion fuels creativity (Figure 6-1). Passion comes in many forms, and leaders can help their employees make the link between personal enthusiasm and work.

Passion for the Job

Not all of us have passion for our jobs, perhaps because we've chosen poorly or been assigned arbitrarily. As Teresa Amabile has written, "Of all the things managers can do to stimulate creativity, perhaps the most efficacious is the deceptively simple task of matching people with the right assignments. Managers can match people with jobs

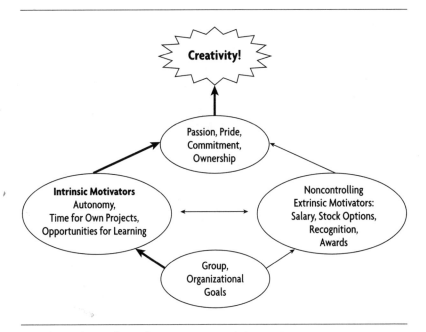

Creativity!

Passion, Pride, Commitment, Ownership

Intrinsic Motivators
Autonomy, Time for Own Projects, Opportunities for Learning

Noncontrolling Extrinsic Motivators: Salary, Stock Options, Recognition, Awards

Group, Organizational Goals

6 1 The Relationship of Motivation and Creativity

that play to their expertise and their skills in creative thinking, *and* ignite intrinsic motivation."[18]

How do you become a successful matchmaker? Sometimes it's a matter of selecting people who match the values of the organization. Southwest Airlines, whose 7 percent turnover rate was the lowest in the industry in 1990, hired 1,400 that year from 62,000 applicants. CEO Herb Kelleher provides the formula:

> What we are looking for, first and foremost, is a sense of humor. Then we are looking for people who have to excel to satisfy themselves and who work well in a collegial environment. We don't care that much about education and expertise, because we can train people to do whatever they have to do. We hire attitudes.[19]

At other times, the matchmaking requires more finesse, such as pairing people's natural strengths or passions with particular jobs

---

MATCHING CREATIVE PEOPLE TO THEIR JOBS

Successful matching may require a rather refined sense of what really turns creative people on. Cummings and Oldham studied 171 employees in two manufacturing facilities. The employees were drawn from various divisions, including design and manufacturing engineers, technicians, and draftsmen. Each person's creativity was assessed (using the Gough Creative Personality Scale), as were the contributions each made to the firm's formal suggestion program. The creativity of each suggestion was determined by a committee that accepted ideas that were novel and useful. How did the more creative employees fare? Well, if you guessed that their suggestions would, overall, be judged more creative than those of their less creative colleagues, you would be wrong. Instead, the creative people produced more creative ideas only when they had a more complex job and were allowed freedom to pursue that job by a supportive, non-controlling supervisor.[20]

---

within the same company. Running a binational company can present an unusual challenge when cultural differences enter the matchmaking equation. CoWare's Guido Arnout wanted his engineers in Belgium and the marketers in the United States because of the good match between national/regional strengths, in this case an orientation toward risk, and needs of the company. "You have Marketing to sell the idea, Sales to sell what you actually have, Engineering to be skeptical about what the customer really wants and needs. You need those natural tensions, to have good arguments." Arnout sees the strength of Belgian engineers as being system thinkers, very methodical and quality oriented. On the American side, sales and marketing play to the more entrepreneurial, risk-taking preferences of the employees—and the needs of the company.

Some managers have creatively redefined the job so as to stimulate the passion. When Russell Herndon designed a new regulatory group for Genzyme Corporation, he advertised inside and outside the organization for people who wanted to carry a product and process all the way from inception to use—not just oversee some small step in regulatory procedures. As a consequence, he attracted a highly unusual group of people from varied backgrounds. They saw an exciting opportunity quite unlike the usual regulatory affairs job.

Passion for the Innovation (Product, Service)

Can people be motivated by their passion for a product? The team that brought us the powerful advertisements for Dove soap loves their product and feels good about promoting it. "Dove has always had a component of honesty," observes Nancy Vonk, a creative director for ad agency Ogilvy & Mather. Her teammate, Creative Director Janet Kestin adds, "We've tried to make truth at the heart of everything we have done." Among much other information given them by their client, Lever, was an intriguing fact. Dove, unlike the face soaps with which it competed, was so mild that it affected litmus paper just as distilled water did, namely not at all, whereas the competitive products turned the paper dark, indicating high alkalinity. (Dove is not, at a molecular level, really a soap; rather it is a soap alternative invented during World War II.) Vonk and Kestin, who had backgrounds as an art director and a writer, and neither of whom had technical expertise, ran out and purchased all the necessary components to replicate the litmus test in their office. What they saw "totally knocked [them] out." They were shocked that even soaps reputed to be mild in fact contained ingredients harsh to the skin. Their loyalty to the brand was strengthened by the "armwash test," in which they, like other subjects in a test of mildness, washed an inner arm in a circular direction, for sixty seconds, three times a day with soap and the other inner arm the same way, with Dove. After three days, the inner arm subjected to soap was marked with a tender red spot; the Dove arm was not.

The product was "a dream come true—a product with a provable technical advantage," because both women are "somewhat cynical about advertising," and want to "sell products based on their merits rather than some snow-job."[21]

Real enthusiasm is contagious. And Fisher-Price's Lisa Mancuso's is highly infectious. "I love the product; I feel passion for what I do. . . . I couldn't champion something I didn't love. . . . People want to be on your team when you yourself believe in what you are doing and you yourself are successful. I really love what I do, so I can get people excited, because I'm not faking it."[22]

Passion for the Organization

Maybe the passion is for the organization as a whole—for its overall mission. Susan Schilling of Lucas Learning says of her enthusiastic employees, "If they wanted money, they'd be somewhere else. They work here because they are excited about what we are doing" (making entertaining and educational products for children).[23] And original Apple Computer team member Randy Wigginton describes the group's zeal in those early days: "Everyone who worked there identified totally with their work—we all believed we were on a mission from God."[24]

Those are start-up companies. How about one that was originated in 1903? Harley-Davidson employees are so dedicated to their company that a four-day rally for 150,000 people on Harley's ninety-fifth anniversary could be run with just one additional employee, and otherwise entirely with volunteer labor. Moreover, the volunteers had worked hard to improve this rally over the highly successful ninetieth anniversary gathering. Former CEO Richard Teerlink explains the reason why his employees were both passionate and innovative.

> We didn't want people who just come to work. We wanted people to be excited about what they do, to have an emotional attachment to our company. They didn't necessarily have to ride the motorcycle. It was the excitement they got

when they were standing in line in the supermarket wearing a Harley T-shirt and someone said, "Do you work at Harley? Wow!" We got people who wanted to work for this kind of company, who wanted to make a difference. I call it the "Harley Ether." They knew the environment generally would encourage them to make a difference, to challenge [themselves] to be continuously better.

This enthusiasm for bettering their organization has translated into important innovations. Harley's labor relations are the envy of other companies because of the constant improvements wrought by largely self-managed work teams.[25]

Now, you may ask, how do I get my employees or group members to feel that way? Maybe you can't. But leaders of creative groups have discovered a number of managerial levers that certainly increase the likelihood that group members will feel passion, commitment, and pride. The first step is understanding how to set goals so that they don't destroy motivation.

Intrinsic Motivators: Motivating from the Inside Out

Intrinsic motivation is the difference between "you couldn't pay me enough to . . . " and "I can't believe I'm getting *paid* to do this, it's so much fun!" It is the difference between hiring peoples' hands and head, and engaging their heart. GE's Jack Welch believes that "the idea flow from the human spirit is absolutely unlimited. All you have to do is tap into that well . . . It's creativity. It's a belief that every person counts."[26] James Vincent, former CEO of Biogen, notes, "The issue is always, how do you combine motivation and mission?"[27] That is, how do you get people to enjoy working for an organizational goal? Obviously, you can't just tell them, "enjoy," but that doesn't mean you are helpless. There are a number of ways to build the creative ecology that instills passion.

Autonomy

Debbie Herd, J.C. Penney's college relations manager, says, "It occurred to us that Gen Xers will work ninety hours a week if they have their own business. So we decided we needed to make them think they are entrepreneurs."[28] Bruce Tulgan of Rainmaker, Inc., reflects the culture of the Generation X "non-organizational" person in his answer to the question: What does this generation want? "That's easy. They want to be handed the remote control."[29] And Mark Levin, CEO and founder of Millennium Pharmaceuticals in Cambridge, Massachusetts, notes: "If you hire outstanding people, you have to give them authority."[30] This means (as noted in Chapter 4) converging on the mission, the goals of the organization—but giving as much freedom as possible in *how* the goals are achieved; channeling the human energy flows, but not micromanaging those flows. Said Anthony Rucci, then chief administrative officer at Sears, "When people get a chance to accomplish something themselves, they build self-esteem. They just come to life."[31]

David Witte, CEO of the Ward Howell International executive search firm, says, "freedom and responsibility are the very best golden handcuffs there are." For example, in the oil business, says Witte, "I can easily take people from bureaucratic companies like Amoco or Exxon, but there's no way in hell I can steal from Joe Foster." Foster, when he was at Tenneco Oil, was one of the first in the energy business to offer employees the freedom and authority of self-managing teams.[32] So helping the creative groups set the goals and then granting as much autonomy as possible in *how* the goal is reached, building in some time and resources for learning and creative offshoots—these are ways not only to motivate but to retain members of your creative groups.

Time for Personal Projects

3M gives employees 15 percent of work time for individual projects. HP gives 10 percent, plus continuous access to labs and equipment.[33] In recent years it has become increasingly difficult for employees to *find* those hours, but both these companies have multiple stories

---

SELF-ESTEEM AND PRODUCTIVITY

Research on a nationwide survey of several thousand workers showed that in addition to education and experience, feeling good about oneself had a strong effect on productivity (as reflected in wages). "The researchers found both that self-esteem affected the acquisition of human capital and that human capital and its payoff via higher wages tended to enhance self-esteem. . . . A 10 percent rise in self-esteem boosted wages more than a 10 percent increase in education or work experience."[34]

---

about the important innovations that came out of "skunkworks," groups working on undeclared projects in their spare time. Small companies, especially start-ups, can afford even less to give their employees some segment of time for individual or small group innovation, but they have less need to do so. After all, their employees are usually at the company because they are excited about the particular project or product that is dominating organizational attention.

Opportunities to Learn

One motivator applies equally to large or small companies, and is so important that it is often written into many new employees' job contract. At Price Waterhouse, John Waterman, 30, says: "I'm here because I keep learning. Whenever I start to get a little bored, a new project comes along with opportunities for learning." Tracy Amabile, 33, echoes the sentiment: "The people and the learning are what's primary. I've been provided a lot of opportunities, lots of challenging work in different industries."[35] Hewlett-Packard has half the average attrition of labor markets in its industries; in the 1990s attrition fell by a third. "I get benchmarked on this frequently," says Sally Dudley, a manager of human resources. "We don't do anything special. We're 'among the leaders' on pay. Our total compensation package is fairly traditional for a large company." So there's no different *extrinsic* motivation at work here. But then she reveals what *is* unusual at Hewlett-Packard. In her twenty-four years at HP, she has held fourteen different jobs. "Those who have spent most of their careers at HP—and most of us have—don't identify with doing the same thing."[36] Similarly, when asked about their reasons for working at Oracle computer company in Silicon Valley, California, employees "all start talking about the challenges, the chance to do interesting work on the cutting edge."[37] This attitude is typical of that innovation-driven geography, where changing jobs for software engineers often involves no more than walking across the street. Losing the excitement can mean losing your best people. Employees talk about the fun of working on a "cool" project, and their anticipation of finding the next "way cool" one. The challenge for managers is to keep that excitement in-house, lest their creative groups disintegrate.

Extrinsic Motivators: Motivating from the Outside In

What besides the challenge of meeting goals motivates people? As Woody Allen has observed, money is good, if only for financial reasons. Money and rank can motivate. "Six-figure salary." "Reports directly to the CEO." "Stock options." "Company car." "Company car in private parking space." But will such incentives lead to the passion, commitment, and sense of ownership that drive creativity? The answer seems to be (as in most of life): it depends. If all those great incentives align with peoples' own interests or at least support some of the internal motives discussed later—yes. If on the other hand, such overt incentives serve to control people or deprive them of autonomy—no.

Feeling your wallet fatten when the company's stock goes up helps create a sense of belonging and ownership. At some of the most admired corporations in the United States, a high percentage of the workforce is eligible for stock ownership, options, and bonuses. At Federal Express and Intel, for instance, all employees qualify.

This variable pay accounts for a much bigger than average piece of everybody's total compensation.[38]

In some cases, it is possible to tie financial motivators directly to project outcome, rather than to the performance of the entire company. Walter Noot, head of production for Viewpoint DataLabs International, a company in Salt Lake City that makes three-dimensional models and textures for film production houses, video game companies, and car manufacturers, came up with a novel way to reward his creative groups when he found they were asking for raises every six months. Instead of giving them salaries, he paid them as if they were contract workers. They were still full-time Viewpoint employees, with benefits, but every project team split 26 percent of the money Viewpoint expected to receive from a client. Salaries jumped 60 to 70 percent, but productivity almost doubled. Moreover, the group members have no set hours—they work when they please.[39]

Unexpected rewards, not tied to the expectation of performance, but delivered after special effort, are also—perhaps especially—motivating. During the 1997 UPS strike, Federal Express had to deal with 800,000 extra packages a day.

Thousands of employees voluntarily poured into the hubs a little before midnight—on weekdays this was after working a regular job—to sort the mountain of extra packages for several hours. Their toil demonstrated a dedication beyond any slogans. When the strike had ended, [CEO Frederick] Smith congratulated them in 11 full-page newspaper ads that ended with the salute: "Bravo Zulu!" The military phrase is prized because employees learn during training that it is the highest compliment: "Job well done, your performance rose above and beyond the call of duty." Smith also ordered special bonuses."[40]

Even if you don't have control over the budget and you can't afford a page in the *New York Times*, you can still provide extrinsic motivation in the form of recognition. A simple "way-to-go!" energizes people. The manager who submits his annual report to the vice president of the organization listing all the innovations and accomplishments of his department, but without naming a single

---

INTRINSIC AND EXTRINSIC MOTIVATION

Teresa Amabile has identified *intrinsic motivation* as crucial to creativity. Intrinsic motivation "arises from the individual's positive reaction to qualities of the task itself; this reaction can be experienced as interest, involvement, curiosity, satisfaction, or positive challenge." Amabile defines *extrinsic motivation* as arising "from sources outside of the task itself; these sources include expected evaluation, contracted-for-rewards, external directives, or any of several similar sources." The intrinsically motivated person will find pleasure in the task itself, and will, on his or her own, seek creative ways to approach it. The extrinsically motivated person might work hard, but is unlikely to seek creative solutions. This does not mean that all incentives extrinsic to the task necessarily inhibit creativity. Amabile proposes that "informational" or "synergistic" extrinsic motivators, those such as recognition and bonuses that confirm competence, will enhance creativity. Or an extrinsic reward, such as more sophisticated equipment for a scientist or special travel opportunities, that helps people do more exciting work on later projects can be a powerful enabler of intrinsic motivation and creativity. But those extrinsic motivators such as surveillance, unrealistic goals, and an emphasis on criticism and compensation will undermine creativity. Workers will simply do what they need to do to meet the external expectations.[41]

---

one of the subordinates who was responsible for those achievements, misses an inexpensive, obvious opportunity to motivate more creativity.

And then there are special awards. We never outgrow the fun of winning. At Electronic Arts, half of the quarterly awards are given to groups. One of the company values is integrity, and a quarterly award is given to those who have "changed the course of the company to doing something based on high integrity at high personal cost. They're taking a risk . . . like an employee in the middle of the organization . . . going over their boss and saying, 'I think we're about to do something that just isn't right.'"[42] The Integrity trophy is a cookie jar with one plastic cookie inside (symbolic of not taking the last cookie!), and the winners are expected to keep the jar filled all quarter with real cookies for everyone's consumption.[43] Motorola has a Total Customer Service team competition. In 1994, the gold medal was won by a team of lawyers and engineers that succeeded in trimming fifteen pages of invention disclosure forms to two—a process that saved Motorola the equivalent of forty-four years of engineering time in one year. A field of 4,300 teams from eleven countries competed.

Not all leaders believe formal awards are necessary—or even desirable. Notes Richard Teerlink, former CEO of Harley-Davidson,

> We don't have a suggestion system, but we encourage people always to look at what is the right thing to do rather than just how to do the thing right. . . . We are involved in a continuous improvement environment. . . . so how do we put in front of people the opportunity to challenge routines? We don't want to make a big deal out of it, because if you do a lot of awarding, there are losers. We want everybody just to say "this is part of the culture, part of my job, it's fun, it adds excitement to my job because I can be the instigator of change."[44]

So which is it, awards or no awards? Well, it depends a lot on the purpose of those awards and how they are viewed by their recipients. If they are seen as confirming competence and creating a climate of excellence, they may contribute to creativity. If, however, they are viewed as a necessary token of recognition or promotion ("Anyone hoping to make senior manager had better win at least one quarterly award!"), then they will be controlling and undermining of intrinsic motivation. Underlying both extrinsic and intrinsic reward are the organizational goals—not only what they are but how they are set.

Goal Setting

Suppose you allow a group to set its own objectives. What is your guess about how aggressive those goals will be? If you thought "quite aggressive," you are right. People tend to select objectives that are difficult but attainable—"aspirational" or "stretch" goals. If peoples' goals are too low, of course, leaders can push the group to achieve more. When either a group leader or an outside observer indicates to group members that they are capable of doing better, the group tends to set higher goals for itself.[45] One source of passion comes from the adrenaline rush people experience as they pursue stretch goals—and attain them.

However, if managers arbitrarily ratchet up the bar after people have already set goals as high as they believe reasonable, disillusionment sets in and group members may decide to game the system. When the merger of Ciba and Sandoz created Novartis, the world's second largest pharmaceutical company, country managers were challenged to give their "best shot"—that is, the most ambitious possible objectives. "After they did, they were basically told that they were expected to do X% more. They were furious."[46] "Impossible goals demotivate," says Randy Komisar, one of several highly experienced Silicon Valley entrepreneurs who has gone into the business of mentoring the CEOs of innovative start-up businesses.

> If the sales goals are unachievable, everyone is miserable. If after the salespeople don't reach them, you reward them anyway—that is demotivating, because they have no sense of accomplishment. They need to feel successful, to reach the goals so that they feel good about it. It is important to the momentum of the business that they have continued, sustained success, goal after goal—not episodic.[47]

NEED FOR ACHIEVEMENT AND GOAL SETTING

People vary in the extent to which they are driven to succeed (achievement), to be in charge (power), and to have close relationships with others (affiliation). Psychologists have long been interested in these variations among people and have developed standardized ways of determining how strongly the motives for achievement, power, and affiliation direct people's behavior. In particular, those high in the need for achievement (who, one might reasonably assume, would predominate in many managerial positions) tend to prefer moderate levels of risk. If they are given low goals, success would feel meaningless and failure catastrophic; if goals are set very high, then success would be unlikely. A moderately high level of risk, on the other hand, would present the achievement-motivated person with a challenge that has a good chance of success and a feeling of accomplishment. Those high in this "entrepreneurial" orientation also strongly desire feedback so they can adjust their goals accordingly.[48]

Optimism

Remember Eeyore, the gloomy donkey in the Winnie the Pooh stories, who always saw only the negative side of affairs? There was no silver lining to the clouds over his head, no possible good outcome from any venture. "I shouldn't be surprised if it hailed a good deal tomorrow," Eeyore observed. "Blizzards and what-not. Being fine today doesn't Mean Anything."[49] Eeyore would not have been a good member, much less leader, of a creative group. He was a small black hole, sucking in the energy of those around him as he plodded toward (and created) a bleak future.

Passion and enthusiasm thrive in an atmosphere of optimism and confidence in the future. Ann Winblad, partner in Winblad Hummer, a venture capital firm specializing in start-up software companies, says that leaders need to look for ways that a company can succeed, not just ways that a company can fail. Leaders can inspire their groups to look at the glass as half full instead of half empty—and that optimism can be critical when the group encounters the inevitable problems of innovation.[50] Randy Komisar, the "virtual CEO" in Silicon Valley who nurses many start-ups through their initial days, makes a similar point about management teams who are optimistic and confident:

> I find that teams motivated principally by the pot of gold find it too elusive when the going gets tough and sheer tenacity is required. There's nothing better in my mind than watching a team's reaction to being rejected by a VC [venture capital] firm. If they turn their tails and run for the hills, then I know it's not a good fit. If, instead, they say "that VC is going to rue the day it turned us down"—that's a team I want to help."[51]

Guido Arnout, the CEO of CoWare, finds some differences across culture in this respect. In the heady gold rush environment of Silicon Valley, he finds that people concentrate on the *cheese* in Swiss cheese. Some of his European colleagues, he says, ignore the cheese and focus on the holes, which they find threatening. But, "holes," he observes, "are opportunities."[52]

Encouraging Serendipity

In fact, many an innovation began as an opportunity seen in one of those holes—in a possibility no one else saw. In the "Three Princes of Serendip," the fairy tale from which Horace Walpole coined the term *serendipity*, their Highnesses "were always making discoveries, through accidents & sagacity, of things which they were not in quest of."[53] One enormous (thousand incident) catalog of serendipitous events is divided into three types: (1) positive—a surprising discovery correctly understood, (2) negative—a surprising discovery not capitalized upon by the discoverer, and (3) pseudo-serendipity—finding what you were looking for, but in a surprising way.[54] Here, we are interested in only the first and third types.

Often the first step in the creative process, the identification of an opportunity, appears by chance, as a problem or at least a puzzle. You may think that aiding such serendipitous events is a logical impossibility. Not really. Isn't it intriguing that some people and some companies are consistently "lucky"? Is it in their stars? Or do they have a knack for preparing for serendipity, recognizing the unusual moment when it occurs, and encouraging it? Many innovations have probably been lost because someone was in too much of a hurry or too browbeaten to be curious. What if Alexander Fleming had just cursed and tossed out his bacteria culture that had been contaminated with mold? No penicillin. Just as physical space can be designed to enhance the probability of random meetings between people, the psychological environment can be created to encourage the chance collision of ideas and the redirection of "failures." If managers train their employees to narrow their vision to the usual, the routine, the approved way of doing things, who in their organizations will ever follow an intriguing puzzle, an unexpected outcome? History is full of scientific discoveries that occurred serendipitously—often because an experiment "went wrong." Alexander Fleming has written, "One sometimes finds what one is not looking for."[55]

For instance, a Du Pont scientist working on Freon accidentally polymerized several gases into a white powder that became Teflon. Or how about the vial that college student Ralph Wily, hired by Dow Chemical to scrub glassware, couldn't get clean? The substance was eventually made into a greasy, dark green film. First used by military on fighter planes to guard against corrosive sea spray, it was also used for upholstery in cars. After Dow rid the film of its green color and unpleasant odor, the company marketed it as Saran Wrap.

Moreover, many creative discoveries involved the fortuitous juxtaposition of events, observations, or contacts with individuals other than the original scientist. In 1929, a B.F. Goodrich organic chemist, Waldo Semon, was trying to bind rubber to metal when he stumbled on a polymer called polyvinyl chloride (PVC). It was a lousy adhesive, but when Semon molded it into a ball, it bounced down the hall-way—unusual behavior for a synthetic rubber. "I knew I had something different," says Semon. But he didn't know what to do with it until he happened to see his wife sewing a shower curtain from rubber-lined cotton. Realizing that PVC would make perfect water-proof coating, he took a sample of PVC-coated fabric into his boss's office, placed it on top of the in/out basket, and dumped a decanter of water over it. "It scared him stiff," recalls Semon, but the papers stayed dry. The vinyl thus created could be molded, was inexpensive, and had the added benefit of being fire resistant.[56]

Having time to follow their own projects (mentioned earlier as motivating) not only kept these scientists interested and committed to their organizations, but enabled them to capitalize on serendipitous discoveries. None of these inventions would have made it to the market unless the environment encouraged curiosity, persistent investigation, and the shared perception that failure in one realm may translate into success in another. Moreover, each invention did take more than one person's initial "aha" to become profitable. These organizations provided the resources for groups to explore and follow through.

Sometimes serendipity involves having others point out what's under your nose, as a new product development team at Halliburton Energy Services found. In the world of oil drilling equipment, vendors identify their drill bits by a distinctive color. Schlumberger products are blue, Smith International's are green and Halliburton Energy Services drill bits traditionally are fire engine red. In January of 1999, Halliburton launched a new product line. Wanting to signal to the world that their product was distinctive and improved, the thirty-person team in charge decided to break with tradition and select a new color. They circulated to the entire company digital photographs of the first bit off the production line and in addition posted two alternative color schemes (red-gray and bronze-silver) for everyone to evaluate. To the surprise of the team, their colleagues favored the natural steel color of the unpainted bit, which had not been intended as an alternative, and credited the team with changing the paradigm of the industry! Also serendipitously, because clear paint highlighted rather than obscured the craftsmanship of the bit, the morale of employees in the manufacturing plant soared as they saw their work displayed. A 60 percent increase in performance in the field demonstrated that the pride was well placed.[57]

Lady Luck also has a home in Hollywood. In companies in the explicit business of creativity, such as film production houses, serendipity is recognized as an important and continuous source of inspiration. A spontaneous contribution from any quarter may end up as part of the final product. Alan Horn, chairman and CEO of Castle Rock Entertainment, tells the story of how a famous line originated in the movie *When Harry Met Sally*. In the middle of lunch at a diner, Sally (Meg Ryan) astonishes and embarrasses Harry (Billy Crystal) with a very convincing demonstration of how a woman can fake an orgasm. After the performance, a matronly figure sitting nearby gives her luncheon order to the waiter: "I'll have what she's having!" Not in the script, the line was ad-libbed by Crystal while the film crew was shooting cut-aways in the scene. It drew such a huge laugh that it was incorporated into the film. The screenplay, notes Horn, is "an open process that takes as long as it takes" and undergoes changes right up to the last minute. It is part of the creative process to remain alert to the possibilities of serendipitous contributions from anyone with a good idea.[58]

Serendipity sometimes involves recognizing and leveraging existing knowledge at a crucial time; to the purist, this may be *pseudo-serendipity*—finding what you sought, but in unexpected ways (e.g., under your nose). Whatever we call it, it can provide benefits straight to the bottom line. Data General Corporation experienced a decade of losses totaling more than half a billion dollars and a close brush with bankruptcy when personal computers triumphed over mini-computers in the late 1980s. The development project that eventually produced one of the two product lines that brought the company back to profitability had been killed by CEO Ronald Skates; however, the product development team had already produced a cutting-edge fault-tolerant storage system. Only when a financial analyst at a product announcement meeting in New York in 1991 noticed the system and commented to Mr. Skates that "this is a phenomenal product," did the CEO realize what he had. "Data General had the right product at the right time to catch an opportunity," commented a marketing manager for Hewlett-Packard's Enterprise Storage Solutions Business, which became an OEM partner.[59]

When Lars Kolind took over the Danish hearing aid company Oticon, he faced a situation not unlike Data General's. By 1990, the company was in crisis, losing market share and with little apparent advantage over competitors. However, Kolind identified a potential product in the pipeline—one that had lain dormant since 1979! Although it was a large "behind-the-ear" model (as opposed to a small one in the ear), it compressed sounds to a very narrow comfortable band. Users found it unnecessary to use the volume control. Recognizing the competitive advantage that this, the "world's first fully automatic hearing aid" offered, Kolind took it to market with great fanfare and reestablished the company as a technology leader. Certainly it was "lucky" that the technology existed within the company. But it took leadership, optimism, and drive to identify the opportunity and capitalize on it.

Paradoxes

The Western mind is accustomed to asking: "So, which is it?" We don't like the answer "both." "Either/or" is often a lot cleaner and easier to manage than "it depends." Creativity involves inherent paradoxes. Managing creativity requires a tolerance for ambiguity and a love of the unexpected. Managers are not trained for this. From earliest education, we are encouraged to resolve contradictions and make decisions in manly, authoritative fashion. Moreover, the myths with which we opened the book have grown up for good reason, often in the perhaps unconscious effort to avoid some of the messiness of managing creativity in groups. Innovation would be easier if, as those myths suggest, we could delegate creativity to a few flamboyant individuals who would work in isolation and if we didn't need to worry about creativity at all except for a few really big projects—and then only at their very early stages.

We hope it is now clear that creativity is a multistage, complex process that we must visualize as a whole. We must keep eventual convergence and implementation in mind even as we are creating options. The process is made even more complex by differences in thinking styles, cultures, and backgrounds of group members, and by group dynamics. We are constantly balancing individual against group needs and group needs against organizational. Most important, though, we recognize that creativity is inherently paradoxical. Throughout this book, we have hinted at these paradoxes. Let's take a closer look at some of the most vexing—and exciting—ones:

* expertise and beginner's mind

* encouraging creative abrasion and maintaining cohesiveness

* freedom and structure

* professionalism and play

Expertise and Beginner's Mind

Creativity draws on both the highly prepared mind and on the fresh perspective of newcomers.[60] In Chapter 2, we emphasized the need for a variety of deep knowledge bases from which to generate creative abrasion. Even in a group of experts, each member will be a beginner when treading on another expert's turf. In Chapter 3, we suggested the importance of visits *from* "aliens"—individuals who would ask "dumb" (i.e., unexpected) questions—and visits *to* alien environments, so that developers could cultivate their own beginner's mind. Expertise and beginner's mind challenge the manager, who must encourage both of them and tolerate hearing the often contradictory messages they give.

Recall the "Dove Team" discussed earlier in this chapter. The Ogilvy & Mather advertising team—two women without chemical expertise—exemplified the value of two such approaches when they were employed to advertise Lever's Dove soap. They teamed up with technical people and started down a path that would result in the rarest of advertisements—one that directly, visibly, and dramatically increased sales and blew the competition out of the bathtub. Moved by their personal experience of testing Dove's pH and conducting the armwash test, they pursued other technical details that would convey to the public their own conviction that Dove was, by objective criteria, superior to competitive products. The pair kept asking the technical people with their "beginner's mind," "are we getting this right?" "We wanted to be truthful, without scaring or boring people. We needed to show people some simple science that was incredibly relevant."[61]

Encouraging Creative Abrasion and Maintaining Cohesiveness

This paradox is probably the hardest challenge facing all leaders of creative groups. As we discussed in Chapter 2, certain kinds of individual differences are essential for generating the variability that is the raw material for innovation. But differences can lead to stereotyping, to disliking and disaffection within the group, which can dampen the willingness to work creatively together. Moreover, even when it is achieved, cohesiveness has several undesirable side effects, most notably loss of members who don't cohere, and elitism among those who do.

Teamwork and Cohesiveness In our much-splintered world, because we like people like us, we tend to avoid or dislike people with dissimilar backgrounds, beliefs, and values. A group of similar people will be more likely to develop interpersonal bonds that will promote group cohesiveness; dissimilar people will be less attracted to the other members and to the group—even when the difference is simply tenure in the organization. The result? Those individuals who feel most "different" from the other group members are more likely to leave. So you not only have to work hard to select and recruit people who are different from you and other team members, but you also have to work at retaining them.

Group Cohesiveness and Elitism Another problem is that the more cohesive the group, the more likely members are to feel and act like organizational elite. The sense of belonging to a special group engenders pride and ownership and all those good things. It also makes snobs (esprit de corps; us versus the rest of them). Group members expect to be allowed to break rules (that's part of being creative, after all) and to be rewarded more lavishly (not just money, but in terms of opportunity or freedom) than groups working on routine projects. They likely expect, and receive, more top management attention. They enjoy the excitement, the camaraderie, et cetera. Your "mission impossible" is to keep these elite folks happy without alienating everyone else in the organization. A starting point is to be sure that the group members realize how their status may affect others in the organization.

Moreover, after a special project is over, these elite folks may have to go "back to the ranch"—return to more routine assignments. Cross-functional teams constantly face this issue. The trick is to configure the assignments back in the functional groups to allow individuals to renew their knowledge base. Therefore, managers have to consider rotation, rewarding people to renew their expertise as well as to serve on teams. These goals are not incompatible. Since people are intrinsically motivated, what better way to accomplish both objectives than to allow people time to work on a special project, spend a sabbatical with experts in their field, or in some other way refresh their knowledge base?

Freedom and Structure

Creativity that will result in useful innovation thrives in a partially controlled ecology—like wild animals in large nature reserves. There is ample freedom for ideas to roam, to flourish and interact uninhibitedly, but there are also boundaries and fences. The balance is a delicate one. Allow too much freedom, and the ideas are novel but without relevance. Tighten the boundaries too much and there is no inspiration. The larger the organization grows, the more visible becomes this paradox. "How to maintain our guerrilla flavor when we've become the great corporate moneymaker is a real challenge," says Jeff Dunn, chief operating officer of Nickelodeon.[62] As suggested in prior chapters, it is up to the leader to determine the appropriate boundaries. "Do you know what I really like about your management," one team member asked the group leader. "No, but I can see you are going to tell me," the leader smiled. "You helped us clarify exactly what needed to be done," the team member said, "and then you got out of the way."

That wasn't really the way the manager remembered it. "Out of the way" suggested a mental if not actual vacation from the project. He had spent long hours talking both individually and collectively with group members on the project. He had presided over exhaustingly argumentative group meetings, negotiated compromises, assuaged hurt pride, and reminded team members about the value of their differences. He had provided resources and support, protected them from upper management, and checked on progress unobtrusively. But he knew what the team member meant. He had pushed structure when the decisions involved *what* to do, and he had pushed freedom when the decisions involved *how* the tasks were to be accomplished.

A related tension is between planning and improvisation. Miles Davis could have made a living with a microphone instead of a trumpet today, had he devoted his famous lung power on the management speech circuit to explaining jazz improvisation. Jazz artists understand that a key element in successful group improvisation is flexible communication with one another within a minimal set of specific rules—and jazz is increasingly recognized as a good metaphor for creativity in business. Jazz musicians all play the same basic piece of music, but not by the book, slavishly following the sheet music. Rather, they react to each other, introduce new themes, take off in complementary directions and then return to weave their contribution into the group performance and set the stage for the next excursion by a colleague. As John Kao has observed, "The (creative) role of the manager is to work the central paradox, or tension, of the jam session: to locate the ever-mobile sweet spot somewhere between systems and analysis on the one hand and the free-flowing creativity of the individual on the other."[63] In Brown and Eisenhardt's study of computer firms, the most successful "relied on structures that were neither too extensive . . . nor chaotic."[64] An improvisation metaphor is useful, "in which projects are adapted to changing circumstances even as they are being developed."[65]

Even war requires a balance between planning and improvisation. During the 1990 Persian Gulf War, commanding General Schwarzkopf continually confounded his underlings by tearing up computer projections and rearranging tactics. He was able to do so in no small part because he was given his mission by U.S. President Bush and Joint Chief of Staff Head Colin Powell, and then left relatively free to carry it out. "That's the corporate equivalent of the board of directors vesting a lot of authority in their operational theatre manager," says David Francis, executive recruiter and West Point grad.[66]

Professionalism and Play

As Chapters 3 and 5 suggested, creative groups usually indulge in a lot of playground behavior. Joanne Carthey, founder of NctPro, a utility software producer in Phoenix, has four rules: "We make promises, we keep our word, we clean up our messes, and we *have*

INNOVATION, COMMUNITY, AND AUTONOMY

William Judge, Gerald Fryxell, and Robert Dooley conducted extensive interviews at eight U.S. biotechnology firms. Innovation
was assessed through an analysis of the "cycle times" of the
companies' patents—the shorter the cycle time, the faster the
new technology is being brought to market. On the basis of this
analysis, the eight companies were divided into high and low
innovation groups. There were striking differences between the
cultures of the two groups. The "ability of management to
create a sense of community in the workplace was the key differ-
entiating factor. Highly innovative units behaved as focused commu-
nities, while less innovative units behaved more like traditional
bureaucratic departments."[67] Specifically, in the innovative companies, leaders provided overarching goals, but allowed the scientists autonomy in reaching them. In the less innovative firms,
there was either too much or too little
autonomy.

---

fun" (italics added).[68] Sometimes top management leads the way.
Herb Kelleher, CEO of Southwest Airlines, does impersonations of
Elvis Presley and Roy Orbison at company parties. On Halloween,
he came to Southwest's hangar in a dress, impersonating Corporal
Klinger (from the popular television show M*A*S*H), to thank
mechanics for working overtime.[69]

Of course, merely engaging in practical jokes doesn't ensure that
employees will think coming to work is fun. One company we know
of was led by a CEO who took entertainment to great lengths. The
annual company parties were elaborate affairs, with expensive and
prominent entertainers, practical jokes played on the audience (such
as having an extremely boring speaker, ostensibly a well-known
professor from a local, prestigious university, drone on until he
was noisily booted off the stage by upper management). When the

company was small, the spirit of fun was genuine; the CEO's personal informality and habit of managing by walking around reinforced a sense of egalitarianism and a "family" ethos. However, when the company grew rapidly, a layer of management brought in from the outside did not share the original culture. A number of these people were perceived by employees as police rather than coaches. The employees began to view with cynicism the increasingly expensive entertainment and gags intended to extend the spirit of a start-up. "Who cares if the annual party is a blast, when your daily work is miserable because of inexperienced, insecure, even stupid supervisors?" asked one employee. The CEO had not changed his norms, but he was so insulated from the rest of the organization that he did not realize that playfulness had become a thin frosting on a cake of mud.

However, when playfulness pervades the entire group, the *members* sometimes take the lead. Just ask Jerry Hirshberg about how painful *that* can be! At Nissan Design International, employees set up elaborate mechanisms to simulate a major earthquake at their site in tremor-prone San Diego. Then they lured their unsuspecting leader into the building to experience the "quake"—huge corrugated metal warehouse doors that rattled and violently shook, ceiling-mounted heating and air-conditioning pipes that decoupled and spewed out steam, twenty-foot steel tubes that tumbled to the floor. They even videotaped the whole episode and have never allowed Hirshberg to forget that his reaction was less heroic than he himself had expected. But he has the good grace to tell the story on himself, in no small part because it exemplifies the playfulness he believes is important to creativity.[70]

Members of creative groups find little contradiction in introducing an element of play into their serious commitment to their work. They are extremely professional, but they balance their hard work with hard play. As we suggested above, working in an organization that admits, even appreciates, that your life consists of more than the hours at work, attracts the whole person—including the creativity expressed in play. As always, it is the leader's job to set the tone and decide the balance between the paradoxical dynamics.

To return to Ted...

Clearly, he must have read a draft of this book, because he did everything we suggest! (Okay, so maybe he learned some of it on his own.) May we all do so well.

Key Points

* Just as physical environments can be managed to promote creativity, so can the psychological climate.

* Failing forward implies intelligent failures and group learning. The organization can expect to benefit from failure when the effort results from known risks, is supported by management, and has contingency plans in place.

* Creativity flourishes in a climate of open communication. Effective managers of creativity should welcome dissent and good and bad news; respond to the needs of members; scan the larger environment for ideas; and develop ways to communicate honestly and openly.

* Perhaps the most crucial way to tap the creativity of groups is to promote passion among members—passion for the organization, for the job, and for the product. Passion can be promoted in a variety of ways:

  * By setting difficult but attainable goals.

  * By managing extrinsic motivators in such a way that they confirm competence and create a climate of excellence.

  * By granting people autonomy, time for personal projects, and opportunities for further learning.

  * By matching people with the jobs within the organization most likely to kindle their passions.

  * By creating a climate of optimism and confidence in the future.

* Many innovations are the result of recognizing creative opportunities and acting on them. Serendipity can be managed by providing opportunities for chance interactions, then encouraging those interactions when they take place.

* The complexity of the creative process in groups is reflected in a number of paradoxes. Such paradoxes represent opportunities for managers to make creative resolutions:

  * While groups must draw on deep wells of knowledge, they also need pairs of naive eyes to see things from fresh perspectives.

  * Creative abrasion springs from group differences. But heterogeneity can also result in interpersonal conflict and fragmentation. Leaders must promote both creative abrasion and cohesiveness.

  * Groups need freedom and autonomy to function creatively, but the larger organization has specific, structured needs that must be met.

  * Creativity is serious work—but must be balanced by play.

Conclusion

We have said that creativity is a *process*—and that it can be encouraged and influenced. Since we all have more than we can do in the time available, however, it is difficult if not impossible to add new duties and tasks. But we all can manage *differently* what we already do. Dozens of times during the week and on many different fronts, you make decisions that affect the potential creativity of your group. Some of those decisions could be nudged in a slightly different direction to remove barriers to creativity: altering the list of invitees to a given meeting so as to encourage divergence, scheduling some "time-outs" so as to allow incubation, bringing in a facilitator to aid convergence. Other decisions are far more weighty and require serious consideration of all the systemic ramifications: hiring differently, revising incentive systems, questioning one's own leadership style.

Thinking of creativity as a process removes, we hope, some of the mystery—and the temptation to step back from the challenge. You *can* affect the creativity of your group. Practice may not make perfect, but it sure as heck helps. Managers who are continuously improving can identify those stages and steps in the messy, dynamic, and nonlinear process of innovation that they have managed better than the last time they led a group to higher levels of creativity. They aim for an upward spiral, revisiting issues and points in the process at ever-higher levels of understanding and sophistication. Whether they manage a small group or thousands of people, they use every opportunity to prototype and experiment in building a more creative group. While it is unlikely that any manager can follow *all* the suggestions in this book, it is equally unlikely that he or she could not follow *some*.

Creativity, like learning, is not only a process but also an attitude. An attitude that promotes creativity is a kind of alertness to innovation opportunities—a constant mental challenge to routine and an openness to change. Many chances to enhance creativity do not come neatly packaged in a clear decision point but are diffused over time, in tiny acts or omissions of action. Casual comments. Body language. Unexamined assumptions. Feelings—unexpressed or made obvious. So much depends on what we, as managers, honestly *believe* about the creative potential of those around us and of the situation. Managing creativity is all about the values we enact.

Some individuals thrive on the challenge of constant change and improvement; others recoil from the implicit chaos. We suspect that you are one of the former, because you chose to read this book. In truth, we don't believe any of us has much choice about becoming more creative. The problems faced by society are so large that only innovativeness of the highest order will overcome them. But it takes only a small spark to ignite a large fire. Let the sparks fly!

Notes

Chapter 1: What Is Group Creativity?

1. Quoted in Hal Lancaster, "Getting Yourself in a Frame of Mind to Be Creative," *Wall Street Journal*, 16 September 1997, B1.

2. Warren Bennis and Patricia Biederman. *Organizing Genius: The Secrets of Creative Collaboration* (Reading, Mass.: Addison-Wesley, 1997), 199.

3. Sharon Begley, "The Transistor," *Newsweek* (special issue on "2000: The Power of Invention") (winter 1997): 25–26.

4. Frank Barron, *Creativity and Psychological Health: Origins of Personality and Creative Freedom* (Princeton, N.J.: Van Nostrand, 1963).

5. Walter Swap, ed., *Group Decision Making* (Beverly Hills, Calif.: Sage, 1984), 16–17.

6. M. I. Stein, "Creativity and Culture," *Journal of Psychology* 36 (1953): 311–322.

7. Teresa M. Amabile, *Creativity in Context* (Boulder, Colo.: Westview, 1996), 35.

8. Alan G. Robinson and Sam Stern, *Corporate Creativity* (San Francisco: Berrett-Koehler, 1997), 11.

9. Robert Rothenberg, *Creativity and Madness* (Baltimore: Johns Hopkins Press, 1990), 5.

10. Donald W. MacKinnon, "IPAR's Contribution to the Conceptualization and Study of Creativity," in *Perspectives in Creativity*, ed. Irving A. Taylor and J. W. Getzels (Chicago: Aldine, 1975), 68.

11. Henry Petroski, "Form Follows Failure," *Invention & Technology* (Fall

1992): 54–61, passim. See also Petroski's 1992 book, *The Evolution of Useful Things* (New York: Alfred A. Knopf).

12. John Seely Brown, "Introduction: Rethinking Innovation in a Changing World," in *Seeing Differently: Insights on Innovation*, ed. John Seely Brown (Boston: Harvard Business School Press, 1997), xii.

13. Mihaly Csikszentmihalyi and Keith Sawyer, "Creative Insight: The Social Dimension of a Solitary Moment," in *The Nature of Insight*, ed. Robert Sternberg and Janet Davidson (Cambridge, Mass.: MIT Press, 1995), 348.

14. See Steven C. Wheelwright and Kim B. Clark. *Revolutionizing Product Development: Quantum Leaps in Speed, Efficiency, and Quality* (New York: Free Press, 1992).

15. See Dorothy Leonard-Barton, *Wellsprings of Knowledge* (Boston: Harvard Business School Press, 1995), especially Chapter 4, pp. 104 ff.

Chapter 2: Creative Abrasion

1. Jerry Hirshberg, *The Creative Priority: Driving Innovative Business in the Real World* (New York: Harper Business, 1998).

2. Kathleen M. Eisenhardt, Jean L. Kahwajy, and L. J. Bourgeois III, "How Management Teams Can Have a Good Fight," *Harvard Business Review* 75 (July–August 1997): 84.

3. See also Kathleen M. Eisenhardt, Jean L. Kahwajy, and L. J. Bourgeois III, "Conflict and Strategic Choice: How Top Management Teams Disagree," *California Management Review* 39 (Winter 1997): 42–62.

4. R. J. Berg, interview, 20 May 1998.

5. Joseph Haggin, "Illinois' Beckman Institute Targets Disciplinary Barriers to Collaboration," *Chemical & Engineering News* (6 March 1995): 32–39.

6. Quoted in Sharon Begley, with B. J. Sigesmund, "The Houses of Invention," *Newsweek* (special issue on "2000: The Power of Invention") (winter 1997): 26.

7. David Liddle, interview quoted in Dorothy Leonard, *Wellsprings of Knowledge* (1995), 81.

8. Marilyn Wilson-Hadid and Peter Pook, interview, 2 June 1998.

9. M. E. Shaw, *Group Dynamics: The Psychology of Small Group Behavior* (New York: McGraw-Hill, 1976).

10. Susan E. Jackson, "Team Composition in Organizational Settings: Issues in Managing an Increasingly Diverse Work Force," in *Group Process and Productivity*, ed. Stephen Worchel, Wendy Wood, and Jeffry Simpson (Beverly Hills, Calif.: Sage, 1992).

11. Jackson, "Team Composition in Organizational Settings," 150.
12. Russell Herndon, Senior Vice President of Genzyme Corporation, interview, 18 January 1998.
13. Donn Byrne, *The Attraction Paradigm* (New York: Academic Press, 1971).
14. Wendy Wood, "Meta-analytic Review of Sex Differences in Group Performance," *Psychological Bulletin* 102, no. 1 (1987): 53–71.
15. Katherine Y. Williams and Charles A. O'Reilly III, "Demography and Diversity in Organizations: A Review of 40 Years of Research," *Research in Organizational Behavior* 20 (1998): 77–140.
16. J. F. O. McAllister, "Civil Science Policy in British Industrial Reconstruction, 1942–51" (Ph.D. diss., Oxford University, 1986), 27.
17. G. Hofstede, *Culture's Consequences: International Differences in Work-Related Values* (Newbury Park, Calif.: Sage, 1980).
18. Fons Trompenaars and Charles Hampden-Turner, *Riding the Waves of Culture*, 2d. ed. (New York: McGraw-Hill, 1998).
19. Mihaly Csikszentmihalyi, *Creativity* (New York: Harper Collins, 1966), 8–9.
20. Jerry Hirshberg, *The Creative Priority: Driving Innovative Business in the Real World* (New York: HarperBusiness, 1998).
21. Guido Arnout, interview, 18 June 1998.
22. Quoted in Malcom Gladwell, "Annals of Style: The Coolhunt," *The New Yorker*, 17 March 1997, 78.
23. Kevin Curran, interview, 2 June 1998.
24. For an article describing the application of two thinking-style diagnostics to the issue of composing creative groups, see Dorothy Leonard and Susaan Straus, "Putting Your Company's Whole Brain to Work," *Harvard Business Review* 75 (July–August 1997): 110–121.
25. Jerry Hirshberg, quoted in Leonard-Barton, *Wellsprings of Knowledge*, 79.
26. Jerry Hirshberg, interview, 25 February 1994.
27. Jerry Hirshberg, interview, 10 December 1993.
28. See Hirshberg, *The Creative Priority*.
29. Lisa Mancuso, interview, 2 June 1998.
30. Robert Sternberg, *Successful Intelligence* (New York, Simon & Schuster, 1996), 191–192.
31. Paul Horn, "Creativity and the Bottom Line," *Financial Times*, 17 November 1997, 12.
32. Reported in Williams and O'Reilly, "Demography and Diversity in Organizations," 77–140.
33. Carol Snyder, interview, 2 June 1998.
34. Rosabeth Moss Kanter has called the organizational bias that results from

selecting people in our own images "homosocial reproduction." See Rosabeth Moss Kanter, *Men and Women of the Corporation* (New York: Basic Books, 1993).

35. Anne Fisher, "Key to Success: People, People, People," *Fortune,* 27 October 1997, "The World's Most Admired Companies" section, 232.

36. Kenneth Labich, "Is Herb Kelleher America's Best CEO?" *Fortune,* 2 May 1994, 50.

37. Kevin Curran, interview, 2 June 1998.

38. Marco Thompson, interview, 11 August 1998.

39. Advertisement in *Fortune,* 16 February 1998, 118.

40. Solomon E. Asch, "Opinions and Social Pressure," *Scientific American* 193 (1955): 31–35.

41. Stuart Valins and Richard Nisbett. "Attribution Processes in the Development and Treatment of Emotional Disorders," in *Attribution: Perceiving the Causes of Behavior,* ed. Edward E. Jones, David Kanouse, Harold Kelley, Richard Nisbett, Stuart Valins, and Bernard Weiner (Morristown, N.J.: General Learning Press, 1971), 139.

Chapter 3: Generating Creative Options

1. Gregory Moorhead, Richard Ference, and Chris Neck, "Group Decision Fiascoes Continue," *Human Relations* 44, no. 6 (1991): 539–549.

2. David Halberstam, *The Reckoning* (New York: William Morrow & Co., 1986), 610.

3. Matie L. Flowers, "A Laboratory Test of Some Implications of Janis's Groupthink Hypothesis," *Journal of Personality and Social Psychology* 35 (1997): 888–896.

4. Donald Pelz and Frank Andrews, *Scientists in Organizations* (New York: John Wiley, 1966).

5. Daniel Gigone and Reid Hastie, "The Common Knowledge Effect: Information Sharing and Group Judgment," *Journal of Personality and Social Psychology* 65, no. 5 (1993): 959–974.

6. Donn Byrne, *The Attraction Paradigm* (New York: Academic Press, 1971).

7. Susan Saegert, Walter Swap, and Robert B. Zajonc, "Exposure, Context, and Interpersonal Attraction," *Journal of Personality and Social Psychology* 25, no. 2 (1973): 234–242.

8. Irving Janis, *Groupthink,* 2d. ed. (Boston: Houghton Mifflin, 1982).

9. Janis, *Groupthink,* 9.

10. Janis, *Groupthink,* 14.

11. Arthur Schlesinger, quoted in Janis, *Groupthink,* 39.

12. Oscar Wilde, *The Remarkable Rocket* (1888; reprint, Charlottesville, Va.: Graham-Johnston, 1978).

13. Les Vadasz, interview, 7 July 1998.

14. S. Moscovici and E. Lage, "Studies in Social Influence IV: Minority Influence in a Context of Original Judgments," *European Journal of Social Psychology* 8, no. 3 (1976): 349–365.

15. Charlan Nemeth and Pamela Owens, "Making Work Groups More Effective: The Value of Minority Dissent," in *Handbook of Work Group Psychology,* ed. M. A. West (New York: John Wiley, 1996).

16. Charlan Jeanne Nemeth and Joel Wachtler, "Creative Problem Solving as a Result of Majority vs. Minority Influence," *European Journal of Social Psychology* 13, no. 1 (1983): 45–55.

17. Susan Schilling, interview, 12 December 1997.

18. Hal Lancaster, "Learning Some Ways to Make Meetings Slightly Less Awful," *Wall Street Journal,* 26 May 1998, B1.

19. J. Hall and W. Watson, "The Effects of a Normative Intervention on Group Decision-Making Performance," *Human Relations* 23, no. 4 (1970): 304.

20. Hall and Watson, "The Effects of a Normative Intervention," 312.

21. P. C. Wason, "On the Failure to Eliminate Hypotheses in a Conceptual Task," *Quarterly Journal of Experimental Psychology* 12, no. 3 (1960): 129–140.

22. See, for example, Eugene Borgida and Richard Nisbett, "The Differential Impact of Abstract vs. Concrete Information on Decisions," *Journal of Applied Social Psychology* 7, no. 3 (1977): 258–271.

23. Brian Mullen, Craig Johnson, and Eduardo Salas, "Productivity Loss in Brainstorming Groups: A Meta-analytic Integration," *Basic and Applied Social Psychology* 12, no. 1 (1991): 3–23.

24. Joseph Valacich, Alan Dennis, and Terry Connolly, "Idea Generation in Computer-Based Groups: A New Ending to an Old Story," *Organizational Behavior and Human Decision Processes* 57, no. 3 (1994): 448-467.

25. W. M. Williams, and R. J. Sternberg, "Group Intelligence: Why Some Groups Are Better Than Others," *Intelligence* 12, no. 4 (1988): 351–377.

26. Marc Gunther, "This Gang Controls Your Kids' Brains," *Fortune,* 27 October 1997, 172–182, passim.

27. Interval Research video.

28. Interviews at IDEO in Palo Alto, California, 21 April 1998.

29. Gene Bylinsky, "Mutant Materials," *Fortune,* 13 October 1997, 144.

30. Stephanie Forrest, quoted in Gautam Naik, "Back to Darwin: In Sunlight and Cells, Science Seeks Answers to High-Tech Puzzles," *Wall Street Journal,* 16 January 1996, A1.

31. John Hiles, president of Thinking Tools, Inc., quoted in Naik, "Back to Darwin."

32. Paul Kantor, quoted in *EXEC* (summer 1998), 4.

33. Deborah Ancona and David Caldwell, "Bridging the Boundary: External Activity and Performance in Organizational Teams," *Administrative Science Quarterly* 37, no. 4 (1992): 634–665.

34. Paul Horn, "Creativity and the Bottom Line," *Financial Times*, 17 November 1997, 12.

35. Hal Lancaster, "Getting Yourself in a Frame of Mind to Be Creative," *Wall Street Journal*, 16 September 1997, B1.

36. Quoted in Shona L. Brown and Kathleen M. Eisenhardt, "The Art of Continuous Change: Linking Complexity Theory and Time-Paced Evolution in Relentlessly Shifting Organizations," *Administrative Science Quarterly* 42, no. 1 (1997): 9.

37. William Taylor "The Business of Innovation: An Interview with Paul Cook," *Harvard Business Review* 68, (March–April 1990): 102.

38. Richard Nisbett and Timothy Wilson, "Telling More than We Can Know: Verbal Reports on Mental Processes," *Psychological Review* 84, no. 4 (1977): 231-259.

39. See Dorothy Leonard-Barton, *Wellsprings of Knowledge* (Boston, Harvard Business School Press, 1995). See also Dorothy Leonard and Jeffrey Rayport, "Sparking Innovation through Empathic Design," *Harvard Business Review* 75 (November–December 1997): 103–113.

40. Eugene Webb, Donald Campbell, Richard Schwartz, and Lee Sechrest, *Unobtrusive Measures: Non-Reactive Research in the Social Sciences* (Chicago: Rand-McNally, 1972).

41. Personal communication with Curt Bailey, president of Sundberg-Ferar, Walled Lake, Michigan, 26 August 1998.

42. See Gerald Zaltman, "Rethinking Market Research: Putting People Back In," *Journal of Marketing Research* 34 (November 1997): 424–437.

43. Dorothy Leonard and Jeffrey Rayport, "Sparking Innovation through Empathic Design," *Harvard Business Review* 75 (November–December 1997): 103–113.

44. Gunther, "This Gang Controls Your Kids' Brains," 176.

45. Quoted in Malcom Gladwell, "Annals of Style: The Coolhunt," *The New Yorker*, 17 March 1997, 78.

46. Roy Furchgott, "For Cool Hunters, Tomorrow's Trend Is the Trophy," *New York Times*, 28 June 1998, 10.

47. Gladwell, "The Coolhunt," 86.

48. Clayton Christensen and Dorothy Leonard-Barton, "Ceramics Process

Systems Corporation," Case 9-691-028 (Boston: Harvard Business School, 1990).

Chapter 4: Converging on the Best Options

1. Quoted in Mihalyi Csikszentmihalyi, *Creativity: Flow and the Psychology of Discovery and Invention* (New York: Harper Collins, 1996), 99.
2. Sandra Weintraub, "Cultivate Your Dreams to Find New Solutions," *R&D Innovator* 4, no. 10 (1995): 1–3.
3. Weintraub, "Cultivate Your Dreams."
4. Colleen Seifert, David Meyer, Natalie Davidson, Andrea Patalano, and Ilan Yaniv, "Demystification of Cognitive Insight: Opportunistic Assimilation and the Prepared-Mind Perspective," in *The Nature of Insight*, ed. Robert Sternberg and Janet Davidson (Cambridge, Mass.: MIT Press, 1995), 66–124.
5. Randy Komisar, interview, 15 June 1998.
6. Yvonne Daley, "Writer Relies on Memory as Sight Fails," *Boston Sunday Globe*, 28 June 1998, A8.
7. Jerry Hirshberg, *The Creative Priority: Driving Innovative Business in the Real World* (New York: HarperBusiness, 1998), 88–89
8. Hirshberg, *The Creative Priority*, 88.
9. Hirshberg, *The Creative Priority*, 82
10. Sharon Arad, Mary Ann Hanson, and Robert Schneider, "A Framework for the Study of Relationships between Organizational Characteristics and Organizational Innovation," *Journal of Creative Behavior* 31, no. 1 (1997): 42–58.
11. Alan Horn, interview, 27 July 1998.
12. Guido Arnout, interview, 18 June 1998.
13. Rosabeth Moss Kanter, *On the Frontiers of Management* (Boston: Harvard Business School Press, 1997), 275.
14. Marilyn Wilson-Hadid and Peter Pook, interviews, 2 June 1998.
15. Steven E. Prokesch, "Unleashing the Power of Learning: An Interview with British Petroleum's John Browne," *Harvard Business Review* 75 (September–October 1997): 150.
16. J. F. O. McAllister, "Civil Science Policy in British Industrial Reconstruction 1942-51." (Ph.D. thesis, Oxford University, 1986), 27.
17. Thomas Petzinger, Jr., "A Hospital Applies Teamwork to Thwart an Insidious Enemy," *Wall Street Journal*, 8 May 1998, B1.
18. Chana R. Schoenberger, "Mission Statements Are Job 1—For Some," *Boston Globe*, 14 July 1998, D1, D7.

19. Jim Billington, "The Three Essentials of an Effective Team." *Management Update* 2, no. 1 (1997): 4.
20. Steve Perlman, interview, 19 June 1998.
21. Steve Perlman, interview, 19 June 1998.
22. Randy Komisar, interview, 15 June 1998.
23. Dorothy Leonard-Barton, *Wellsprings of Knowledge* (Boston: Harvard Business School Press, 1995), 86–87.
24. Lisa Mancuso, interview, 3 June 1998.
25. Bing Gordon, Chief Creative Officer, interview, 19 May 1998.
26. Bing Gordon, interview, 19 May 1998.
27. See J. Richard Hackman, "Why Teams Don't Work," in *Applications of Theory and Research on Groups to Social Issues,* ed. R. S. Tindale, J. Edwards, and E. J. Posavac (New York: Plenum, 1998).
28. Paul Horn, "Creativity and the Bottom Line," *Financial Times,* 17 November 1997, 12.
29. Hirshberg, *The Creative Priority,* 58.
30. Larry Shubert, Director IDEO and Product Development, interview, 21 April 1998.
31. For more information on core capabilities, see Leonard-Barton, *Wellsprings of Knowledge.* See also Gary Hamel and C. K. Prahalad, *Competing for the Future* (Boston: Harvard Business School Press, 1994).
32. Leonard-Barton, *Wellsprings of Knowledge.*
33. See Marco Iansiti, "Real-world R&D: Jumping the Product Generation Gap," *Harvard Business Review* 71 (May–June 1993): 138–147.
34. Susan Schilling, interview, 12 December 1997.
35. Tom Corddry, interview at Microsoft, 28 February 1994.
36. Susan Schilling, interview, 12 December 1997.
37. Betsy Pace, interview, 5 February 1998.
38. Based on the work of Chris Argyris. See Chris Argyris, *Reasoning, Learning, and Action: Individual and Organizational* (San Francisco: Jossey-Bass, 1982).

Chapter 5: Designing the Physical Environment
1. Fritz Steel, *Making and Managing High-Quality Workplaces: An Organizational Ecology* (New York: Teachers College Press, 1986), 55.
2. Robert Campbell, "End of the 'Magic Incubator,'" *Boston Globe,* 5 June 1998, D1.
3. Campbell, "End of the 'Magic Incubator,'" D1.
4. Thomas J. Allen, *Managing the Flow of Technology* (Cambridge, Mass.: MIT Press, 1977), 235–240.

5. John Kao, "Oticon (A)," Case 9-395-144 (Boston: Harvard Business School), 1995.

6. Meg Carter, "Design: The Office—It's a Place to Relax; Arthur Andersen's Sixth Floor Offers a Glimpse of How Tomorrow's Workspaces Will Be Designed," *The Independent* (London), 26 March 1998.

7. Frank H. Mahnke, *Color, Environment and Human Response: An Interdisciplinary Understanding of Color and Its Use as a Beneficial Element in the Design of the Architectural Environment* (New York: Van Nostrand Reinhold, 1996).

8. Michael A. Veresej, "Welcome to the New Workspace," *Industry Week*, 15 April 1996, 24–27.

9. Quoted in Mihaly Csikszentmihalyi, *Creativity* (New York: Harper Collins, 1966), 66.

10. Described in Franklin Becker, *The Successful Office: How to Create a Workspace That's Right for You* (Reading, Mass.: Addison-Wesley, 1982), 115.

11. Leonard K. Eaton, *Two Chicago Architects and Their Clients* (Cambridge, Mass.: MIT Press, 1969).

12. Jilly Welch, "Creature Comforts: Innovations in Office Design," *People Management*, 19 December 1996, 47

13. Georg von Krogh, and Philipp Käser, "Knowledge Navigation for Future Earnings Capabilities" (unpublished paper), 4.

14. Irving A. Taylor, "Creative Production in Gifted Young (Almost) Adults Through Simultaneous Sensory Stimulation," *Gifted Child Quarterly* 14, no. 1 (1970): 46–55.

15. Welch, "Creature Comforts," 20.

16. Franklin Becker and Fritz Steele, *Workplace by Design* (San Francisco: Jossey-Bass Publishers, 1995).

17. S. Cohen and N. Weinstein, "Nonauditory Effects of Noise on Behavior and Health," *Journal of Social Issues* 37 (1981): 36–70.

18. David Glass and Jerome Singer, "Experimental Studies of Uncontrollable and Unpredictable Noise," *Representative Research in Social Psychology* 4, no. 1 (1973): 165–183.

19. Dorothy A. Leonard, Paul A. Brands, Amy Edmondson, and Justine Fenwick, "Virtual Teams: Using Communications Technology to Manage Geographically Dispersed Development Groups," in *Sense and Respond*, ed. Stephen P. Bradley and Richard L. Nolan (Boston: Harvard Business School Press, 1998), 285–298.

20. Quoted in Gregory Witcher, "Steelcase Hopes Innovation Flourishes Under Pyramid," *Wall Street Journal*, 26 May 1989, B1.

21. Peter Pook, interview, 3 June 1998.

22. Marc Gunther, "This Gang Controls Your Kids' Brains," *Fortune*, 27 October 1997, 172–182, passim.

23. Becker, and Steele, *Workplace by Design.*

24. Kathleen M. Eisenhardt, Jean L. Kahwajy, and L. J. Bourgeois III, "How Management Teams Can Have a Good Fight," *Harvard Business Review* 75 (July–August 1997): 81.

25. Leonard, et al., "Virtual Teams."

Chapter 6: Designing the Psychological Environment

1. Larry Ellison, interview, 26 May 1998.

2. Quoted by Tom Peters, "Prometheus Barely Unbound," *Academy of Management Executive* 4, no. 4 (1990): 79.

3. For detailed examples of both innovative and noncreative companies, see Rosabeth Moss Kanter, *The Change Masters* (New York: Simon and Schuster, 1983). See especially the section, "Rules for Stifling Innovation."

4. Alison Lawton, interview, 5 August 1998.

5. Quoted in Dorothy Leonard-Barton, *Wellsprings of Knowledge*, 119.

6. Amy Edmondson, "Psychological Safety and Learning Behavior in Work Teams," *Administrative Science Quarterly* (forthcoming, 1999).

7. Alan Horn, interview, 27 July 1998.

8. Quoted in William L. Shanklin, *Six Timeless Marketing Blunders* (Lexington, Mass.: Lexington Books, 1989), 111.

9. Steve Lohr, "IBM Opens the Doors of Its Research Labs to Surprising Results," *New York Times*, 13 July 1998, D1, D3.

10. Marc Gunther, "This Gang Controls Your Kids' Brains," *Fortune*, 27 October 1997, 172.

11. Jeffrey R. Beir, "*Managing Creatives,*" speech given on 13 March 1995 at "Managing for Innovation" Conference sponsored by *Industry Week*. In *Vital Speeches* 61, no. 16 (1995): 501-507.

12. Barbara Waugh, Hewlett-Packard Human Resources Director, interview, 15 June 1998.

13. Barbara Waugh, interview, 15 June 1998.

14. Joseph Bower, with Dorothy Leonard and Sonja Ellingson Hout, "Teradyne: Corporate Management of Disruptive Change," Case 9-398-121 (Boston: Harvard Business School, 1998).

15. Kathleen M. Eisenhardt, Jean L. Kahwajy, and L. J. Bourgeois III, "How Management Teams Can Have a Good Fight," *Harvard Business Review* 75 (July–August 1997): 81.

16. Lawrence L. Knutson, "Oldest U.S. Worker, at 102, Says His Job Still a 'Pleasure,'" *Boston Globe*, 13 March 1998.

17. Quoted in Nina Munk, "The *New* Organization Man," *Fortune*, 16 March 1998, 65.

18. Teresa A. Amabile, "How to Kill Creativity," *Harvard Business Review* 76 (September–October 1998): 81.

19. Kenneth Labich "Is Herb Kelleher America's Best CEO?" *Fortune*, 2 May 1994, 50.

20. Anne Cummings and Greg R. Oldham, "Enhancing Creativity: Managing Work Contexts for the High Potential Employee," *California Management Review* 40 (fall 1997): 22–38.

21. Nancy Vonk and Janet Kestin, interview, 5 August 1998.

22. Lisa Mancuso, interview, 3 June 1998.

23. Susan Schilling, interview, 12 December 1997.

24. Quoted in Warren Bennis and Patricia Biederman, *Organizing Genius: The Secrets of Creative Collaboration* (Reading, Mass.: Addison-Wesley, 1997), 83.

25. Richard Teerlink, interview, 2 September 1998.

26. John A. Byrne, "Jack: A Close-up Look at How America's #1 Manager Runs GE," *Business Week*, 8 June 1998, 102.

27. Edward Prewitt, "What You Can Learn from Managers in Biotech," *Management Update*, 2 May 1997, 3.

28. Quoted in Munk, "The *New* Organization Man," 74.

29. Bruce Tulgan, founder of Rainmaker, Inc., a consulting firm in New Haven, Connecticut. Quoted in Munk, "The *New* Organization Man," 74.

30. Prewitt, "What You Can Learn from Managers in Biotech," 3.

31. Anthony Rucci, Interview, "Bringing Sears into the New World," in "From the Front," *Fortune*, 13 October 1997, 184.

32. Thomas A. Stewart, "Gray Flannel Suit? Moi?" *Fortune*, 16 March 1998, 82.

33. Ashok K. Gupta and Arvind Singhal, "Managing Human Resources for Innovation and Creativity," *Research Technology Management* 36, no. 3 (1993): 44.

34. Gene Koretz, "The Vital Role of Self-Esteem," *Business Week*, 2 February 1998, 26.

35. Quoted in Stewart, "Gray Flannel Suit?" 79.

36. Quoted in Stewart, "Gray Flannel Suit?" 82.

37. Quoted in Stewart, "Gray Flannel Suit?" 79.

38. Anne Fisher, "Key to Success: People, People, People," *Fortune*, 27 October 1997, 232.

39. Munk, "The New Organization Man," 62–82.

40. Linda Grant, "Why FedEx Is Flying High," *Fortune*, 10 November 1997, 160.

41. Teresa M. Amabile, *Creativity in Context* (Boulder, Colo.: Westview Press, 1996).

42. Bing Gordon, interview, 19 May 1998.

43. Bing Gordon, interview, 19 May 1998.

44. Richard Teerlink, interview, 2 September 1998.

45. Alvin Zander, *Groups at Work* (San Francisco: Jossey-Bass, 1977).

46. Carin Knoop and Srikant Datar, "*Novartis (A): Being a Global Leader,*" Case 9-198-041 (Boston: Harvard Business School, 1998) 1.

47. Randy Komisar, interview, 15 June 1998.

48. David McClelland, *The Achieving Society* (Princeton, N.J.: Van Nostrand, 1961).

49. A. A. Milne, *The House at Pooh Corner* (New York: E.P. Dutton and Co., 1928).

50. Ann Winblad, interview, 16 June 1998.

51. Randy Komisar, quoted in Michael Roberts and Nicole Tempest, "*Randy Komisar: Virtual CEO,*" Case N9-898-078 (Boston: Harvard Business School, 1998).

52. Guido Arnout, interview, 18 June 1998.

53. Letter by Horace Walpole, reproduced in Theodore Remer, *Serendipity and the Three Princes* (Norman: University of Oklahoma Press, 1965).

54. Pek Van Andel, "Serendipity: 'Expect also the unexpected.'" *Creativity and Innovation Management* 1 (March 1992): 20–32.

55. *People's Almanac* 2 (1978) as quoted in Ira Flatow, *They All Laughed: From Light Bulbs to Lasers, the Fascinating Stories Behind the Great Inventions that Have Changed Our Lives* (New York: HarperCollins, 1992), 57.

56. These examples (vinyl and Saran) from Debra Rosenberg, "Plastics," *Newsweek* (special issue on "2000: The Power of Invention") (winter 1997): 45.

57. Lee Smith, interview, 25 February 1999.

58. Alan Horn, interview, 27 July 1998.

59. Glenn Rifkin, "Data General Comeback Built on Cost-Cutting and Innovation," *New York Times*, 17 March 1997, D5.

60. For a discussion of "beginner's mind," see John Kao, *Jamming: The Art and Discipline of Business Creativity* (New York: HarperBusiness, 1996).

61. Nancy Vonk and Janet Kestin, interview, 5 August 1998.

62. Gunther, "This Gang Controls Your Kids' Brains," 174.

63. Kao, *Jamming*, 41.
64. Shona Brown and Kathleen Eisenhardt, "The Art of Continuous Change," *Administrative Science Quarterly* 42 (1997): 16.
65. Brown and Eisenhardt, "The Art of Continuous Change."
66. Larry Reibstein with Dody Triantar, Marcus Mabry, Michael Mason, Carolyn Friday, and Bill Powell, "The Gulf School of Management," *Newsweek* 1 April 1991, 35.
67. William Q. Judge, Gerald E. Fryxell, and Robert S. Dooley, "The New Task of R and D Management," *California Management Review* 39, no. 3 (1997): 72-85.
68. Joanne Carthey, quoted in Lila Booth, "The Change Audit: A New Tool to Monitor Your Biggest Organizational Challenge," *Harvard Management Update* 3, no. 3 (1998): 3
69. Edward O. Welles, "Captain Marvel," *INC,* January, 1992, 2.
70. Jerry Hirshberg, *The Creative Priority: Driving Innovative Business in the Real World* (New York: HarperBusiness, 1998): 117-118.

Bibliography

Allen, Thomas J. 1977. *Managing the Flow of Technology.* Cambridge, Mass.: MIT Press.

Amabile, Teresa M. 1996. *Creativity in Context.* Boulder, Colo.: Westview.

———. 1998. "How to Kill Creativity." *Harvard Business Review* 76 (September–October): 76–87.

Ancona, Deborah, and David Caldwell. 1992. "Bridging the Boundary: External Activity and Performance in Organizational Teams." *Administrative Science Quarterly* 37, no. 4: 634–665.

Arad, Sharon, Mary Ann Hanson, and Robert Schneider. 1997. "A Framework for the Study of Relationships between Organizational Characteristics and Organizational Innovation." *Journal of Creative Behavior* 31, no. 1: 42–58.

Argyris, Chris. 1982. *Reasoning, Learning, and Action: Individual and Organizational.* San Francisco: Jossey-Bass.

Asch, Solomon E. 1955. "Opinions and Social Pressure." *Scientific American* 193: 31–35.

Barron, Frank. 1963. *Creativity and Psychological Health: Origins of Personality and Creative Freedom.* Princeton, N.J.: Van Nostrand.

Becker, Franklin. 1982. *The Successful Office: How to Create a Workspace That's Right for You.* Reading, Mass.: Addison-Wesley.

Becker, Franklin, and Fritz Steele. 1995. *Workplace by Design.* San Francisco: Jossey-Bass.

Begley, Sharon. 1997. "The Transistor." *Newsweek* (special issue on "2000: The Power of Invention" (winter): 25–26.

Begley, Sharon, with B. J. Sigesmund. 1997. "The Houses of Invention." *Newsweek* (special issue on "2000: The Power of Invention") (winter): 26.

Bennis, Warren, and Patricia Biederman. 1997. *Organizing Genius: The Secrets of Creative Collaboration.* Reading, Mass.: Addison-Wesley.

Billington, Jim. 1997. "The Three Essentials of an Effective Team." *Management Update* 2, no. 1: 4.

Booth, Lila. 1998. "The Change Audit: A New Tool to Monitor Your Biggest Organizational Challenge." *Harvard Management Update* 3, no. 3: 3.

Borgida, Eugene, and Richard Nisbett. 1977. "The Differential Impact of Abstract vs. Concrete Information on Decisions." *Journal of Applied Social Psychology* 7, no. 3: 258–271.

Bower, Joseph, with Dorothy Leonard and Sonja Ellingson Hout. 1998. "Teradyne: Corporate Management of Disruptive Change." Case 9-398-121. Boston: Harvard Business School.

Brown, John Seely. 1997. "Introduction: Rethinking Innovation in a Changing World. " In *Seeing Differently: Insights on Innovation,* edited by John Seely Brown. Boston: Harvard Business School Press.

Brown, Shona L., and Kathleen M. Eisenhardt. 1997. "The Art of Continuous Change: Linking Complexity Theory and Time-Paced Evolution in Relentlessly Shifting Organizations." *Administrative Science Quarterly* 42, no. 1: 1–34.

Bylinsky, Gene. 1997. "Mutant Materials." *Fortune,* 13 October, 144.

Byrne, Donn. 1971. *The Attraction Paradigm.* New York: Academic Press.

Byrne, John A. 1998. "Jack: A Close-up Look at How America's #1 Manager Runs GE." *Business Week,* 8 June, 102.

Campbell, Robert. 1998. "End of the 'Magic Incubator'." *Boston Globe,* 5 June, D1.

Carter, Meg. 1998. "Design: The Office—It's a Place to Relax; Arthur Andersen's Sixth Floor Offers a Glimpse of How Tomorrow's Workspaces Will Be Designed." *The Independent (London),* 26 March.

Christensen, Clayton, and Dorothy Leonard-Barton. 1990. "Ceramics Process Systems Corporation " Case 9-691-028. Boston: Harvard Business School.

Cohen, Sheldon, and Neil Weinstein. 1981. "Nonauditory Effects of Noise on Behavior and Health." *Journal of Social Issues* 37: 36–70.

Cummings, Anne, and Greg R. Oldham. 1997. "Enhancing Creativity: Managing Work Contexts for the High Potential Employee." *California Management Review* 40 (Fall): 22–38.

Csikszentmihalyi, Mihalyi. 1996. *Creativity: Flow and the Psychology of Discovery and Invention.* New York: Harper Collins.

Csikszentmihalyi, Mihaly, and Keith Sawyer. 1995. "Creative Insight: The Social

Dimension of a Solitary Moment." In *The Nature of Insight*, edited by Robert Sternberg and Janet Davidson. Cambridge, Mass.: MIT Press.

Daley, Yvonne. 1998. "Writer Relies on Memory as Sight Fails." *Boston Sunday Globe*, 28 June, A8.

Eaton, Leonard K. 1969. *Two Chicago Architects and Their Clients*. Cambridge, Mass.: MIT Press.

Edmondson, Amy. 1998. "Psychological Safety and Learning Behavior in Work Teams." Working Paper 98-093. Harvard Business School, Division of Research.

Eisenhardt, Kathleen M., Jean L. Kahwajy, and L. J. Bourgeois III. 1997. "Conflict and Strategic Choice: How Top Management Teams Disagree." *California Management Review* 39 (Winter): 42–62.

———. 1997. "How Management Teams Can Have a Good Fight." *Harvard Business Review* 75 (July–August): 77–85.

Fisher, Anne. 1997. "Key to Success: People, People, People." *Fortune*, 27 October, The World's Most Admired Companies, 232.

Flowers, Matie L. 1977. "A Laboratory Test of Some Implications of Janis's Groupthink Hypothesis." *Journal of Personality and Social Psychology* 35: 888–896.

Furchgott, Roy. 1998. "For Cool Hunters, Tomorrow's Trend Is the Trophy." *New York Times*, 28 June, 10

Gigone, Daniel, and Reid Hastie. 1993. "The Common Knowledge Effect: Information Sharing and Group Judgment." *Journal of Personality and Social Psychology* 65, no. 5: 959–974.

Gladwell, Malcom. 1997. "Annals of Style: The Coolhunt." *New Yorker* 72, 17 March, 78–88.

Glass, David, and Jerome Singer. 1973. "Experimental Studies of Uncontrollable and Unpredictable Noise." *Representative Research in Social Psychology* 4, no. 1: 165–183.

Grant, Linda. 1997. "Why FedEx Is Flying High." *Fortune*, 10 November, 160.

Gunther, Marc. 1997. "This Gang Controls Your Kids' Brains." *Fortune*, 27 October, 172–182, passim.

Gupta, Ashok. K., and Arvind Singhal. 1993. "Managing Human Resources for Innovation and Creativity." *Research Technology Management* 36, no. 3: 41–48.

Hackman, J. Richard. 1998. "Why Teams Don't Work." In *Applications of Theory and Research on Groups to Social Issues*, edited by R. S. Tindale, J. Edwards, and E. J. Posavac. New York: Plenum.

Haggin, Joseph. 1995. "Illinois' Beckman Institute Targets Disciplinary Barriers to Collaboration." *Chemical & Engineering News*, 6 March, 32–39.

Halberstam, David. 1986. *The Reckoning*. New York: William Morrow & Co.

Hall, Jay, and W. H. Watson. 1970. "The Effects of a Normative Intervention on Group Decision-Making Performance." *Human Relations* 23, no. 4: 299–317.

Hamel, Gary, and C. K. Prahalad. 1994. *Competing for the Future*. Boston: Harvard Business School Press.

Hirshberg, Jerry. 1998. *The Creative Priority: Driving Innovative Business in the Real World*. New York: HarperBusiness.

Hofstede, Greert. 1980. *Culture's Consequences: International Differences in Work-Related Values*. Newbury Park, Calif.: Sage.

Horn, Paul. 1997. "Creativity and the Bottom Line." *Financial Times*, 17 November, 12.

Iansiti, Marco. 1993. "Real-world R&D: Jumping the Product Generation Gap." *Harvard Business Review* (May–June): 138–147.

Jackson, Susan E. 1992. "Team Composition in Organizational Settings: Issues in Managing an Increasingly Diverse Work Force." In *Group Process and Productivity*, edited by Stephen Worchel, Wendy Wood, and Jeffry Simpson. Beverly Hills, Calif.: Sage.

Janis, Irving. 1982. *Groupthink*. 2d ed. Boston: Houghton Mifflin.

Judge, William Q., Gerald E. Fryxell, and Robert S. Dooley. 1997. "The New Task of R and D Management," *California Management Review* 39, no. 3: 72–85.

Kanter, Rosabeth Moss. 1983. *The Change Masters*. New York: Simon and Schuster.

———. 1993. *Men and Women of the Corporation*. New York: Basic Books.

———. 1997. *On the Frontiers of Management*. Boston: Harvard Business School Press.

Kantor, Paul. Quoted in *EXEC*, Summer, 1998.

Kao, John. 1995. "Oticon (A)." Case 9-395-144. Boston: Harvard Business School.

———. 1996. *Jamming: The Art and Discipline of Business Creativity*. New York: HarperBusiness.

Knoop, Carin, and Srikant Datar. 1998. "Novartis (A): Being a Global Leader." Case 9-198-041. Boston: Harvard Business School.

Knutson, Lawrence L. 1998. "Oldest US Worker, at 102, Says His Job Still a 'Pleasure.'" *Boston Globe*, 13 March.

Koretz, Gene. 1998. "The Vital Role of Self-Esteem." *Business Week*, 2 February, 26.

Labich, Kenneth. 1994. "Is Herb Kelleher America's Best CEO?" *Fortune*, 2 May, 50.

Lancaster, Hal. 1997. "Getting Yourself in a Frame of Mind to Be Creative." *Wall Street Journal,* 16 September, B1.

———. 1998. "Learning Some Ways to Make Meetings Slightly Less Awful." *Wall Street Journal,* 26 May, B1.

Leonard, Dorothy A., Paul A. Brands, Amy Edmondson, and Justine Fenwick. 1998. "Virtual Teams: Using Communications Technology to Manage Geographically Dispersed Development Groups." In *Sense and Respond,* edited by Stephen P. Bradley and Richard L. Nolan, 285–298. Boston: Harvard Business School Press.

Leonard, Dorothy, and Jeffrey Rayport. 1997. "Sparking Innovation through Empathic Design." *Harvard Business Review* 75 (November–December): 103–113.

Leonard-Barton, Dorothy. 1995. *Wellsprings of Knowledge.* Boston: Harvard Business School Press.

Lohr, Steve. 1998. "IBM Opens the Doors of Its Research Labs to Surprising Results." *New York Times,* 13 July, D1, D3.

MacKinnon, Donald W. 1975. "IPAR's Contribution to the Conceptualization and Study of Creativity." In *Perspectives in Creativity,* edited by Irving A. Taylor and J. W. Getzels. Chicago: Aldine.

Mahnke, Frank H. 1996. *Color, Environment and Human Response: An Interdisciplinary Understanding of Color and Its Use as a Beneficial Element in the Design of the Architectural Environment.* New York: Van Nostrand Reinhold.

McAllister, J. F. O. 1986. "Civil Science Policy in British Industrial Reconstruction, 1942–51." Ph.D. diss., Oxford University.

McClelland, David. 1961. *The Achieving Society.* Princeton, N.J.: Van Nostrand.

Milne. A. A. 1928. *The House at Pooh Corner.* New York: E. P. Dutton and Co.

Moorhead, Gregory, Richard Ference, and Chris Neck. 1991. "Group Decision Fiascoes Continue." *Human Relations,* 44, no. 6: 539–549.

Moscovici, Serge and Elizabeth Lage. 1976. "Studies in Social Influence IV: Minority Influence in a Context of Original Judgments." *European Journal of Social Psychology* 8, no. 3: 349–365.

Mullen, Brian, Craig Johnson, and Eduardo Salas. 1991. "Productivity Loss in Brainstorming Groups: A Meta-analytic Integration." *Basic and Applied Social Psychology* 12 no. 1: 3–23.

Munk, Nina. 1998. "The *New* Organization Man." *Fortune,* 16 March, 65.

Naik, Gautam. 1996. "Back to Darwin: In Sunlight and Cells, Science Seeks Answers to High-Tech Puzzles." *Wall Street Journal,* 16 January, A1.

Nemeth, Charlan Jeanne, and Joel Wachtler. 1983. "Creative Problem Solving as a Result of Majority vs. Minority Influence." *European Journal of Social Psychology* 13, no. 1: 45–55.

Nemeth, Charlan, and Pamela Owens. 1996. "Making Work Groups More Effective: The Value of Minority Dissent." In *Handbook of Work Group Psychology*, edited by M. A. West. New York: John Wiley.

Nisbett, Richard, and Timothy Wilson. 1977. "Telling More Than We Can Know: Verbal Reports on Mental Processes." *Psychological Review* 84, no. 4: 231–259.

Pelz, Donald, and Frank Andrews. 1966. *Scientists in Organizations.* New York: John Wiley.

People's Almanac. 1978. Vol. 2.

Peters, Tom. 1990. "Prometheus Barely Unbound." *Academy of Management Executive* 4, no. 4: 70–84.

Petroski, Henry. 1992. *The Evolution of Useful Things.* New York: Alfred A. Knopf.

Petroski, Henry. 1992. "Form Follows Failure." *Invention & Technology*, Fall: 54–61, passim.

Petzinger, Jr., Thomas. 1998. "A Hospital Applies Teamwork to Thwart an Insidious Enemy." *Wall Street Journal*, 8 May, B1.

Prewitt, Edward. 1997. "What You Can Learn From Managers in Biotech." *Management Update*, 2 May, 3.

Prokesch, Steven E. 1997. "Unleashing the Power of Learning: An Interview with British Petroleum's John Browne." *Harvard Business Review* 75 (September–October): 146–168.

Reibstein, Larry, with Dody Triantar, Marcus Mabry, Michael Mason, Carolyn Friday, and Bill Powell. 1991. "The Gulf School of Management." *Newsweek*, 1 April, 35.

Remer, Theodore. 1965. In *Serendipity and the Three Princes.* Norman: University of Oklahoma Press.

Rifkin, Glenn. 1997. "Data General Comeback Built on Cost-Cutting and Innovation." *New York Times*, 17 March, D5.

Roberts, Michael, and Nicole Tempest. 1998. "Randy Komisar: Virtual CEO." Case N9-898-078. Boston: Harvard Business School.

Robinson, Alan G., and Sam Stern. 1997. *Corporate Creativity.* San Francisco: Berrett-Koehler.

Rosenberg, Debra. 1997. "Plastics." *Newsweek* (special issue on "2000: The Power of Invention") (winter): 45.

Rothenberg, Robert. 1990. *Creativity and Madness.* Baltimore: Johns Hopkins Press.

Rucci, Anthony. 1997. Interview, "Bringing Sears into the New World." In "From the Front" *Fortune,* 13 October, 184.

Saegert, Susan, Walter Swap, and Robert B. Zajonc. 1973. "Exposure, Context, and Interpersonal Attraction." *Journal of Personality and Social Psychology* 25, no. 2: 234–242.

Schoenberger, Chana R. 1998. "Mission Statements Are Job 1—For Some." *Boston Globe,* 14 July, D1, D7.

Seifert, Colleen, David Meyer, Natalie Davidson, Andrea Patalano, and Ilan Yaniv. 1995. "Demystification of Cognitive Insight: Opportunistic Assimilation and the Prepared-Mind Perspective." In *The Nature of Insight,* edited by Robert Sternberg and Janet Davidson, 66–124. Cambridge, Mass.: MIT Press.

Shanklin, William L. 1989. *Six Timeless Marketing Blunders.* Lexington, Mass.: Lexington Books.

Shaw, Marvin E. 1976. *Group Dynamics: The Psychology of Small Group Behavior.* New York: McGraw-Hill.

Steel, Fritz. 1986. *Making and Managing High-Quality Workplaces: An Organizational Ecology.* New York: Teachers College Press.

Stein, Morris I. 1953. "Creativity and Culture." *Journal of Psychology* 36: 311–322.

Sternberg, Robert. 1996. *Successful Intelligence.* New York: Simon & Schuster.

Stewart, Thomas A. 1998. "Gray Flannel Suit? Moi?" *Fortune,* 16 March, 82.

Swap, Walter, ed. 1984. *Group Decision Making.* Beverly Hills, Calif.: Sage.

Taylor, Irving A. 1970. "Creative Production in Gifted Young (Almost) Adults through Simultaneous Sensory Stimulation." *Gifted Child Quarterly* 14, no. 1: 46–55.

Taylor, William. 1990. "The Business of Innovation: An Interview with Paul Cook." *Harvard Business Review* 68 (March–April): 96–107.

Trompenaars, Fons, and Charles Hampden-Turner. 1998. *Riding the Waves of Culture.* 2d ed. New York: McGraw-Hill.

Valacich, Joseph, Alan Dennis, and Terry Connolly. 1994. "Idea Generation in Computer-Based Groups: A New Ending to an Old Story." *Organizational Behavior and Human Decision Processes* 57, no. 3: 448–467.

Valins, Stuart, and Richard Nisbett. 1971. "Attribution Processes in the Development and Treatment of Emotional Disorders." In *Attribution: Perceiving the Causes of Behavior,* edited by Edward E. Jones, David Kanouse, Harold Kelley, Richard Nisbett, Stuart Valins and Bernard Weiner. Morristown, N.J.: General Learning Press.

Van Andel, Pek. 1992. "Serendipity: 'Expect also the Unexpected.'" *Creativity and Innovation Management* 1 (March): 20–32.

Veresej, Michael A. 1996. "Welcome to the New Workspace." *Industry Week*, 15 April, 245, 24–27.

Wason, P. C. 1960. "On the Failure to Eliminate Hypotheses in a Conceptual Task." *Quarterly Journal of Experimental Psychology* 12, no. 3: 129–140.

Weintraub, Sandra. 1995. "Cultivate your Dreams to Find New Solutions." *R&D Innovator* 4, no. 10: 1–3.

Welch, Jilly. 1996. "Creature Comforts: Innovations in Office Design." *People Management* 19 (December): 20–24.

Welles, Edward O. 1992. "Captain Marvel." *INC*, January, 2.

Wheelwright, Steven C., and Kim B. Clark. 1992. *Revolutionizing Product Development: Quantum Leaps in Speed, Efficiency, and Quality*. New York: Free Press.

Wilde, Oscar. (1888)1978. *The Remarkable Rocket*. Charlottesville, Va.: Graham-Johnston.

Williams, Katherine Y., and Charles A. O'Reilly, III. 1998. "Demography and Diversity in Organizations: A Review of 40 Years of Research." *Research in Organizational Behavior* 20: 77–140.

Williams, Wendy M., and Robert J. Sternberg. 1988. "Group Intelligence: Why Some Groups Are Better than Others." *Intelligence* 12, no. 4: 351–377.

Witcher, Gregory. 1989. "Steelcase Hopes Innovation Flourishes Under Pyramid." *Wall Street Journal*, 26 May, B1.

Wood, Wendy. 1987. "Meta-analytic Review of Sex Differences in Group Performance." *Psychological Bulletin* 102, no. 1: 53–71.

Zaltman, Gerald. 1997. "Rethinking Market Research: Putting People Back In." *Journal of Marketing Research* 34 (November): 424–437.

Zander, Alvin. 1977. *Groups at Work*. San Francisco: Jossey-Bass.

Index

creativity (*continued*)
  structuring of, 9
  studies of, 81
Csikszentmihalyi, Mihaly, 31
cultural diversity, 28–35
  pitfalls from, 28–31
  and work attitudes and values,
    30–31
cultural icons, 158
Cummings, Anne, 180
Curran, Kevin, 44
customers. *See* empathic design

Data General, serendipity at, 195–196
deadlines, 53, 56
design, cultural aspects of, 30–33
design firms, innovation at, 11. *See
    also* GVO; IDEO; Nissan Design
    International; Sundberg-Ferar,
    information gathering by
detail, importance of, 103
deviates. *See* aliens; minority influ-
    ence
devil's advocate, 61, 69–70
Disney, hiring policy at, 43
dissent
  group reaction to, 61–62
  power of, 63
  process rules for, 65
  value of, 62, 64–65
dissenters. *See* aliens
distance, and communication, 141
divergence, 6–7, 41
  balancing with convergence, 55–57
  managing, 63–64
divergent thinking
  communication styles for, 150–153
  stimuli for, 146–150
diversity, 24, 27
  age, 29

and creative abrasion, 20–22
cultural, 28–35
intellectual, 43–44
limits of, 49
of thinking styles, 35–41
Dooley, Robert, 202
Dove soap, 181–182, 198
dreaming, creativity in, 97–98
dress codes, 43
driving forces, 118, 119
  interaction with core capabilities,
    119–121
Dyson, Freeman, 145

Eaton, Leonard, 146
Edmondson, Amy, 168
Edvinsson, Leif, 148, 149
Eisenhardt, Kathleen, 21, 79
Electronic Arts
  motivators at, 188–189
  playful objects as aids to creativity
    at, 159
  priority setting at, 109
  sports simulations at, 110
electronic brainstorming, 73
Ellison, Larry, 164
e-mail, usefulness of, 160
empathic design, 80
  defined, 82
  observation and, 83
  premise behind, 82–83
enthusiasm, importance of, 191–192
environment
  physical, importance of, 135–162
  psychological, importance of,
    163–205
erosion measures, of information
    gathering, 84
ethnographic studies. *See* empathic
    design

About the Authors

Dorothy Leonard, the William J. Abernathy Professor of Business Administration, joined the Harvard Business School faculty after teaching at the Sloan School of Management, Massachusetts Institute of Technology. At Harvard, MIT, and Stanford, and for corporations such as Kodak, AT&T, and Johnson & Johnson, she has conducted executive courses on a wide range of innovation-related topics such as designing work groups, structuring new product development, and technology transfer during new product and process development. She is a faculty member of Harvard executive programs and served as faculty chair for two courses: Enhancing Corporate Creativity and Leading Product Development.

Dr. Leonard's major research interests and consulting expertise are in organizational innovation and technology strategy and commercialization. She is currently studying the generation, identification, and management of knowledge assets in companies. She has consulted with and taught about innovation for governments (of such countries as Sweden, Jamaica, and Indonesia) and major corporations (such as IBM and Nielsen Media Research), and she serves on the corporate board of directors for American Management Systems and for Guy Gannett Communications.

Her numerous publications appear in academic journals, practitioner journals, and books on innovation management. She has also written dozens of field-based cases used in business school classrooms around the world. Her previous book, *Wellsprings of Knowledge: Building and Sustaining the Sources of Innovation,* was published in hardback in 1995 and reissued in paperback in 1998.

Walter Swap is a Professor of Psychology and former Chairman of the Psychology Department at Tufts University. He is also a Professor in the Gordon Institute, which offers a degree in engineering management to practicing engineers and scientists. Dr. Swap served for nine years as the Dean of the Colleges, responsible for all aspects of undergraduate academic life at Tufts.

At Tufts, Dr. Swap's professional life has been divided among teaching, research, and administration. He was accorded Tufts' most prestigious teaching prize, the Lillian Leibner Award, in 1983. He was a founding member of the university's innovative Center for Decision Making, where he introduced undergraduates to the complexities of choice and group dynamics, and conducted workshops for midlevel managers from a variety of industries. He has helped create several additional centers, including the Center for Teaching Excellence, the Center for Interdisciplinary Studies, and the Center for Writing, Thinking and Speaking.

Among Dr. Swap's publications are *Group Decision Making* and chapters in *Environmental Decision Making: A Multidisciplinary Perspective* and *International Multilateral Negotiation: Approaches to the Management of Complexity.* In addition to other book chapters, he has authored numerous articles in professional journals, including *The Journal of Personality and Social Psychology* and *Personality and Social Psychology Bulletin,* on topics including attitude change, personality theory, altruism, and aggression. Dr. Swap is also a pianist, a singer, and an amateur composer.